Praise for Best Places® Guidebooks

"Best Places *covers must-see portions of the West Coast with style and authority. In-the-know locals offer thorough info on restaurants, lodgings, and the sights.*"
—NATIONAL GEOGRAPHIC TRAVELER

"Best Places *are the best regional restaurant and guide books in America.*"
—THE SEATTLE TIMES

"*. . . travelers swear by the recommendations in the Best Places guidebooks . . .*"
—SUNSET MAGAZINE

"*Known for their frank yet chatty tone . . .*"
—PUBLISHERS WEEKLY

"... e not

" eed ds."

"Bes od, and

"Eat, Diego."

"F takes
precedence over all similar guides."
—BOOKLIST

"The best guide to Seattle is the locally published Best Places Seattle . . ."
—JONATHAN RABAN, MONEY MAGAZINE

TRUST THE LOCALS

The original insider's guides, written by local experts

COMPLETELY INDEPENDENT

- No advertisers
- No sponsors

EVERY PLACE STAR-RATED & RECOMMENDED

★★★★ The very best in the region

★★★ Distinguished; many outstanding features

★★ Excellent; some wonderful qualities

★ A good place

NO STARS Worth knowing about, if nearby

MONEY-BACK GUARANTEE

We're so sure you'll be satisfied, we guarantee it!

HELPFUL ICONS

Watch for these quick-reference symbols throughout the book:

 FAMILY FUN

 GOOD VALUE

 ROMANTIC

 UNIQUELY NORTHERN CALIFORNIA

BEST PLACES®

NORTHERN CALIFORNIA

The Locals' Guide to the Best Restaurants,
Lodgings, Sights, Shopping, and More!

Edited by
MATTHEW RICHARD POOLE

EDITION 5

SASQUATCH BOOKS
SEATTLE

Printed in the United States of America
Published by Sasquatch Books
Distributed by Publishers Group West

Fifth edition
09 08 07 06 05 04   6 5 4 3 2 1

ISBN: 1-57061-407-5
ISSN: 1533-3981

Cover photograph: Ron Watts/Corbis
Cover and interior design: Nancy Gellos
Maps: GreenEye Design
Interior composition: Bill Quinby
Production editor: Cassandra Mitchell
Copyeditor: Karen Parkin
Proofreader: Sherri Schultz
Indexer: Michael Ferreira

SPECIAL SALES

BEST PLACES® guidebooks are available at special discounts on bulk purchases for corporate, club, or organization sales promotions, premiums, and gifts. Special editions, including personalized covers, excerpts of existing guides, and corporate imprints, can be created in large quantities for specific needs. For more information, contact your local bookseller or Special Sales, Best Places Guidebooks, 119 S Main Street, Suite 400, Seattle, Washington 98104, 800/775-0817.

SASQUATCH BOOKS
119 South Main Street, Suite 400
Seattle, WA 98104
(206) 467-4300
custserv@sasquatchbooks.com
www.sasquatchbooks.com

CONTENTS

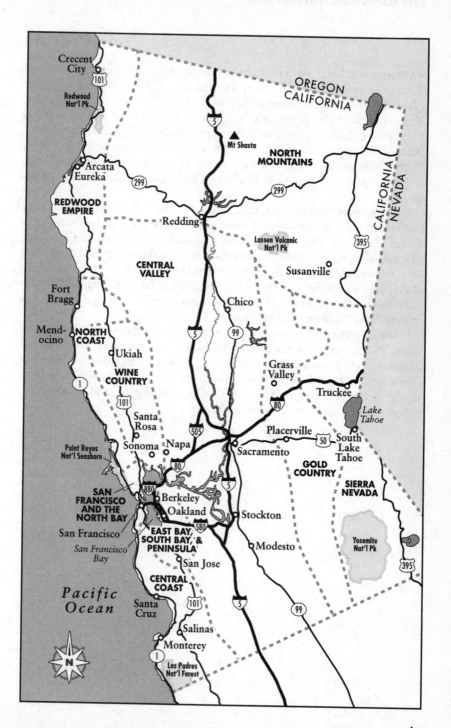

Crecent City
101
Redwood Nat'l Pk

▲ Mt Shasta

OREGON
CALIFORNIA

NORTH MOUNTAINS

5

299

Arcata
Eureka

REDWOOD EMPIRE

299

Redding

Lassen Volcanic Nat'l Pk

Susanville

395

CALIFORNIA
NEVADA

CENTRAL VALLEY

Fort Bragg

Mend-ocino

NORTH COAST

Ukiah

WINE COUNTRY

Chico

5   99

Grass Valley

Truckee

Lake Tahoe

1

101

Santa Rosa

Point Reyes Nat'l Seashore

Sonoma   Napa

505

80

Placerville

50

Sacramento

South Lake Tahoe

GOLD COUNTRY

SIERRA NEVADA

SAN FRANCISCO AND THE NORTH BAY

880

Berkeley
Oakland

San Francisco

San Francisco Bay

EAST BAY, SOUTH BAY, & PENINSULA

580

5

Stockton

Modesto

Yosemite Nat'l Pk

395

San Jose

CENTRAL COAST

Pacific Ocean

Santa Cruz

101

Salinas

Monterey

1

5

99

Los Padres Nat'l Forest

N

Contributors

MATTHEW RICHARD POOLE, a native Northern Californian, has authored more than two dozen travel guides to California and abroad, including *Best Places San Francisco*, *Frommer's California*, *ACCESS Hawaii*, and *Berlitz Las Vegas*. Matthew also is a regular contributor to radio and television travel programs, including numerous guest appearances on *Bay Area Backroads*. Before becoming a full-time travel writer and photographer, he worked as an English tutor in Prague, ski instructor in the Swiss Alps, and scuba instructor in Maui. He currently lives in Northern California, but spends most of his time on the road.

MARY ANNE MOORE and **MAURICE READ** are freelance writers and editors, and contributors to several other travel guides including *Northern California Cheap Sleeps* and *The Unofficial Guide to Bed & Breakfasts in California*. Mary Anne is also a legislative consultant at the California State Capital and loves to travel. Maurice is a Sacramento-based lobbyist and gourmet chef who's always on the lookout for dog-friendly lodgings, great fly fishing, and memorable meals. Mary Anne and Maurice have also contributed to previous editions of *Best Places Northern California*.

TANYA HENRY has been eating her way around the Bay Area for almost ten years. She has written for a number of publications including *San Francisco Magazine*, *San Francisco Best Places*, and, most recently, the *San Francisco Chronicle*. She has a two-year-old son who has given up mac and cheese for a steady diet of free range chicken bathed in a ragout of wild mushrooms, pancetta, and gorgonzola. She lives in Marin.

About Best Places® Guidebooks

People trust us. Best Places® guidebooks, which have been published continuously since 1975, represent one of the most respected regional travel series in the country. Our reviewers know their territory and seek out the very best a city or region has to offer. We are able to provide tough, candid reports about places that have rested too long on their laurels, and to delight in new places that deserve recognition. We describe the true strengths, foibles, and unique characteristics of each establishment listed.

Best Places Northern California is written by and for locals, and is therefore coveted by travelers. It's written for people who live here and who enjoy exploring the region's bounty and its out-of-the-way places of high character and individualism. It is these very characteristics that make *Best Places Northern California* ideal for tourists, too. The best places in and around the region are the ones that denizens favor: independently owned establishments of good value, touched with local history, run by lively individuals, and graced with natural beauty. With this fifth edition of *Best Places Northern California*, travelers will find the information they need: where to go and when, what to order, which rooms to request (and which to avoid), where the best music, art, nightlife, shopping, and other attractions are, and how to find the region's hidden secrets.

We're so sure you'll be satisfied with our guide, we guarantee it.

NOTE: *The reviews in this edition are based on information available at press time and are subject to change. Readers are advised that places listed in previous editions may have closed or changed management, or may no longer be recommended by this series. The editors welcome information conveyed by users of this book. Feedback is welcome via email: books@sasquatchbooks.com.*

How to Use This Book

This book is divided into ten major regions, encompassing the Sierra Nevada, the San Francisco Bay Area, the Central Valley, and all destinations north to the Oregon border. All evaluations are based on numerous reports from local and traveling inspectors. Final judgments are made by the editors. **EVERY PLACE FEATURED IN THIS BOOK IS RECOMMENDED.**

STAR RATINGS Restaurants and lodgings are rated on a scale of zero to four stars (with half stars in between), based on uniqueness, loyalty of local clientele, performance measured against the establishment's goals, excellence of cooking, cleanliness, value, and professionalism of service. Reviews are listed alphabetically.

★★★★ The very best in the region

★★★ Distinguished; many outstanding features

★★ Excellent; some wonderful qualities

★ A good place

NO STARS Worth knowing about, if nearby

(For more on how we rate places, see the Best Places® Star Ratings box on page xiv.)

PRICE RANGE Prices for restaurants are based primarily on dinner for two, including dessert, tax, and tip (no alcohol). Prices for lodgings are based on peak season rates for one night's lodging for two people (i.e., double occupancy). Peak season is typically Memorial Day to Labor Day; off-season rates vary but can sometimes be significantly less. Call ahead to verify, as all prices are subject to change.

$$$$ Very expensive (more than $100 for dinner for two; more than $200 for one night's lodging for two)

$$$ Expensive (between $65 and $100 for dinner for two; between $120 and $200 for one night's lodging for two)

$$ Moderate (between $35 and $65 for dinner for two; between $75 and $120 for one night's lodging for two)

$ Inexpensive (less than $35 for dinner for two; less than $75 for one night's lodging for two)

RESERVATIONS (FOR RESTAURANTS ONLY) We used one of the following terms for our reservations policy: reservations required, reservations recommended, no reservations. "No reservations" means either reservations are not necessary or are not accepted.

ACCESS AND INFORMATION At the beginning of each chapter, you'll find general guidelines about how to get to a particular region and what types of transportation are available, as well as basic sources for any additional tourist information you might need. Also check individual town listings for specifics about visiting those places.

THREE-DAY TOURS In every chapter, we've included a quick-reference, three-day itinerary designed for travelers with a short amount of time. Perfect for weekend getaways, these tours outline the highlights of a region or town; each of the establishments or attractions that appear in boldface within the tour are discussed in greater detail elsewhere in the chapter.

ADDRESSES AND PHONE NUMBERS Every attempt has been made to provide accurate information on an establishment's location and phone number, but it's always a good idea to call ahead and confirm. If an establishment has two area locations, we list both at the top of the review. If there are three or more locations, we list only the main address and indicate "other branches."

CHECKS AND CREDIT CARDS Many establishments that accept checks also require a major credit card for identification. Note that some places accept only local checks. Credit cards are abbreviated in this book as follows: American Express (AE); Carte Blanche (CB); Diners Club (DC); Discover (DIS); Japanese credit card (JCB); MasterCard (MC); Visa (V).

EMAIL AND WEB SITE ADDRESSES Email and web site addresses for establishments have been included where available. Please note that the web is a fluid and evolving medium, and that web pages are often "under construction" or, as with all time-sensitive information, may no longer be valid.

MAPS AND DIRECTIONS Each chapter in the book begins with a regional map that shows the general area being covered. Throughout the book, basic directions are provided with each entry. Whenever possible, call ahead to confirm hours and location.

HELPFUL ICONS Watch for these quick-reference symbols throughout the book:

 FAMILY FUN Family-oriented places that are great for kids—fun, easy, not too expensive, and accustomed to dealing with young ones.

 GOOD VALUE While not necessarily cheap, these places offer you the best value for your dollars—a good deal within the context of the region.

 ROMANTIC These spots offer candlelight, atmosphere, intimacy, or other romantic qualities—kisses and proposals are encouraged!

 UNIQUELY NORTHERN CALIFORNIA These are places that are unique and special to Northern California and beyond, such as a restaurant owned by a beloved local chef or a tourist attraction recognized around the globe.

♿ Appears after listings for establishments that have wheelchair-accessible facilities.

INDEXES All restaurants, lodgings, town names, and major tourist attractions are listed alphabetically in the back of the book.

BEST PLACES® STAR RATINGS

Any travel guide that rates establishments is inherently subjective—and Best Places® is no exception. We rely on our professional experience, yes, but also on a gut feeling. And, occasionally, we even give in to a soft spot for a favorite neighborhood hangout. Our star-rating system is not simply a checklist; it's judgmental, critical, sometimes fickle, and highly personal.

For each new edition, we send local food and travel experts out to review restaurants and lodgings, and then to rate them on a scale of one to four, based on uniqueness, loyalty of local clientele, performance measured against the establishment's goals, excellence of cooking, cleanliness, value, and professionalism of service. That doesn't mean a one-star establishment isn't worth dining or sleeping at—far from it. When we say that all the places listed in our books are recommended, we mean it. That one-star pizza joint may be just the ticket for the end of a whirlwind day of shopping with the kids. But if you're planning something more special, the star ratings can help you choose an eatery or hotel that will wow your new clients or be a stunning, romantic place to celebrate an anniversary or impress a first date.

We award four-star ratings sparingly, reserving them for what we consider truly the best. And once an establishment has earned our highest rating, everyone's expectations seem to rise. Readers often write us letters specifically to point out the faults in four-star establishments. With changes in chefs, management, styles, and trends, it's always easier to get knocked off the pedestal than to ascend it. Three-star establishments, on the other hand, seem to generate healthy praise. They exhibit outstanding qualities, and we get lots of love letters about them. The difference between two and three stars can sometimes be a very fine line. Two-star establishments are doing a good, solid job and gaining attention, while one-star places are often dependable spots that have been around forever.

The restaurants and lodgings described in *Best Places Northern California* have earned their stars from hard work and good service (and good food). They're proud to be included in this book—look for our Best Places® sticker in their windows. And we're proud to honor them in this, the fifth edition of *Best Places Northern California*.

SAN FRANCISCO AND THE NORTH BAY

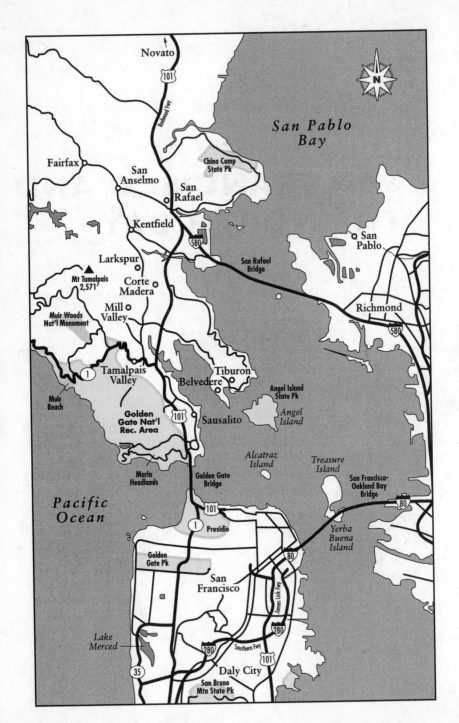

SAN FRANCISCO AND THE NORTH BAY

San Francisco

Please don't call it Frisco. It's San Francisco. Locals call it "the city," using the shorthand with confidence because they know they have something special. In no other city in the country is the meeting of land and sea so spectacular or the combination of nature and culture so enticing. Surrounded by ocean and bay, crinkled into hill after hill, the city sits under a downy layer of fog one moment and sparkles in the clear Northern California sunlight the next.

But the attraction isn't just the setting; San Francisco's neighborhoods exude a personality that makes this place much more than a pretty collection of natural gifts. The city's neighborhoods are as varied as its topography. A trendy energy radiates from the Marina on summer days, with residents and visitors jogging, cycling, and inline skating along the Marina Green. The alternative lifestyle is alive and thriving in the Haight. The Mission District moves to a multiethnic beat, stirring the cultural pot in its eateries and its public artwork. And while it's true that on some days the fog never clears, it's a small price to pay to play in one of the world's greatest cities.

ACCESS AND INFORMATION

Two major airports serve the city—**SAN FRANCISCO INTERNATIONAL AIRPORT (SFO)** (650/821-8211; www.flysfo.com) and **OAKLAND INTERNATIONAL AIRPORT (OAK)** (510/563-3300; www.oaklandairport.com). Most travelers use SFO, which is located 14 miles south of downtown San Francisco via Highways 101 or 280. Fares to either airport are often identical, so if a flight to SFO is sold out, there may still be available seats on flights to OAK. Trips to or from SFO are easy with one of the fast, reliable **SHUTTLE SERVICES,** such as SuperShuttle (415/558-8500; www.supershuttle.com) or Quake City (415/255-4899); fares are around $17. Bayporter Express (877/467-1800 in the Bay Area or 415/467-1800 elsewhere; www.bayporter.com) is a popular Oakland Airport shuttle service that charges $23 per person for rides to San Francisco. **BAY AREA RAPID TRANSIT (BART;** 510/464-6000; www.bart.gov) trains run daily from the SFO terminal to downtown San Francisco and cost only about $5 one way; BART also services OAK, but you'll need to take a free shuttle from the airport. **TAXIS** wait at each SFO terminal's arrival area and will relieve you of $35 for the 20-minute trip downtown.

PARKING in San Francisco can be an ordeal; many neighborhoods limit nonresidents to only 2 hours, and most downtown meters have a maddening maximum time limit of 30 minutes. To make things even more frustrating, traffic cops are quick, ruthless, and in abundance (almost 30 percent of all parking tickets issued statewide are issued in San Francisco). If you see a tow-away warning, take it seriously. Public parking garages abound, and if you look hard enough, you can find some garages or park-and-pay lots that don't charge Manhattan rates. If you park in a disabled zone, the violation alone will cost $250 to $275, not to mention the towing fees and hassle of getting the car back.

Major hotels have taxi stands; otherwise, telephone for a cab, since taxis usually cruise along only the most populated streets.

Public transportation reaches every neighborhood but grows sparse after midnight. **MUNI**, the **SAN FRANCISCO MUNICIPAL RAILWAY** (415/673-6864; www.sfmuni.com), includes buses, above-ground/underground streetcars, and cable cars. Exact change is required ($1 bills are OK), and free transfers (except for cable cars) grant two more rides within the next 1½ hours (be sure to ask for a transfer as soon as you board the bus). Short-term (one-, three-, and seven-day) and monthly MUNI passes allowing unlimited rides are available at the Visitor Information Center (see below) and at City Hall during weekday business hours. (For information on cable cars, see the Major Attractions section, below.)

BART (510/464-6000; www.bart.gov) is a clean, reliable, high-speed underground commuter train system that runs through the southeastern side of the city, with routes to Daly City and the East Bay, including Berkeley and Oakland.

San Franciscans have become masters at dressing in layers, never sure exactly what the day's **WEATHER** holds. Sunny afternoons can be warm and spectacular, but are often preceded by foggy mornings or followed by cool evenings. The climate is mild, rarely rising above 70°F or falling below 40°F, but bring a sweater or coat—chances are you'll need it. Spring and fall months are warmest, as the fog makes its most frequent appearances in summer.

For more details on San Francisco sites and attractions, visit the helpful staff at the Convention and Visitors Bureau's **VISITOR INFORMATION CENTER** (lower level of Hallidie Plaza at Market and Powell Sts; 415/391-2000; www.sfvisitor.org), open seven days a week, Monday through Friday 9am to 5pm, Saturday and Sunday 9am to 3pm. Free information is available by fax 24 hours a day (800/220-5747). The bureau has a hotel reservation service (888/782-9673; www.sfvisitor.org) with photos, descriptions, and features of more than 200 Bay Area hotels.

MAJOR ATTRACTIONS

San Francisco, like Paris, is a great walking town, and one of the city's most spectacular scenic walks is along the **GOLDEN GATE PROMENADE**, a 4-mile stretch from **AQUATIC PARK** in front of the Cannery through the beautiful **MARINA GREEN** and **CRISSY FIELD** to historic **FORT POINT**, a fortification built in 1861 that's nestled under the south end of the Golden Gate Bridge. If you have the energy, continue your tour with a walk across the bridge for a breathtaking view of the Bay Area and the Pacific. Another gorgeous waterfront stroll follows the Embarcadero north from Market Street. Be sure to take a stroll through the newly restored Ferry Building Marketplace—tenants within this historic landmark include several cafés, wine shops, and some of Northern California's finest artisan food producers, including Cowgirl Creamery, Ricchiuti Confections, and Scharffen Berger Chocolate. At Pier 7, you'll get a good look at **TREASURE ISLAND** and the yachts and freighters sailing beneath the San Francisco–Oakland Bay Bridge. A hop on the **F LINE**, which runs vintage trolleys up the palm-filled center of the Embarcadero, takes you to touristy Pier 39. There you can watch the hundreds of barking **SEA LIONS** playing and basking in the sun on the west side of the pier.

The third-most-visited amusement attraction in the nation, **PIER 39** (415/981-PIER; www.pier39.com) is packed with kitschy shops and overpriced, touristy restaurants, but it boasts beautiful views of Angel Island, Alcatraz, and the bay. It has great entertainment for kids with its **VENETIAN CAROUSEL**, jugglers, mimes, big-screen **CINEMAX THEATER**, and an arcade stocked with every gizmo and quarter-sucking machine the young-at-heart could dream of. Once you've had your fill of the tourist-packed pier, jump aboard the ferry for the **ISLAND HOP TOUR** and make your way around both Angel Island and Alcatraz (make advance reservations), or take a **SAN FRANCISCO BAY CRUISE** or a scenic trip to the pretty towns across the bay, **SAUSALITO** and **TIBURON**. For tour information and ferry schedules, call the Blue & Gold Fleet (415/705-5555; www.blueandgoldfleet.com).

Just a short jaunt west of Pier 39 are world-famous **FISHERMAN'S WHARF, THE CANNERY**, and **GHIRARDELLI SQUARE**. They're always mobbed with tourists, but they offer some interesting shops. It's also still a working waterfront—stroll along the north side of Jefferson Street, between Taylor and Jones Streets, to see the colorful fishing boat fleet. And from mid-November through June, this is where you'll see the city's highly touted (and delicious) **DUNGENESS CRABS** boiling in large metal pots on the sidewalks lining the wharf.

While tourists flock to Fisherman's Wharf and Pier 39, locals often take their kids in the other direction to the **EXPLORATORIUM** (415/561-0360; www.exploratorium.edu), a unique interactive museum that brings scientific concepts to vivid life—it's a blast at any age. The Exploratorium's marvelous **TACTILE DOME**, where visitors must feel their way through a maze of hurdles in total darkness, requires a certain amount of nerve. The Exploratorium is housed within the magnificent **PALACE OF FINE ARTS** (3601 Lyon St, between Jefferson and Bay Sts; 415/563-7337), designed by renowned architect Bernard Maybeck for the 1915 Panama-Pacific International Exposition. Surrounded by a natural lagoon, the Palace is an ideal spot for a picnic.

In the southwest corner of the city, near the ocean and Lake Merced, is the popular **SAN FRANCISCO ZOO** (45th Ave and Sloat Blvd; 415/753-7061; www.sfzoo.org). Don't miss the famed Primate Discovery Center, where several species of apes and monkeys live in glass-walled condos. The zoo also has rare Sumatran and Siberian tigers, African lions (visit during their mealtimes), a children's petting zoo, and even an insect zoo. On the other side of the Golden Gate Bridge, in Sausalito, is the **BAY AREA DISCOVERY MUSEUM** (East Fort Baker; 415/487-4398; www.badm.org), a wonderland of hands-on science, art, and multimedia exhibits designed for kids. Go north across the bridge, exit at Alexander Avenue, and follow the signs.

For a sweeping view of the Pacific Ocean, visit the historic **CLIFF HOUSE** (415/386-3330) and sip a cocktail at a window-side table, then climb around the neighboring ruins of the once-spectacular **SUTRO BATHS** (1090 Point Lobos Ave).

To explore some of the city's multiethnic neighborhoods and architectural masterpieces, strap on your heavy-duty walking shoes and hike around the **RUSSIAN HILL** neighborhood, starting at the top of the crookedest street in the world, **LOMBARD STREET** (at Hyde St). Wind your way down Lombard's multiple, flower-lined curves and continue east until Lombard intersects with Columbus Avenue, then turn right and stay on Columbus for a tour of charming **NORTH BEACH**—a predominantly Italian and Chinese neighborhood where residents practice tai chi in **WASHINGTON SQUARE** on weekend mornings or sip espresso as they peruse Proust or the San Francisco *Bay Guardian*'s really racy personal ads (guaranteed to make you blush). You can extend this tour by turning right off Columbus onto Grant Avenue, which will take you through the heart of the ever-bustling and fascinating **CHINATOWN**—the only part of the city where vendors sell live, 3-foot-long slippery eels next to X-rated fortune cookies and herbs meant to cure whatever ails you.

If you're in need of an aerobic workout, take a different tour: instead of turning off Lombard onto Columbus, keep following Lombard Street east all the way up to **COIT TOWER** (415/362-0808) on the top of **TELEGRAPH HILL,** then reward yourself for making the steep ascent (gasp, gasp) with an elevator trip to the top of the tower for a panoramic view of the Bay Area.

If you'd rather ride than walk the hills of San Francisco, an outside perch on one of the city's famed **CABLE CARS** is always a kick. The three cable car routes are named after the streets on which they run (you can take them in either direction), operate daily from 6:30am to 12:30am, rain or shine, and cost only $3 one-way. The Powell-Mason line starts at Powell and Market Streets and terminates at Bay Street near Fisherman's Wharf; the Powell-Hyde line also begins at Powell and Market Streets but ends at Victorian Park near Aquatic Park and the bay, making it the most scenic route; and the California line runs from California and Market Streets through Chinatown to Van Ness Avenue. Expect very long lines during peak travel times, especially when the weather is warm. For more information on the cable cars, call MUNI or visit their website (415/673-6864; www.sfmuni.com).

MUSEUMS

The **SAN FRANCISCO MUSEUM OF MODERN ART** (151 3rd St, between Mission and Howard Sts; 415/357-4000; www.sfmoma.org), housed in a dramatic modernist building designed by Swiss architect Mario Botta, offers works by Picasso, Matisse, O'Keeffe, Rivera, Pollock, Warhol, Klee, De Forest, and Lichtenstein, among others. The **ASIAN ART MUSEUM** (415/581-3500; www.asianart.org) is the largest museum outside of Asia devoted exclusively to Asian art, housed in a new 165,000-square-foot home in the 1917 Beaux Arts building that used to be the city's main library.

The **CALIFORNIA PALACE OF THE LEGION OF HONOR** (in Lincoln Park near 34th Ave and Clement St; 415/863-3330 or 415/750-3600; www.legionof honor.com), a three-quarter-scale replica of Paris's grand Palais de la Légion d'Honneur, features European paintings (including works by Monet, Cézanne, and Rembrandt), sculptures (a large collection of Rodin), and decorative art. It also has a small collection of ancient art and hosts a constant stream of interesting international exhibits. Galleries for established San Francisco artists are located primarily on lower Grant Avenue and near Union Square; up-and-coming artists tend to exhibit in SoMa (the South of Market Street area).

Fantastic **MURALS** decorate many public spaces in the city, particularly in the **MISSION DISTRICT,** the city's vibrant, primarily Hispanic neighborhood; for maps outlining self-guided walks or for very good two-hour guided tours, contact the **PRECITA EYES MURAL ARTS CENTER** (2981 24th St at Harrison St; 415/285-2287; www.precitaeyes.org). If you don't have time for a tour, at least stroll down narrow

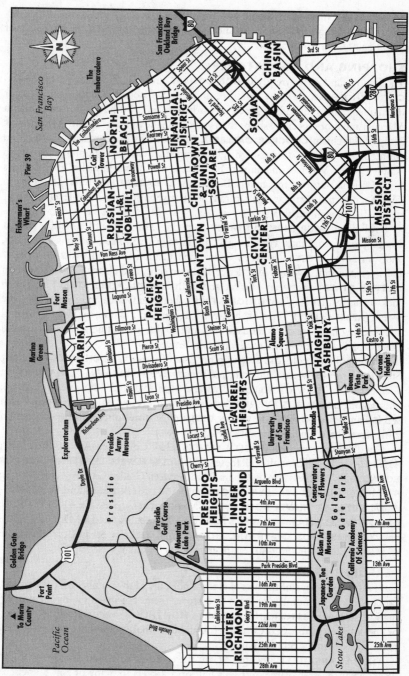

DOWNTOWN SAN FRANCISCO

BALMY ALLEY (near Harrison and 25th Sts), which is lined with about 30 incredibly colorful murals on the garages and fences of the homes and is the birthplace of mural painting in San Francisco.

SHOPPING AND BOOKSTORES

The famous and oh-so-trendy **UNION SQUARE** area and the nearby **SAN FRANCISCO SHOPPING CENTRE** (Market and 5th Sts) together boast many major department stores (including Macy's, Nordstrom, Saks Fifth Avenue, and Neiman Marcus) and more specialty shops than you can shake a credit card at. A short walk away is the chichi **CROCKER GALLERIA** (bounded by Post, Kearny, Sutter, and Montgomery Sts), a 70-foot-high, glass-domed, three-level shopping mall with Ralph Lauren, Versace, and similar boutiques, which was modeled after Milan's 1867 Galleria Vittoria Emmanuelle II. The vast **EMBARCADERO CENTER** (between Clay, Sacramento, Battery, and Drumm Sts) is a sophisticated three-level, open-air neo-mall also well worth a spree.

Stroll down **SACRAMENTO STREET** (between Lyon and Spruce Sts) for elegant clothing and furnishings. For vintage, cutting-edge, and folksy fashions and crafts, shop on **24TH STREET** (between Castro and Church Sts) and **HAIGHT STREET** (between Masonic Ave and Shrader St). Hip, eclectic, and classic items abound on **CASTRO STREET** (between Market and 19th Sts), **FILLMORE STREET** (between Jackson and Sutter Sts), and **UNION STREET** (between Gough and Steiner Sts). The 5-acre **JAPAN CENTER** (Post St, between Laguna and Fillmore Sts) houses several shops selling Japanese crafts, housewares, and books, with numerous sushi bars and other Japanese-style eateries sandwiched in between.

Cosmopolitan cooks can stock up on Asian foodstuffs in **CHINATOWN** along Stockton Street (between California and Broadway Sts) or in **NEW CHINATOWN** on Clement Street (between Arguello Blvd and 10th Ave, and 18th and 25th Aves). Shops along **COLUMBUS AVENUE** (between Broadway and Bay Sts) in North Beach sell Italian treats, while the **MISSION DISTRICT**'s stores offer Latin specialties on 24th Street (between Guerrero St and Potrero Ave).

Good bookstores include **CITY LIGHTS** (261 Columbus Ave at Broadway; 415/362-8193), still Beat after all these years; **A CLEAN WELL-LIGHTED PLACE FOR BOOKS** (601 Van Ness Ave, in Opera Plaza between Golden Gate Ave and Turk St; 415/441-6670); and **STACEY'S BOOKSTORE** (581 Market St at 2nd St; 415/421-4687). **GET LOST TRAVEL BOOKS** (1825 Market St at Guerrero St; 415/437-0529); **RAND MCNALLY MAP & TRAVEL STORE** (595 Market St at 2nd St; 415/777-3131); and **THOMAS BROS. MAPS AND BOOKS** (550 Jackson St at Columbus Ave; 415/981-7520 or 800/969-3072) are great stops for any traveler.

PERFORMING ARTS

San Franciscans' love of the arts is evident not only in the number of artsy goings-on but also in the number of ways to discover them. For up-to-the-moment information, surf to the **SAN FRANCISCO ARTS MONTHLY** Web site (artsmonthlysf.org) or check the *San Francisco Chronicle*'s Datebook (more commonly known as "the pink section") in the Sunday paper.

TIX BAY AREA (251 Stockton St, on the east side of Union Square; 415/433-7827; www.theatrebayarea.org) sells half-price tickets to many of San Francisco's dance, music, and theater events on the day of the performance only (tickets for Sunday and Monday events are sold on Saturday). You must purchase the tickets in person and pay in cash or with traveler's checks. Advance full-price tickets are sold here, too, and may be purchased with Visa, MasterCard, traveler's checks, or cash. Tickets to most dance and theater events are also sold by phone through the **CITY BOX OFFICE** (415/392-4400; www.cityboxoffice.com) and **BASS TICKETMASTER** (510/762-2277; www.tickets.com).

MUSIC: San Francisco's bountiful music scene has a 24-hour-a-day tempo. The accordion is the city's official musical instrument, but don't look for the squeeze box in the venues below. It makes most of its appearances in street performances.

The world-class **SAN FRANCISCO OPERA** (415/864-3330, box office; or 415/861-4008, general information; www.sfopera.com) alternates warhorses with rarities from September through January at the War Memorial Opera House. This beloved Beaux Arts beauty was modeled on Garnier's Paris Opéra and opened on October 15, 1932, with a production of Puccini's *Tosca*. Sixty-five years later, on September 5, 1997, the same Puccini production launched the reopening after an 18-month, $86.5 million renovation that included seismic retrofitting, regilding of the 530 rosettes on the lobby's barrel-vaulted ceiling, and replacing of the old stage curtain with an elaborate 3,000-pound, gold silk organza number. Subscribers grab up most of the red velvet seats, but fans with smaller bankrolls can stand in line early on performance mornings to buy one of the 200 standing-room tickets, which go on sale at 10am (50 of these inexpensive tickets are held until two hours before the performance). The **SAN FRANCISCO SYMPHONY** (415/864-6000; www.sfsymphony.org), under the heralded baton of music director Michael Tilson Thomas, performs from September through July at the modern Louise M. Davies Symphony Hall (201 Van Ness Ave at Grove St), a gorgeous $38 million construction with a wraparound glass facade.

On summer Sundays, families and couples tote blankets and picnic baskets to free outdoor performances (everything from jazz to opera to symphony) at the pretty **STERN GROVE** (Sloat Blvd and 19th Ave; 415/252-6252, www.sterngrove.org). The **SAN FRANCISCO JAZZ FESTIVAL** (415/788-7353; www.sfjazzfest.org), one of the largest in the country, toots its horn every fall with concerts, dances, films, and lectures. (For the scoop on the city's best nightclub performances, see Nightlife, below.)

THEATER AND COMEDY: AMERICAN CONSERVATORY THEATER (415/749-2ACT; www.act-sfbay.org), the city's best-known theater company, presents solid productions of new works and classics under the artistic direction of Carey Perloff from September through July in the Geary Theater (415 Geary St). Broadway shows on tour are performed at the **GOLDEN GATE, CURRAN,** and **ORPHEUM THEATERS** (415/551-2000; www.bestofbroadway-sf.com). **THEATRE ON THE SQUARE** (450 Post St, between Powell and Mason Sts; 415/433-9500) and **MARINES MEMORIAL THEATRE** (609 Sutter St at Mason St; 415/771-6900; www.marinesmemorial theatre.com) showcase off-Broadway acts.

Among the small local theater companies offering wonderful performances are the **LORRAINE HANSBERRY THEATRE** (620 Sutter St at Mason St; 415/474-8800 or 415/288-0336); the **LAMPLIGHTERS MUSIC THEATER** (415/227-4797; www.lamplighters.org), which performs primarily Gilbert and Sullivan comic operas at Yerba Buena Gardens' Center for the Arts (701 Mission St at 3rd St) and the Ira & Leonore S. Gershwin Theater (2350 Turk St at Masonic St); and the **MAGIC THEATRE** (Fort Mason Center, Building D, off Marina Blvd at Buchanan St; 415/441-8822; www.magictheatre.org). **THEATRE RHINOCEROS** (2926 16th St at South Van Ness Ave; 415/861-5079) specializes in gay and lesbian drama. Summer and early autumn bring free outdoor performances at various venues by America's oldest political musical-comedy theater group, the Tony award–winning **SAN FRANCISCO MIME TROUPE** (415/285-1717; www.sfmt.org). The more serious **SHAKESPEARE IN THE PARK** (415/422-2222; www.sfshakes.org) theater group also performs for free in the summer in Golden Gate Park. **BEACH BLANKET BABYLON**, the longest-running musical revue in the world, is a cabaret-style show full of silly jokes that's famous for its wild costumes and humongous hats. It remains a favorite of residents and visitors alike, so be sure to reserve seats in advance at Club Fugazi (678 Green St near Powell St; 415/421-4222; www.beachblanketbabylon.com).

San Francisco has launched the careers of many comedians, including Robin Williams and Whoopi Goldberg. See the latest talents at the **PUNCHLINE** (444 Battery St, 2nd Fl, between Clay and Washington Sts; 415/397-4337 or 415/397-7573 for recorded information; www.punchlinecomedyclub.com).

DANCE: The internationally renowned **SAN FRANCISCO BALLET** (415/865-2000; www.sfballet.org), led by artistic director Helgi Tomasson, leaps into its season in December with the classic Nutcracker and begins its repertory season in February; performances are held at the beautiful War Memorial Opera House (301 Van Ness Ave at Grove St). For modern and contemporary performances, see the **ODC/SAN FRANCISCO** dance troupe (415/863-6606); for contemporary ballet, **LINES** (415/863-3040; www.linesballet.org) is a local favorite and often performs at Yerba Buena Gardens' Center for the Arts (701 Mission St at 3rd St). Modern dance recitals also are frequently held at **THEATER ARTAUD** (450 Florida St at 17th St; 415/626-DOME).

FILM: The **SAN FRANCISCO INTERNATIONAL FILM FESTIVAL** (415/931-FILM; www.sfiff.org) attracts film fanatics for a fortnight every spring; screenings are held at various venues in San Francisco, Berkeley, and Marin County. Another popular event is the **SAN FRANCISCO INTERNATIONAL LESBIAN AND GAY FILM FESTIVAL** (415/703-8650; www.frameline.org), which takes place in June. For rare revivals and premieres, check out the palatial **CASTRO THEATRE** (429 Castro St off Market St; 415/621-6120; www.thecastrotheatre.com), a flamboyant Spanish baroque-style movie palace designed by Timothy Pflueger in 1923; the funky (but finely programmed) **ROXIE CINEMA** (3117 16th St at Valencia St; 415/863-1087); and the homey **RED VICTORIAN MOVIE HOUSE** (1727 Haight St, between Cole and Shrader Sts; 415/668-3994).

PARKS, GARDENS, AND BEACHES

GOLDEN GATE PARK, encompassing 1,017 acres of lush grounds dotted with magnificent museums, lakes, and gardens, is a masterpiece of park design. For a good introduction to its attractions, join one of the **FREE GUIDED WALKING TOURS** offered by Friends of Recreation and Parks (415/263-0991 or 415/750-5105) every weekend from May through October. Plant enthusiasts mustn't miss the **STRYBING**

ARBORETUM AND BOTANICAL GARDENS (near 9th Ave and Lincoln Wy; 415/661-1316; www.strybing.org), home to more than 7,000 plant and tree varieties. Free guided walks are given daily at 1:30pm. A somewhat more Zen-like experience is offered by the lovely **JAPANESE TEA GARDEN,** the oldest Japanese-style park in the United States, which always attracts crowds but particularly when the cherry blossoms and azaleas bloom in March and April (pssst . . . to avoid the hordes, visit when it's raining). In the northeast corner of the park is the spectacular **CONSERVATORY OF FLOWERS** (John F. Kennedy Dr, near Conservatory Dr; 415/831-2700; www.conservatoryofflowers.org), an 1879 Victorian fairyland hothouse full of tropical flora. It's an architectural beauty worth admiring both inside and out. In the middle of the park, serene **STOW LAKE** compels you to rent a rowboat, paddleboat, or electric boat (415/752-0347) and circle the 430-foot-high artificial island known as **STRAWBERRY HILL,** the highest peak in the park. Look for the hill's waterfall and Chinese moon-watching pavilion as well as the numerous turtles and ducks that live on the lake. If you have youngsters in tow, don't skip the **CHILDREN'S PLAYGROUND** (off Kezar Dr), which has a dazzling Golden Age 1912 carousel (the oldest one in a public park) that's guaranteed to make every child's heart go pitter-patter. Every Sunday, Golden Gate Park's main drag is closed to auto traffic so skaters and joggers can let loose on the tree-lined street. **SKATE RENTALS** are readily available on Fulton and Haight Streets.

The city's entire northwest corner is part of the **GOLDEN GATE NATIONAL RECREATION AREA (GGNRA),** the largest urban park in the world. Take a hike along its gorgeous wildflower-laced **COASTAL TRAIL,** which hugs the headlands for more than 10 miles and offers fantastic views of the Pacific Ocean; start at Point Lobos (at the end of Point Lobos Ave, near the Sutro Baths) and wind your way to the Golden Gate Bridge. **THE PRESIDIO,** a lush 1,480-acre former military base, has become part of the GGNRA and offers superb views to hikers (and drivers) as well as historic buildings, a scenic golf course, walking and biking tours, and a national cemetery. Also part of the GGNRA are **CRISSY FIELD,** a fabulous windsurfing spot, and the **MARINA GREEN,** prime kite-flying and jogging territory; both are located off Marina Boulevard, near the on-ramp to the Golden Gate Bridge. For maps and more details on the GGNRA, call the National Park Information Center (415/556-0560).

In the heart of the city, across from the Museum of Modern Art, is **YERBA BUENA GARDENS** (Mission St between 3rd and 4th Sts), San Francisco's 5-acre urban park featuring a walk-through waterfall enclosing a beautiful memorial for Martin Luther King Jr., a sculpture garden, and terrace cafes. The Yerba Buena **CHILDREN'S CENTER,** cleverly situated on the roof of the Moscone Convention Center, has plenty of diversions for little tykes, including a carousel, an ice-skating rink, a bowling alley, an arts and technology center, and a children's garden. For consumers of all ages, Sony's **METREON** Entertainment Complex has shops, restaurants, a 15-screen cinema, an IMAX theater, and a children's play center designed by author-illustrator Maurice Sendak.

Riptide-ridden and blustery **OCEAN BEACH** is a haven for seasoned surfers as well as for families, dog walkers, joggers, and lovers who enjoy the long, sandy beach located off the Great Highway on the far west side of the city. On warm days, sun

SAN FRANCISCO THREE-DAY TOUR

DAY ONE: The streets of San Francisco. Get your walking shoes on, because we're going to attempt to see the majority of San Francisco's most famous attractions in a single day. Start your day off in high style with a light breakfast of tea and scones at the **GARDEN COURT** within the **PALACE HOTEL**, one of the most elaborate and beautiful dining rooms ever built. Since you're in the neighborhood, it's time to do a little window shopping at **UNION SQUARE**—with a mandatory stop at **NEIMAN MARCUS** to chuckle at the absurd price tags and then a stroll through the gilded lobby of the **WESTIN ST. FRANCIS**. Next, hop on either the **POWELL-MASON** or **POWELL-HYDE CABLE CAR** to **FISHERMAN'S WHARF** and head to Pier 41 to catch the fantastic **ALCATRAZ ISLAND TOUR**; be sure to make a reservation far in advance and ask for the headphone tour. After the prison tour, walk west along the water near Fisherman's Wharf to the intersection of Jefferson and Taylor Streets and buy a fresh **DUNGENESS CRAB COCKTAIL** from the boisterous street vendors. Continue west along the wharf, making a few optional side trips to the **CANNERY**, **GHIRARDELLI SQUARE**, and the **SAN FRANCISCO MARITIME NATIONAL HISTORICAL PARK**. You're probably in need of a pickerupper by now, so head for the intersection of Beach and Hyde Streets to have a worldfamous **IRISH COFFEE** at the **BUENA VISTA CAFE**. If you don't mind the long but beautiful walk (if you do, take the number 28 or 29 bus, or hail a taxi), continue west along the shoreline, past **AQUATIC PARK**, along the **GOLDEN GATE PROMENADE** to the **GOLDEN GATE BRIDGE** for an at-least-once-in-your-lifetime stroll across the world's most famous bridge. OK, you've walked the bridge and now you're starving. Take a bus or taxi back to **NORTH BEACH** and head for **ENRICO'S**. It's not the best restaurant in the city, but it has one of the best San Francisco vibes, and live jazz nightly. Get a patio seat and order the burger and a rum-and-mint-infused *mojito* (very tasty). Afterward, cruise northwest up **COLUMBUS AVENUE**, soaking up the sights and smells and stopping in at classic San Francisco haunts such as **SPECS' TWELVE ADLER MUSEUM CAFE**, **VESUVIO**, and **CAFFE TRIESTE**. By now it's probably time for the second showing of **BEACH BLANKET BABYLON** at **CLUB FUGAZI**, San Francisco's best and longest-running comedic musical (buy your tickets well in advance). If you're still up for more after the show, head back to **UNION SQUARE** to the **SIR FRANCIS DRAKE HOTEL** and finish the night off in style with some drinking and dancing at the rooftop **HARRY DENTON'S STARLIGHT ROOM**. Now go back to your hotel, take two aspirin, and recover.

DAY TWO: From pastries to Postrio. There are still plenty more quintessential San Francisco sights to see. Even if you have a car, you might want to pick up a bus map and purchase a day pass from a MUNI driver because you'll be adventuring all over the city today. Start the day European-style with a pastery and cappuccino at **CAFÉ DE LA**

PRESSE (352 Grant Ave at Bush St; 415/398-2680). Next, spend a few hours wandering through San Francisco's world-famous **CHINATOWN**, exploring all the funky shops and back alleys; or take a guided **WOK WIZ CHINATOWN WALKING TOUR** (415/981-5588; www.wokwiz.com). This should work up enough of an appetite for lunch at **HOUSE OF NANKING** (919 Kearny St at Columbus Ave; 415/421-1429), another San Francisco landmark. Now that you're refueled on pot stickers and Chinese greens, break out the map and head for **COIT TOWER** on the top of Telegraph Hill for a breathtaking view of the city (and some serious stair-climbing). Catch your breath, reload your camera, and head west to the famous winding block of **LOMBARD STREET** between Hyde and Leavenworth Streets (car or no car, it's still worth a visit). Next, head to the fantastic **SAN FRANCISCO CABLE CAR BARN MUSEUM** to see how those amazing machines work in real time. Afterward, take the **POWELL-MASON** or **POWELL-HYDE CABLE CAR BACK** to **UNION SQUARE**. By now you're probably ready for some well-deserved R&R, so treat yourself to a blowout dinner at **FARALLON**, **POSTRIO,** or the **GRAND CAFE**, three of the best "big-city" restaurants in San Francisco. Order a triple espresso for dessert and walk to **BISCUITS & BLUES** for some toe-tappin' blues or, if you prefer a quieter evening, have a cocktail high above the city in the lounge of the **CARNELIAN ROOM**. Back to the hotel, more aspirin.

DAY THREE: Dim sum and then some. You've seen a lot of the big-name attractions; now it's time to do what you really came to San Francisco for—eat, drink, shop, and repeat. Sleep in late and have a very light breakfast because for lunch you'll be stuffing your face at **YANK SING**, the most popular dim sum restaurant in the city (you can't go to San Francisco and not have a dim sum experience). Since you're already downtown, spend an hour shopping at **EMBARCADERO CENTER** or walking around the **FINANCIAL DISTRICT** marveling at the numerous skyscrapers. Now take a bus, taxi, or long walk to San Francisco's SoMa district. Three must-stops here are the **SAN FRANCISCO MUSEUM OF MODERN ART** and the adjoining **MUSEUMSTORE** for great souvenirs and gifts, the beautiful **YERBA BUENA GARDENS**, and, especially if you have kids tagging along, the **METREON** megaplex entertainment center—all right next to each other. This should take you well into the evening, so now it's time for dinner. If you want small, intimate, and French, make a reservation right now for **FRINGALE**. If you prefer a high-energy, big city–style dining experience, then either walk or take a taxi to the foot of Mission Street to **BOULEVARD**, one of the city's most popular restaurants. When dinner is over, do something really romantic: hail a taxi and ask the driver to take you to the top of **TWIN PEAKS** for a breathtaking view of the city lights. Or, if you're in the mood to party, walk south along the Embarcadero to **PIER 23** for a stiff Long Island Iced Tea and dancing. Now *that's* a San Francisco vacation.

worshippers prefer to bask at **BAKER BEACH** (at the south end of Lincoln Blvd) while gazing at the stupendous view of the Golden Gate (as at most of the city's beaches, however, swimming is unsafe here). The east side of the beach is a popular gay hangout, where sunbathers wear nothing but sunscreen. Other scenic spots include **GLEN CANYON PARK** (Bosworth St and O'Shaughnessy Blvd), which has a playground; the lush **STERN GROVE** (Sloat Blvd at 19th Ave); and **LAKE MERCED** (off Harding Dr between Hwy 35 and Sloat Blvd, near the zoo).

NIGHTLIFE
BARS: San Franciscans need something to cut the chill of those long, foggy nights, so many head to North Beach, which has more than its fair share of popular watering holes, including the funky **SPECS** (Saroyan Alley off Columbus Ave; 415/421-411), an old Beat generation hangout; the charming but rough-around-the-edges **SAVOY TIVOLI** (1434 Grant Ave, between Union and Green Sts; 415/362-7023); and **TOSCA CAFE** (242 Columbus Ave, between Pacific Ave and Broadway; 415/986-9651), where locals hang out (and celebs hide in the back room) sipping the house specialty: coffeeless cappuccinos made with brandy, milk, and chocolate.

When the fog burns off and the weather heats up, grab a chair on the patio of **CAFE FLORE** (2298 Market St at Noe St; 415/621-8579) in the Castro District and order a glass of white wine or a latte. Or get the full array of spirits on the outdoor decks of such local favorites as the **RAMP** (855 China Basin St off 3rd St; 415/621-2378) and **PIER 23** (the Embarcadero between Broadway and Bay Sts; 415/362-5125).

For a more romantic retreat, make your toasts at the lounge of the **CARNELIAN ROOM** restaurant at the top of the 52-story Bank of America building (555 California St, between Kearny and Montgomery Sts; 415/433-7500), which offers a dizzying view of the city when the sky is clear; the plush **CROWN ROOM** in the Fairmont Hotel (950 Mason St at California St, 24th Fl; 415/772-5131); the scenic, glass-walled **TOP OF THE MARK** lounge in the Mark Hopkins Hotel (999 California St at Mason St; 415/392-3434), with dancing to live music after 8:30pm; or **EQUINOX,** the unique revolving rooftop lounge and restaurant at the Hyatt Regency (5 Embarcadero Center; 415/788-1234) that slowly spins in a circle, giving patrons a varying 360-degree panorama.

Union Square's best bustling bars are at **KULETO'S** restaurant (221 Powell St, between Geary and O'Farrell Sts; 415/397-7720) and the **COMPASS ROSE** in the Westin St. Francis Hotel (335 Powell St, between Post and Geary Sts; 415/397-7000), which boasts the largest martini in the city. For the best Irish coffee in town, the **BUENA VISTA** (2765 Hyde St at the corner of Beach St; 415/474-5044) takes top honors.

CLUBS: Great clubs abound in San Francisco, the city that never seems to sleep. Most of San Francisco's clubs present an ever-changing lineup of bands or recorded music, so call ahead for up-to-date recorded listings at each venue. The **BE-AT LINE** (415/626-4087) recorded hotline will also tell you where you can find the night's hot musical acts. Locals tend to pick up a copy of the free *San Francisco Bay Guardian* weekly newspaper (available at cafes and most major street corners) for the straight scoop on the city's wild and ever-changing club scene.

For live blues, jazz, and rock, **SLIM'S** (333 11th St, between Folsom and Harrison Sts; 415/522-0333) can't be beat. The famous **FILLMORE AUDITORIUM** (1805 Geary Blvd at Fillmore St; 415/346-6000) always books top talents, and **BRUNO'S** (2389 Mission St at 20th St; 415/648-7701) is boffo. If you just want to dance and don't care about what to wear or the color of your hair, show up after 10pm at **NICKIE'S BBQ** (460 Haight St, between Webster and Fillmore Sts; 415/621-6508). If dancin' among the teeming masses is more your thing, go to **TEN 15** (1015 Folsom St at 6th St; 415/431-1200). For a mix of live music, the trendy set kicks up its heels at **CAFE DU NORD** (2170 Market St, between Church and Sanchez Sts; 415/861-5016) and the rowdy **LAST DAY SALOON** (406 Clement St, between 5th and 6th Aves; 415/387-6343). If you want to shake, rattle, and roll with the high-fashion crowd, put on your best dancing shoes and go to **HARRY DENTON'S STARLIGHT ROOM** at the top of the Sir Francis Drake Hotel (450 Powell St, between Sutter and Post Sts; 415/392-7755).

To hear the sounds of the city's new bands, stroll Haight Street. Numerous venues line both sides of this famous strip, still populated by dazed youth, the homeless, and various eccentrics. Great cocktails and live swing bands will get you out of your seat and onto the dance floor at **CLUB DELUXE** (1511 Haight St at Ashbury St; 415/552-6949). Elsewhere, the ornate **GREAT AMERICAN MUSIC HALL** (859 O'Farrell St, between Polk and Larkin Sts; 415/885-0750) hosts hundreds of concerts a year, ranging from Motown, rock, and jazz to bluegrass, folk, and zydeco. **PARADISE LOUNGE** (11th and Folsom Sts; 415/861-6906; www.paradiseloungesf.com) offers a stellar lineup of all kinds of music. For a blast of the blues, go to the candlelit **BISCUITS & BLUES** (401 Mason St at Geary St; 415/292-2583). Jumpin' jazz joints include **JAZZ AT PEARL'S** (256 Columbus Ave just N of Broadway; 415/291-8255) and **BUTTERFLY** (1710 Mission St, at Duboce St; 415/864-5575; www.butterflysf.com).

SPORTS AND RECREATION

Bay Area sports buffs are proud of their **SAN FRANCISCO 49ERS** football team (www.sf49ers.com), which plays home games at **3COM PARK** (previously named Candlestick Park, and still called "the Stick" by Bay Area residents). The **SAN FRANCISCO GIANTS** (www.sfgiants.com) play at the home-run-friendly **SBC PARK** (formerly Pacific Bell Park) in China Basin (3rd and King Sts). It's of the "new" intimate ballpark genre, so there are good views of the field even from on high. Perhaps even more enticing, depending on the game, are views of the bay and downtown San Francisco. True to the foodie spirit of the city, regular ballpark fare is enhanced by concession stands and bistros serving pan-Latin and Asian cuisine as well as *bazurros*, salads rolled into fresh flat bread. If none of that appeals, restaurants are springing up all around the park. (Fans of the **OAKLAND A'S** and the **GOLDEN STATE WARRIORS** should turn to the Oakland section in the following pages.)

The **SAN FRANCISCO CHRONICLE MARATHON** (800/698-8699) is usually run in July, but if you'd rather race against two-legged Brillo boxes, centipedes, Snow White and the Seven Dwarfs, and a Whitney Houston clone in drag, sign up for the wild-and-wacky, 7½-mile **BAY TO BREAKERS** race and walk (415/359-2800), held in mid-May.

FESTIVALS

Every winter, the two-week-long **CHINESE NEW YEAR** (415/982-3000; www.chinese parade.com) celebration culminates explosively with an electrifying parade that winds through downtown, Union Square, and Chinatown. In summer and spring, **STREET FAIRS** that typify their neighborhoods pop up (from upscale Union Street to the still-hairy Haight). Japantown launches its **CHERRY BLOSSOM FESTIVAL** with a parade in April; the Mission District draws crowds with its **CINCO DE MAYO PARADE**; and the **SAN FRANCISCO LESBIAN, GAY, BISEXUAL, TRANSGENDER PRIDE CELE-BRATION PARADE** (415/864-3733, www.sfpride.org) attracts thousands of revelers on the last weekend of June.

All heads turn skyward when the U.S. Navy flaunts its amazing acrobatic flight team—the **BLUE ANGELS**—during **FLEET WEEK CELEBRATION** (near Fisherman's Wharf and Pier 39; 415/705-5500; www.fleetweek.com) in early October. Bands, boat rides, and a parade of ships and submarines on the bay round out the festivities.

RESTAURANTS AND LODGINGS BY NEIGHBORHOOD

The city's restaurant scene keeps food reviewers busy inventing new adjectives and diners tottering on the verge of gluttony.

North Beach

Long a neighborhood of immigrants, today North Beach is famous for its Italian food and sidewalk cafes. So charismatic is the area that few notice that there isn't even a beach here. There was one about a hundred years ago, until it was filled in to make room for factories and waterfront activity. Shopkeepers still stand on their stoops chatting in Italian with friends on the sidewalks while cafes and restaurants send up aromatic espresso, focaccia, and saucy pasta greetings. These days, China-town—just to the west—also exerts an influence on the community. **SAINTS PETER AND PAUL ROMAN CATHOLIC CHURCH**, the neighborhood's spiritual anchor, now offers services in English, Italian, and Chinese. Tai chi is as ubiquitous in **WASHINGTON SQUARE PARK** as sunbathing. Always a haven for bohemian society, North Beach residents also treasure a literary history that embraces Beat writers like Allen Ginsberg, Lawrence Ferlinghetti, and Jack Kerouac, and local bars and book-stores still celebrate them.

RESTAURANTS

L'Osteria del Forno / ★★☆

519 COLUMBUS AVE; 415/982-1124 Don't let the touristy Columbus Avenue location fool you: This small eight-table cafe attracts legions of locals who brave lousy parking for anything that comes out of the brick-lined oven, such as fan-tastic focaccia sandwiches, freshly made pizzas and pastas, kick-butt cipolline, and a wondrously succulent roast pork braised in milk (everyone's all-time favorite). Small baskets of warm focaccia bread and Italian wine served by the glass tide you over until the entree arrives. The kitchen is run by two charming Italian women who have successfully combined good food with a homey Italian-bistro atmosphere. Ergo, expect a warm welcome and authentic Italian food at low prices. Darn good espresso, too. *$–$$; cash only; lunch, dinner Wed–Mon; beer and wine; reservations not accepted; between Green and Union Sts.* &

Moose's / ★★

1652 STOCKTON ST; 415/989-7800 OR 800/28-MOOSE Every major city has a place where the prime movers-and-shakers hang out, and this city's is Moose's. Run by well-respected San Francisco restaurateur Ed Moose, the lively, ever-so-friendly establishment facing Washington Square in San Francisco's North Beach district is abuzz every night with lawyers, politicians, and local celebrities who come to sup and schmooze within the spacious, high-energy dining room. The exhibition kitchen offers a monthly changing menu of upscale American dishes that have garnered many a favorable review. The most recommended dishes are anything that's cooked in the wood-burning oven, particularly the famous tender grilled veal chop served with a potato galette or the center-cut pork loin chop served with creamy yellow grits. When in doubt, stick with the roasted chicken or the legendary Caesar salad and juicy Mooseburger combo, washed down with a glass of spicy zinfandel and followed by the butterscotch pot de crème. There's always a jazz combo playing nightly, and the adjacent bar—separated from the main dining room by a frosted-glass partition—stays busy long after the kitchen closes. Moose's hosts a popular weekend brunch as well. *$$–$$$; AE, CB, DC, JCB, MC, V; no checks; lunch Thurs–Fri, dinner every day, brunch Sat–Sun; full bar; reservations recommended; www.mooses.com; between Filbert and Union Sts.* &

Mo's Gourmet Burgers / ★★

1322 GRANT AVE; 415/788-3779 How do you make the perfect hamburger? Well if you're a grillmaster at Mo's Gourmet Burgers, you use only the best-quality center-cut chuck (properly aged, of course), ground fresh daily and hand-formed into big, thick patties. Next, you ignite the volcanic rock underneath the custom-made rotating grill, slap those puppies on, grill 'em exactly to the customer's liking, cover 'em with soft-yet-crusty buns, and serve with a host of accouterments such as fresh tomatoes, onions, lettuce, and house-made mayonnaise. Voilà! Mo's "Best Burger." Other variations include the BBQ, Bacon, Mushroom, Tex-Mex, California (with avocado), Western (with apple-smoked bacon), Belly Buster, and Alpine (with Swiss Gruyère cheese)—each accompanied with a side of French fries, black beans, Spanish rice, or cabbage. Steaks, pork chops, chicken, and a few vegetarian dishes are also on the menu, but it's the burgers that draw carnivores from all around the city to this North Beach bastion for beefaholics. Oh, and don't pass up the mocha shake, served thick and tall in a shimmering steel container. *$; MC, V; no checks; breakfast Sat–Sun, lunch, dinner every day; beer and wine; no reservations; between Vallejo and Green Sts.* &

Peña PachaMama / ★★★

1630 POWELL ST; 415/646-0018 The moment you walk past the neon-orange-clad figure of Kusillo at the door, you are folded into the musical family of Sukay. This Andean ensemble, which has been performing together for more than 20 years, opened Peña PachaMama (Mother Earth, in the ancient Quechua language) to create a center for Bolivian food and music in San Francisco. The Nuevo Latino cuisine—a fusion of traditional Bolivian dishes with the lighter, organic California sensibility—is the perfect opening act for the show; Friday and Saturday nights, the cozy restaurant gets even cozier, as the group plays an invigorating, nonamplified collection of traditional and Bolivian music on a stage next to the dining room. Pan pipes, flutes, guitarlike instruments, drums, masks, festival costumes, and one very large inverted-cone hat made of long feathers and ribbon—all spring around the room under the power of the lively band members. Peña PachaMama's engaging warmth gives it the feel of a neighbor's house, but the kitchen creates savory concoctions that your next-door neighbor might never imagine. Appetizers include Bolivian Rock Soup—a purée of corn tortillas, roasted peppers, tomatoes, and spices—and a wonderful green salad with a dab of ground nut and drizzle of mango-lime sauce. For the main course, Pacha Pollo is a succulent pan-seared chicken with Andean spices, a purée of Peruvian potatoes (they're purple!), and organic greens. Vegetarians can happily put themselves in chef James Canter's hands with the Chef's Vegetarian Selection. An evening here is a full night out on the town—food, culture, and entertainment—all for the very reasonable price of dinner. *$$; AE, MC, V; checks OK; dinner every day, brunch Sat–Sun; beer and wine; reservations recommended; www.penapachamama.com; between Union and Green Sts.* &

Rose Pistola / ★★★

532 COLUMBUS AVE; 415/399-0499 A star has been born in North Beach, and her name is Rose Pistola. The brainchild of Midas-like chef-restaurateur Reed Hearon (who launched the reputations of LuLu and Cafe Marimba), this sleek and sexy addition to the Columbus Avenue promenade is as pleasing to behold as it is to dine in (it's actually named after a popular octogenarian North Beach restaurateur). If you prefer to oversee the preparation of your meal, sit at the counter overlooking the grill; however, the family-style meals are best enjoyed in the large dining room's comfy booths (and tables on the sidewalk offer an alfresco option). The food is rustic Italian with a California flair (less fats, more flavors) inspired by the cuisine of Liguria: roast rabbit with fresh shell-bean ragout and polenta, pumpkin-filled ravioli, or roast pork chop with panzanella, an Italian bread salad infused with onions, basil, and tomatoes. The pastas, wood-fired pizzas, and antipasti are also very well prepared, but the fish dishes (particularly the whole roasted fish) are Hearon's specialty. A late-night menu is served until 1am on weekends. *$$–$$$; AE, DC, MC, V; no checks; lunch, dinner every day; full bar; reservations recommended; between Union and Green Sts.* &

LODGINGS

Hotel Bohème / ★★

444 COLUMBUS AVE; 415/433-9111 Hopelessly chic is perhaps the best way to describe the Hotel Bohème, one of the sexiest small hotels in the city and a favorite retreat of visiting writers and poets. Hovering two stories above Columbus Avenue—the Boulevard Saint-Michel of San Francisco streets—the Bohème artfully reflects North Beach's bohemian flair dating from the late 1950s and early '60s. The time trip starts with a gallery of moody black-and-white photographs lining the hallways and segues into the 16 guest rooms decorated in soothing shades of sage green, cantaloupe, lavender, and black. The rooms feature handmade light fixtures crafted from glazed collages of jazz sheet music, Ginsberg poetry, and old menus and headlines, as well as black iron beds with sheer canopies, European armoires, bistro tables, wicker chairs, and Picasso and Matisse prints. Modern amenities abound, including private baths, remote-control cable TVs, and telephones with modem jacks. A couple of minor caveats: most rooms are quite small, and those facing Columbus Avenue aren't kind to light sleepers (though views of the ever-bustling cafes and shops are entrancing). Otherwise, Hotel Bohème's engaging amalgamation of art, poetry, and hospitality will forever turn you away from America's cookie-cutter corporate hotels. *$$; AE, DC, DIS, MC, V; no checks; mail@hotelboheme.com; www.hotelboheme.com; between Vallejo and Green Sts.*

Chinatown

Chinatown has long been a blend of tacky and traditional. As early as 1893, *Baedeker's Guide to the United States* was advising travelers that "the Chinese Quarter is one of the most interesting and characteristic features of San Francisco and no one should leave the city without visiting it." Today, San Francisco has the second-largest community of Chinese in the United States (about 33 percent of the city's population is Chinese) and Chinatown spreads from Union Square toward North Beach and the Financial District. More than 80,000 people live in Chinatown, making it one of the most densely packed neighborhoods in the country—second only to Harlem. Stores crammed full of poorly made luggage and trinkets rub elbows with those selling elegant jade jewelry. The sidewalks are packed with tourists and locals alike, all moving at a snail's pace past lively fishmongers and produce markets bursting with durian, Asian pears, lychees, Chinese broccoli, and baby bok choy. Other markets specialize in packaged goods like dried shiitake mushrooms, jasmine tea, and crispy rice snacks. Stop by a shop and watch as a merchant measures out a gnarled ginseng root or haggles over the price of fresh armadillo meat. Though not on Stockton Street, another must-see is the **GOLDEN GATE FORTUNE COOKIES** factory (56 Ross Alley at Washington St; 415/781-3956), which sits amid cloistered sweatshops on Ross Alley. Said to be the birthplace of the fortune cookie, the factory is open to tourists.

RESTAURANTS

Great Eastern / ★★

649 JACKSON ST; 415/986-2500 If you love seafood and Chinese food and have an adventurous palate, have we got a restaurant for you. The venerable Great Eastern restaurant in Chinatown is renowned for its hard-to-find seafood, yanked fresh from the myriad huge fish tanks that line the back wall. If it swims, hops, slithers, or crawls, it's probably on the menu. Frogs, sea bass, soft-shell turtles, abalone, sea conch, steelhead, and Lord only knows what else are served sizzling on large, round, family-style tables. Check the neon board in back to peruse the day's catch, which is sold by the pound. Our advice: Unless you're savvy at translating an authentic Hong Kong menu, order one of the set dinners (the crab version is fantastic) or point to another table and say, "I want that." (Don't expect much help from the harried

SAGE ADVICE FOR PARKING IN SAN FRANCISCO

Driving around San Francisco presents a formidable challenge. The combination of hills, traffic, aggressive drivers, and a notable lack of parking will tax your driving skills and patience. To avoid runaway cars on steep hills, *curb your wheels!* Turn the tires *away* from the curb and toward the street when facing uphill, and *toward* the curb when facing downhill—otherwise your car may find itself on a surprise journey or, at best, slapped with a parking ticket. Also, tow-away zones and time limits proliferate, and parking regulations (particularly on street-cleaning days) are strictly enforced. The best way to chalk up tickets is to either ignore parking signs or assume any degree of flexibility. In fact, the city relies on parking citations to augment the government coffers (we're talking *millions* of dollars annually).

As for all those multicolored curbs, here's what the parking department is trying to tell you: A *red* curb means no stopping or parking ever, not even for a second; a

servers.) The crystal chandeliers and glimmering emerald-and-black furnishings make an attempt at elegance, but it's the gaudy fish tanks filled with edible creatures that capture everyone's eye. *$$; AE, MC, V; no checks; lunch, dinner every day; beer and wine; reservations recommended; between Kearny St and Grant Ave.* &

House of Nanking / ★★

919 KEARNY ST; 415/421-1429 This inconspicuous, greasy-looking little dive is one of San Francisco's worst-kept secrets. No joke: The dinnertime waiting line outside this wildly popular hole-in-the-wall starts at 5:30pm; by 6pm, you may face a 90-minute wait for a cramped, crowded, itsy-bitsy table with a plastic menu that lists only half of the best dishes served here. Lunchtime crowds make midday eating just as problematic. Here's a solution: Arrive for a late lunch or a very early dinner (between 2:30pm and 5pm) and walk right in. When owner-chef-head-waiter Peter Fang can give you his full attention, he'll be glad to apprise you of the day's unlisted specials: perhaps succulent chicken or duck dumplings, an exotic shrimp-and-green-onion pancake with peanut sauce, or tempura-like sesame-battered Nanking scallops in a spicy garlic sauce. Or just take a look at what the diners sandwiched around you are eating and point to what looks good (it's hard to go wrong in this place). Nanking, Fang's hometown, is at the inland end of the Shanghai Railroad, making it an exchange point for foods from Sichuan, Peking, Guangdong, and the local coast; Fang is famous for concocting wily revisions of many traditional dishes. While the food is usually very good and the prices are some of the most reasonable in the city, the service is downright terrible (you may not get your beer until 10 minutes after you've started eating), and it's the main reason this restaurant doesn't earn three stars. *$; cash only; lunch Mon–Sat, dinner every day; beer and wine; reservations not accepted; between Columbus Ave and Jackson St.* &

blue curb is reserved for drivers with disabilities who have a California-issued disabled plate or a placard; a *white* curb means there's a five-minute limit *if* the business it fronts is open; a *green* curb indicates a 10-minute limit during business hours; and *yellow* and *yellow-black* curbs are for commercial vehicles only during the day.

Ultimately, the best way to see the city is on your feet or using public transportation. Taxis are few and far between; locals even joke that there are only four or five cabs in the whole city—which doesn't seem so far-fetched when you try to find a free one on a Friday night. Instead of relying on taxis, buy a bus map and a day pass and take MUNI, the sometimes-unreliable-but-essential public transport system of buses, streetcars, and cable cars. For information about the MUNI system, including rates and routes, call 415/673-6864 or visit the MUNI Web site at www.sfmuni.com.

R&G Lounge / ★★

631-B KEARNY ST; 415/982-7877 Situated in limbo between the edge of Chinatown and the edge of the Financial District, the two-story R&G Lounge attracts a mixed crowd of tourists, business people, and local Chinese residents. The restaurant has a loyal following of diners who champion the fresh Cantonese seafood dishes and good prices. The main downstairs dining room has all the charm of a cafeteria, with glaring fluorescent lights and Formica tables. It's harder to get a table in the formal upstairs dining room, where the lighting is a little easier on the eyes. Each dining room offers the same menu, half in English, half in Chinese. But not every item is on the menus, so ask your server for recommendations, or order what we order every time: the very greasy but rich deep-fried salt and pepper crab, the tangy R & G Special Beef, the savory roast duck, the seafood in a clay pot, and for dessert the adzuki bean pudding. Most delicious. *$$; AE, DC, MC, V; no checks; lunch, dinner every day; full bar; reservations not accepted; at Clay St.*

Financial District/Downtown

More than 200,000 people make the pilgrimage to the Financial District's sea of glass and steel skyscrapers every Monday through Friday to work, work, work. They come from as far away as Sacramento and Sebastopol and arrive by bridge, BART, MUNI, ferry, train, bike, or on foot. From seven in the morning to six at night the streets are filled with people, cars, and buses, and the air is filled with a cacophony of horns, the clanging of construction equipment, and the tell-tale bells of the cable cars. Among the towering skyscrapers are two little-known downtown museums that celebrate the city's chaotic growth during the 19th century: the **WELLS FARGO HISTORY ROOM** (800/411-4932) at 420 Montgomery Street (at California St), which has hundreds of genuine vestiges from the company's Wild West days—pistols, posters, photographs, and mining equipment—and the **MUSEUM OF THE MONEY OF THE AMERICAN WEST** in the massive Bank of California building at

400 California Street (at Kearny St). Before you leave the Financial District, be sure to visit the lively **FARMERS MARKET** held in front of the Ferry Building on Saturday mornings. Local restaurants offer breakfast snacks and coffee, but the real stars here are the Northern California farmers and ranchers who fill the market with fabulous fresh produce, organic meats, local oysters, and olive oils.

RESTAURANTS

Aqua / ★★★

252 CALIFORNIA ST; 415/956-9662 When it opened in September 1991, Aqua was the first restaurant in the city to elevate the humble seafood house to a temple of haute cuisine. Huge towering flower arrangements punctuate its spacious high-ceilinged dining room, where slipcovers on the chairs change with the seasons and the large mirrors and dramatic lighting reflect a well-heeled Financial District crowd. You're bound to overhear a lot of oohing and aahing when the artfully presented dishes arrive. Though Aqua's chefs seem to change with the seasons, everyone's favorite dishes still remain on the menu (and for good reason). The ahi tartare, mixed table-side with pears, pine nuts, quail egg, and spices, is the best we've ever had. As is the melt-in-your-mouth glazed Chilean sea bass with mushrooms, scallops, shiso tortellini, and miso broth. Oh, what the heck—we'll have the grilled medallions of ahi tuna with foie gras in pinot sauce as well. If you're really feeling flush, shell out 80 bucks for a parfait of Russian caviar. *$$$–$$$$; AE, DC, DIS, MC, V; no checks; lunch Mon–Fri, dinner Mon–Sat; full bar; reservations recommended; between Battery and Front Sts.* &

Bix / ★★★

56 GOLD ST; 415/433-6300 Somehow the martini never seems to go out of fashion, and neither does Bix, one of the sexiest and most sophisticated supper clubs in the city (and consistently voted best bar in *San Francisco* magazine's readers' poll). It's modeled after a 1920s "New American" supper club, complete with massive silver columns, art deco–style lighting, and oodles of hand-carved Honduran mahogany (it's truly a beautiful room). The restaurant's raison d'être, however, is the top-notch martinis that really sneak up on you. If you manage to make it to a dinner table (the ones on the intimate mezzanine are the best), it's de rigueur to order the crispy chicken hash, a Bix best seller for more than a decade. Other popular choices include the crisp potato pancake with smoked salmon and caviar, classic steak tartare prepared table-side, day-boat scallops with black Périgord truffles pomme purée, and Beluga caviar on toast for a mere $118 a pop (c'mon, live a little). Finish the feast in high fashion with another Bix specialty, the bananas Foster. *$$–$$$; AE, CB, DC, DIS, MC, V; no checks; lunch Mon–Fri, dinner every day; full bar; reservations recommended; between Sansome and Montgomery Sts.* &

Boulevard / ★★★★

1 MISSION ST; 415/543-6084 Nancy Oakes, a self-taught chef whose cooking career began in 1977 at a scruffy San Francisco saloon, teamed up with nationally renowned restaurant designer Pat Kuleto in 1993 and created this glittering jewel that sits squarely in the center of the city's culinary crown.

Hailed as one of the nation's 10 best chefs by *Food & Wine* magazine, Oakes has come a long way from her days of dishing out pub grub to an audience of long-shoremen. These days her patrons tend to be well-heeled gastronomes who have been fans ever since she opened her first restaurant, L'Avenue, in 1988. At big, bustling Boulevard she serves hearty American-style cuisine with French and Italian influences. Before you indulge in her fabulous fare, feast your eyes on Kuleto's fantastic Parisian-inspired interior design, which he has dubbed "industrial art nouveau." After a spin through the revolving entrance door, you'll find yourself standing under an impressive domed brick ceiling offset by a dizzying array of details, including pressed-tin wainscoting, thousands of brightly colored mosaic tiles, and a sea of decorative ironwork that blends elegantly with the dark wood walls and chairs—it's all very romantic. This visual extravaganza is capped with a sweeping view of the Embarcadero and the Bay Bridge. On the seasonal menu you'll find a well-chosen mix of dishes. Oysters, giant beluga caviar, and fresh sautéed Sonoma foie gras served on an apple and fig strudel top the extensive appetizer list. Main courses might include a boneless rabbit stuffed with fresh chicken-and-sun-dried-tomato sausages, roasted to perfection in the wood-fired oven; asparagus risotto accompanied by roasted prawns and shiitake mushrooms filled with herbed goat cheese; and oven-roasted northern halibut resting on a large bed of wilted baby spinach sprinkled with chanterelle mushrooms and a side of buttery potato-chive fritters. For dessert, the ganache-mousse tart with fresh raspberries or pecan pie topped with vanilla ice cream and chocolate sauce push the sated diner over a blissful edge. *$$$; AE, DC, DIS, MC, V; no checks; lunch Mon–Fri, dinner every day; full bar; reservations recommended; www.kuleto.com/boulevard; at Steuart St.* &

Elisabeth Daniel / ★★☆

550 WASHINGTON ST; 415/397-6129 The first thing you notice about this refined restaurant is the quiet. While the streets outside remind you that you're in the heart of a city, Elisabeth Daniel pampers you with the illusion that the world begins and ends within a few feet of your brocade-draped table. The intimate room holds only 16 of them, spaced so that your neighbors' conversation is almost inaudible. Meals are a leisurely affair; for lunch, a three-course meal and a five-course tasting menu compete for your favor. Dinner comprises six tantalizing courses, with three options for each. With alternatives like peppercorn-encrusted venison with spinach and a crisp potato galette; herb-scented black bass on a bed of lobster risotto; and a ragout of mushrooms, herbed gnocchi, and peas, the only disappointment is that you can't try it all. Portions are sized appropriately for the number of courses, leaving room for dessert (chilled tropical fruit soup with passion fruit sorbet, perhaps?). The only caveat here is the service, which ranges from professional to pathetic. *$$$–$$$$; AE, DIS, MC, V; no checks; lunch Mon–Fri, dinner Mon–Sat; wine only; reservations recommended; between Sansome and Montgomery Sts.* &

Kokkari Estiatorio / ★★★☆

200 JACKSON ST; 415/981-0983 Kokkari's owners have done their best to invent a new category—upscale Greek with a California twist. And why not? It worked for

Italian food. Indeed, Kokkari (pronounced koh-CAR-ee) works on many levels, so much so that it's one of our favorites: it's a beautiful, lavishly decorated restaurant (a $5 million investment) with a ritzy country-house ambiance, thanks to the fire crackling in the oversize fireplace, the ornate rugs and plush chairs suitable for royalty, and the large windows and sun-bleached walls. This is a place to relax, soak up the atmosphere, and revel in executive chef Jean Alberti's California-style contemporary Hellenic cuisine. Besides the luxurious front dining room there's a second, larger dining room with exposed wood beams, an open kitchen, and cushy booths lining a walkway between the two dining areas. The usual Greek suspects play well here: avgolemono, the lemony egg, rice, and chicken soup; moussaka, the divinely spiced casserole of eggplant, lamb, and potato; and the quintessential Greek salad—no lettuce, just tomato, olive, red onion, and cucumber. Presentations are stunning, and the flavors are fresh and bright. For starters, don't miss the whole crispy smelt and the octopus salad. The grilled lamb chops with fried potatoes are classic, as are the whole grilled fish. Thick Greek coffee is made in a multiple-step process that involves an elaborate urn of sand (you can even ask the wait staff for a demo). And be sure to leave room for dessert, in particular the velvety *Kalithopita* chocolate cake, the luscious yogurt-granita duo (a dense chocolate cake with nougatine), or the rice pudding with a poached pear and black-currant sauce. *$$$; AE, DC, DIS, MC, V; no checks; lunch Mon–Fri, dinner Mon–Sat; full bar; reservations recommended; www.kokkari.com; at Front St.* &

One Market / ★★★

1 MARKET ST; 415/777-5577 If you enjoy dining in large, high-energy, big-city restaurants—we're talking seating for 220 among a sea of stylish banquettes, polished mahogany, and floor-to-ceiling windows—then you'll really like this one. When it first opened, the fare at One Market was surprisingly inconsistent, bringing both bravos and boos from major restaurant critics. But the ratings improved rapidly when rising-star executive chef Adrian Hoffman took over the open kitchen, presiding over an ever-changing menu that makes the most of California's abundance of farm-fresh products. Hoffman describes his cuisine as "rooted in the classics, but prepared in a contemporary style," which, translated into food, comes out as crispy, spiced soft-shell crab stew, sausage-corn griddle cakes in a sherry honey, whole-roasted snapper stuffed with sausage and fennel in an olive jus, mustard-crusted pork tenderloin in a port-plum glaze with fava bean bread pudding, slow-braised beef shoulder encircled by pearl onions, and similar hunger-inducing dishes. The 300-bottle American wine list is one of the city's best, and live jazz piano music filters through the cavernous dining room every evening. *$$$; AE, DC, MC, V; no checks; lunch Mon–Fri, dinner Mon–Sat; full bar; reservations recommended; at Steuart St.* &

Rubicon / ★★★

558 SACRAMENTO ST; 415/434-4100 Thanks to Rubicon's star-studded cast of financial backers—Robert De Niro, Robin Williams, and Francis Ford Coppola—this Financial District restaurant received so much advance publicity that San Franciscans were setting dates to eat here long before the seismic reinforcements were bolted to the floorboards. Chances are slim that you'll see any Tinseltown talent at the table next to you, but one bite of the foie gras with caramelized rhubarb compote and you couldn't care less who walks in. Other highlights on the monthly-changing menu might include butter-poached Alaskan halibut, seared scallops in a sweet onion puree, venison chops over barley, and roulades of steelhead under a crisp herbal crust. The excellent, extensive, and expensive wine list is literally one of the nation's best. Because of its Financial District location it does a brisk power lunch business, so for a more relaxed meal, opt for dinner. *$$$; AE, DC, MC, V; no checks; lunch Mon–Fri, dinner Mon–Sat; full bar; reservations recommended; between Sansome and Montgomery Sts.* &

The Slanted Door / ★★★

ONE FERRY BUILDING; 415/861-8032 OR 415/693-0996 Chef Charles Phan and his large extended family first opened their restaurant—specializing in country Vietnamese food—in a vacant space on a slightly run-down stretch of Valencia Street in 1995. But Phan's creative cooking and design talents (he's a former UC Berkeley architecture student) eventually made his humble restaurant a nationwide sensation, attracting celebrities like Mick Jagger and former President Clinton. He had no choice but to move it to a larger location in the newly renovated Ferry Building, a 150-seat bay-side restaurant at the northeast corner of the building. Phan's unique fare, based on his mother's recipes, attracts droves of diners for lunch and dinner. The menu changes weekly to reflect the market's offerings, but look for the favored spring rolls stuffed with fresh shrimp and pork, crab and asparagus soup, caramelized shrimp, curried chicken cooked with yams, "shaking" beef sautéed with onion and garlic, any of the terrific clay pot dishes, and, of course, Phan's special Vietnamese crepes. There's also an eclectic collection of teas, which come by the pot for $3 to $5. For dessert, the hands-down favorite is the all-American chocolate cake. Go figure. *$$; AE, DC, DIS, MC, V; no checks; lunch, dinner daily; full bar; reservations recommended; eat@slanteddoor.com; www.slanteddoor.com; at The Embarcadero and Market St.* &

Yank Sing / ★★★

101 SPEAR ST; 415/957-9300 Living on the edge of the Pacific Rim has its advantages. For example, the best dim sum in the United States is probably served in the Bay Area at places like Ton Kiang and Yank Sing. Numerous servers wander past your table with carts bearing steamer baskets, bowls, and tureens. If you want some, just nod. Yank Sing serves more than 90 varieties of dim sum, including such standards as pot stickers, spring rolls, plump shrimp dumplings (dee-licious!), stuffed crab claws, fried eggplant, and *bao* (steamed buns stuffed with aromatically seasoned minced meat). The barbecued chicken is a house specialty, although some find it too sweet; other favorites are Peking duck (served by the slice), minced squab in lettuce cups, and soft-shell crab. Make reservations or prepare to wait and wait and wait, especially for a weekend brunch. Takeout is available, too, and it costs much less. *$$; AE, DC, MC, V; no checks; lunch every day, brunch Sat–Sun; beer and wine; reservations recommended; www.yanksing.com; between Mission and Howard Sts (inside 1 Rincon Center).* &

LODGINGS

Mandarin Oriental / ★★★★

222 SANSOME ST; 415/276-9888 OR 800/622-0404 The rooms at the Mandarin Oriental—currently the only Mobil Five Star–rated hotel in the city—offer some of the most remarkable views in the city. Because it's perched high in the sky (on the top 11 floors of the 48-story 345 California Center Building, San Francisco's third-tallest skyscraper), you're guaranteed a bird's-eye view not only of the city but also of the entire Bay Area, including the Golden Gate Bridge, Alcatraz, and Coit Tower. The 158 guest rooms are comfortable and deceptively austere. Well hidden among the simple blond-wood furniture and fine Asian artwork are deluxe amenities: three two-line speakerphones with fax hookups, cordless phones, Internet access, remote-control televisions with access to videos and DVDs, fully stocked minibars, binoculars, and CD players, as well as jumbo marble bathrooms with stall showers and extra-deep soaking tubs. (If you request a "Signature" room, you can even admire the city's skyline from floor-to-ceiling windows next to the tubs.) Once settled in your room, you'll be treated to complimentary jasmine tea service and your choice of either Thai silk or terry-cloth slippers. Contrary to the policy of many other hotels, the room rates at the Mandarin don't vary according to scenery, so request one of the corner rooms (numbers ending with 6 or 11) or the "Signature" rooms (04 or 14) for the best views. Additional perks include access to numerous business services, valet parking, a continental breakfast and afternoon tea served in the lounge, complimentary shoeshines, concierge, 24-hour room service, and a state-of-the-art fitness center. The hotel's award-winning restaurant, Silks, may be the Maytag repairman of luxury restaurants: it's all gussied up and anxious to serve, but a tad lonely and under appreciated. Regardless, chances are you won't be disappointed if you choose to dine here, but bring plenty of money. *$$$–$$$$; AE, DC, DIS, MC, V; checks OK (for lodgings only); www.mandarinoriental.com; between Pine and California Sts.* &

Omni San Francisco Hotel / ★★★

500 CALIFORNIA ST; 415/677-9494 OR 800/788-6664 After a $100 million renovation, the city's historic 1926 Financial Center Building now houses San Francisco's newest luxury hotel, replete with twinkling crystal chandeliers and an elaborate iron staircase in the lobby that evokes an Old World ambiance. There are just two room types in the 17-story hotel, each featuring classic 1920s decor with mahogany and cherry wood furniture, warm sunset tones, and green-and-gold color schemes. All the standard luxuries are here: in-room high-speed Internet access, safes, minibars, and 27-inch televisions, as well as a fitness center and complimentary luxury car transportation within the downtown area. The "Get Fit" guest rooms are outfitted with portable treadmills, "Get Fit Kits" (including a yoga mat and dumbbells), and even healthy snacks in the refreshment centers—all for just a few extra dollars per day. Sliding doors lead to gleaming marble baths with green and black Chinese granite basins, plush robes, and expensive toiletries you'll want to sneak into your suitcase. The best rooms are the corner suites; each has six huge windows, a large living room, and a king-size bed. Major financial deals are cut over

28-ounce slabs of beef at Bob's Steak and Chop House just off the lobby, and the adjoining bar has been packed with lively locals since the day it opened. *$$$$; AE, DC, DIS, MC, V; checks OK; www.omnisanfrancisco.com; at Montgomery St.* &

The Palace Hotel / ★★★

2 NEW MONTGOMERY ST; 415/512-1111 OR 800/325-3535 (RESERVATIONS ONLY) Reminiscent of more romantic times, this opulent hotel built in 1875 has housed such luminaries as Thomas Edison, D. H. Lawrence, Amelia Earhart, and Winston Churchill, as well as 10 American presidents and numerous aristocrats and royalty from around the world. Hoping to attract a similarly high-class clientele in the future, the management closed the Palace in 1989 for 27 months and poured $170 million into restoring it to its original splendor. And splendid it is. The downstairs decor is truly breathtaking, from the multiple sparkling Austrian-crystal chandeliers, the double row of white Italian marble Ionic columns, and the 80,000-pane stained-glass dome of the Garden Court, to the three grand ballrooms and early 19th-century French tapestry gracing the walls. Unfortunately, all this impressive glitz comes to a screeching halt when you open the door to one of the 551 guest rooms. Although comfortable and attractive, the rooms are more akin to gussied-up generic hotel rooms than to any palace chamber. However, this place does offer all the perks you'd look for in a luxury hotel, including a concierge, 24-hour room service, valet parking, and an elaborate business center, plus a new, palm-embellished health club with an exercise room, a co-ed sauna, a whirlpool, and a stunning white-tiled lap pool capped by a dome of clear glass. Restaurants include the Garden Court, famous for its elaborate breakfast buffet and elegant afternoon tea; Kyo-ya, a rather austere Japanese dining room serving the best (and most expensive) sushi and sashimi in town; and the Pied Piper Bar, which is dominated by a stunning, $2.5 million, 1909 Maxfield Parrish painting of the Pied Piper of Hamelin leading a band of 27 children. Even if you don't have the resources to recline or dine here, this place, like most palaces, is worth a self-guided tour. *$$$$; AE, DC, DIS, MC, V; checks OK (for lodgings only); www.sheraton.com; at Market St.* &

Union Square

For shopping fanatics, this is the heart of it all, the sine qua non for credit card aerobics. But don't despair if Saks Fifth Avenue, Neiman Marcus, Macy's, Gump's, and Tiffany & Co. are not on your top-10 list of vacation destinations. The **THEATER DISTRICT** is right around the corner, and a "French Quarter" hides on Bush Street between Grant and Montgomery Streets, and down tiny Claude and Belden Lanes. Dining options range from relaxed bistros to some of the most elegant restaurants in town. The newly renovated square is named for the fiery pro-Union rallies that took place here during the Civil War; today it provides plenty of free space so you can take a break from power shopping, have snack at the corner cafe, and watch the street performers. The number and quality of the hotels in this area make it the ideal launching pad for excursions into other neighborhoods.

SAN FRANCISCO'S SUNDAY MORNING SENSATION

Ever since the Reverend Cecil Williams took the helm of the **GLIDE MEMORIAL CHURCH** in 1963, San Franciscans of every color, tax bracket, and lifestyle have joined together on Sunday mornings to celebrate life in one of the most high-energy, roof-raising renditions you'll ever witness. As Glide's new reverend, the first thing Williams did was remove all overt religious icons in order to establish a nondenominational setting. He then assembled a 120-member choir accompanied by a blues-style band and opened the doors to every type of person—poor, famous, homeless, wealthy, crazy—of every religion and raised their spirits with uplifting sermons and songs about hope and love.

The Reverend Williams's efforts to help the homeless and poor of the Tenderloin district (one of the city's most poverty-stricken neighborhoods) have attracted nationwide attention and inspired regular appearances by San Francisco local Sharon Stone. Other luminaries either on the stage or in the audience have included Bobby McFerrin, Robin Williams, Maya Angelou, Oprah Winfrey, and Bill Clinton. Even if you've never set foot in a church before, go: you'll be glad you did. Just be sure to arrive a little early to get a first-floor seat (the balcony's view is limited). The church is located at 330 Ellis Street at Taylor Street, west of Union Square (415/771-6300; www.glide.org). Services take place every Sunday at 9am and 11am.

RESTAURANTS

Farallon / ★★★

450 POST ST; 415/956-6969 Diving into the undersea world of chef Mark Franz (of Stars restaurant fame) and master designer Pat Kuleto can leave one breathless. In 1997, the two co-owners opened a dazzling $4 million, 160-seat restaurant offering seafood dishes that are as innovative as Kuleto's elegant aquatic-themed decor. Giant hand-blown jellyfish chandeliers with glowing tentacles seemingly float beneath a sea-blue ceiling in the Jelly Bar cocktail lounge, where sculpted strands of kelp climb up illuminated pillars. Upstairs, the marine motif continues with huge sea-urchin chandeliers dangling from the arched, painted mosaic ceiling—all a dramatic but enchanting stage for Franz's excellent coastal cuisine. For starters, consider delectable asparagus bisque with cardamom cream; truffled mashed potatoes with crab and salmon caviar artfully stuffed into a real sea-urchin shell; Maine lobster and wild-mushroom gnocchi with a leek, tarragon, and champagne lobster sauce; or giant tiger prawns—the best thing on the menu. Entrees change daily and might include ginger-steamed salmon and sea-scallop pillows with a prawn mousse or sautéed gulf prawns with potato risotto, English peas, pearl onions, and truffle portobello coulis. While Franz's forte is fish, he also has a flair for meat dishes such as a juicy grilled filet of beef served with a portobello mushroom and potato galette, haricot verts, and black truffle aioli. The 300-item wine list fits in swimmingly with the menu (though prices are high), and about two dozen wines are available by the glass. The attentive staff helps make Farallon a deep-sea dine to remember. *$$$; AE, DC, DIS, MC, V; no checks; lunch Tues-Sat, dinner every day; full bar; reservations recommended; www.farallon.com; between Mason and Powell Sts.* &

Le Colonial / ★★☆

20 COSMO PL; 415/931-3600 The once-popular Trader Vic's restaurant thrived for many years on this tiny, tucked-away side street near the Tenderloin and Union Square. Today this hideaway is the home of Le Colonial, which serves excellent Vietnamese food that is much more expensive than what you'll find at the usual Asian restaurants around town. But this is no typical Asian restaurant: it's a place to be seen, dress up, and pose along with the other pretty people who arrive here after work to shmooze and flirt. Fashioned after a 1920s Vietnamese plantation, complete with wicker, fans, and rich wood, Le Colonial offers a blend of French and Vietnamese cooking. Upstairs in the lounge, relax with a drink on the cozy couches and choose from an extensive list of appetizers. The dinner menu also offers a wide selection, and most dishes are a tantalizing blend of sweet, spicy, sour, and aromatic flavors. Dishes can be ordered individually as entrees or served family-style. Some good choices include the steamed sea bass wrapped in a banana leaf (their best dish), coconut curry prawns with mango and eggplant; wok-seared beef tenderloin with watercress and onion salad; cold beef salad with tender chunks marinated in lime; ginger roast duck; and the crispy Vietnamese spring rolls. *$$$; AE, DC, MC, V; no checks; dinner every day; full bar; reservations recommended; off Taylor St, between Post and Sutter Sts.* &

Postrio / ★★★

545 POST ST; 415/776-7825 Owned by Southern California superstar chef Wolfgang Puck and the Kimpton Hotel & Restaurant Group, Postrio is a splashy slice of Hollywood set in the heart of San Francisco, with superglitzy decor à la restaurant designer Pat Kuleto, delightful culinary combinations, and the perpetual hope of catching sight of some celeb at the next table. One enters through a spiffy street-level bar that serves tapas and little Puckish pizzas to the unreserving; from there a grand sculpted-iron and copper staircase—on which everybody can at least play the star role—descends dramatically into a crowded, pink-lighted dining room ringed with paintings and plants. It's a lovely, sophisticated setting for some terrific food, prepared by chefs Mitchell and Steven Rosenthal, who proved themselves capable successors when founding chefs Anne and David Gingrass jumped ship to open Hawthorne Lane in '95. Working closely with Puck, the brothers Rosenthal have crafted an exciting hybrid of California-Asian-Mediterranean cuisine that includes such creations as grilled quail accompanied by spinach and a soft egg ravioli with port wine glaze; sautéed salmon with plum glaze, wasabi mashed potatoes, and miso vinaigrette; Chinese duck with mango sauce; and roasted leg of lamb with garlic potato purée and niçoise olives. Tempting choices, indeed, but the dessert menu has its own array of showstoppers—from the potato-pecan pie to the caramel pear tart with Grand Marnier crème fraîche. The wine list is excellent, the service professional, and reservations are essential—make them several weeks in advance. *$$$;*

AE, DC, DIS, MC, V; no checks; dinner every day; full bar; reservations recommended; www.postrio.com; between Mason and Taylor Sts, in the Prescott Hotel. &

LODGINGS

Campton Place Hotel / ★★★☆

340 STOCKTON ST; 415/781-5555 OR 800/235-4300 Almost as soon as Campton Place reopened after an extensive restoration in 1983, its posh surroundings, stunning objets d'art, superlative service, and elegant accommodations began swaying the patrons of the carriage trade away from traditional San Francisco hotels. The lobby, reminiscent of a gallery with its domed ceiling, miles of marble, crystal chandeliers, and striking Asian art, alone is worth the price of admission. The 110 guest rooms are very comfortable, and the custom-built chairs and handsome desks help create a pervasive air of luxury. The limestone bathrooms are equipped with telephones, knitted bathrobes, hair dryers, and French-milled soaps. For the best views, ask for one of the larger deluxe corner rooms on the upper floors. The view from room 1501, which overlooks Union Square, is particularly stunning. For help with your laundry, dry cleaning, shoeshining, or even baby-sitting, just pick up the phone and you'll be accommodated, tout de suite. The concierge will make any and all of your arrangements (a reservation for the hotel's limo, perhaps?), and 24-hour room service will deliver whatever you're craving from the menu at the well-regarded Campton Place restaurant, one of the city's prettiest—and priciest—dining establishments. *$$$–$$$$; AE, DC, MC, V; checks OK (for lodgings only); reserve@campton.com; www.camptonplace.com; between Fillmore and Steiner Sts.* &

Hotel Diva / ★★

440 GEARY ST; 415/885-0200 OR 800/553-1900 Ever since it opened in 1985, Hotel Diva has been the prima donna of San Francisco's modern hotels, winning Best Hotel Design from *Interiors* magazine for its suave, ultramodern design. The hotel's facade is still a veritable work of art, a fashionable fusion of cement, steel, and glass that radiates the aura of a posh 1920s ocean liner. But the high style doesn't stop there: even the 115 guest rooms are works of art, decorated with cobalt blue carpets, sculptured steel furnishings and fireplaces, and haute-design metal headboards fashioned after ocean waves. Standard luxury amenities in each room include invigorating bath products, a remote-control television with interactive multimedia and VCR, designer bathrobes, CD player, two telephones with extra-long cords and voice mail, and global Internet data ports. Guest services include a complimentary breakfast of fresh fruit, breads, yogurt, coffee, and orange juice delivered to your boudoir, as well as room service, a concierge, a 24-hour cardio workout room, four Internet-access guest lounges, and a business center offering free use of computers, software, and a laser printer. Best of all, the Diva is in a prime location, just around the corner from Union Square. Insider tips: Reserve one of the rooms ending in "09," which have extra-large bathrooms with vanity mirrors and makeup tables, and be sure to ask the concierge for Diva's "SF Hot Spots" checklist. *$$$; AE, DC, DIS, MC, V; checks OK; www.hoteldiva.com; between Mason and Taylor Sts.* &

Hotel Monaco / ★★★½

501 GEARY ST; 415/292-0100 OR 800/214-4220 "Wow!" is a common exclamation among first-time guests at Hotel Monaco, one of the hottest hotels in a city brimming with top-notch accommodations. After a $24 million renovation, Monaco reopened in June 1995 and has received nothing but kudos for its sumptuous, stunning decor. Expect a melding of modern European fashion with flourishes of the American Beaux Arts era—the trademark of award-winning designer Cheryl Rowley, who envisioned the 201-room hotel as a "great ship traveling to the farthest reaches of the world, collecting exotic, precious treasures and antiquities." Hence the guest rooms replete with canopy beds, Chinese-inspired armoires, bamboo writing desks, old-fashioned decorative luggage, and a profusion of bold stripes and vibrant colors. The entire hotel is truly a feast for the eyes, particularly the Grand Cafe with its 30-foot ceilings, cascading chandeliers, plethora of stately columns, and many art nouveau frills—all vestiges of its former incarnation as the hotel's grand ballroom. A chic see-and-be-seen crowd typically fills the Grand Cafe's impressive dining room, noshing on trendy California-French cuisine. And of course, there are the requisite hotel toys (health club, steam room, whirlpool spa, sauna), services (massages, manicures, valet parking, business and room service), and complimentary perks (newspaper delivery, morning coffee, afternoon tea and cookies, evening wine reception). You'll like the location as well: in the heart of San Francisco's Theater District, a mere two blocks from Union Square and the cable cars. *$$$–$$$$; AE, DC, DIS, MC, V; no checks; www.monaco-sf.com; at Taylor St.* &

Hotel Rex / ★★★

562 SUTTER ST; 415/433-4434 OR 800/433-4434 The Joie de Vivre hotel company has created another winner with the 94-room Hotel Rex, yet another addition to its cadre of fashionable yet affordable accommodations. The hotel's sophisticated and sensuous lobby lounge is cleverly modeled after a 1920s library, meant to create a stylish sanctuary for San Francisco's arts and literary community (hence the adjoining antiquarian bookstore). To keep costs—and rates—down, many of the site's former Orchard Hotel's imported furnishings have been retained, which adds a bit of authenticity to the European boutique hotel–style ambiance. All of the spacious (for a downtown hotel) guest rooms feature CD players, two-line telephones with voice mail and data port, and electronic key-card systems. The rooms in the back are quieter and overlook a tranquil, shaded courtyard. Perks include room service, same-day laundry/dry cleaning, complimentary newspaper, an evening wine hour, concierge service, and morning car service to the Financial District. The hotel is in a key location as well, within walking distance of Union Square and surrounded by first-rate galleries, theaters, and restaurants. *$$$; AE, DC, MC, V; no checks; www.thehotelrex.com; between Powell and Mason Sts.* &

Hotel Triton / ★★★

342 GRANT AVE; 415/394-0500 OR 800/433-6611 The Hotel Triton has been described as modern, whimsical, sophisticated, chic, vogue, neo-baroque, ultrahip, and retro-futuristic—but words just don't do justice to this unique hostelry-cum-art-gallery that you'll simply have to see to appreciate. The entire hotel, from the bellhop's inverted pyramid–shaped podium to the iridescent throw pillows on the beds and the ashtrays ringed with faux pearls, is the original work of four imaginative (some might say wacky) San Francisco artisans. For a preview of what's behind the bedroom doors, peek into the lobby, where you'll see curvaceous chairs shimmering in gold silk taffeta; an imposing duo of floor-to-ceiling pillars sheathed in teal, purple, and gold leaf; and a pastel mural portraying mythic images of sea life, triton shells, and human figures—all that's missing are Dorothy, Toto, and the ruby slippers. Add to this visual extravaganza all the amenities you'd find in any luxury hotel, including a concierge, valet parking (essential in this part of town), room service, complimentary wine and coffee, business and limousine services, and even a fitness center. The 140 guest rooms and designer suites (designed by such celebs as Carlos Santana, Graham Nash, and the late Jerry Garcia) continue the modern wonderland theme: walls are splashed with giant, hand-painted yellow and blue diamonds, king-size beds feature navy-and-khaki-striped camelback headboards, and armoires that hide remote-control TVs are topped with golden crowns. The treehugger in all of us can embrace the EcoFloor, the Triton's environmentally conscious seventh floor where almost everything is made from recycled, biodegradable, or organically grown materials, and the air and water are passed through fancy filtration systems. Heck, the Triton is so utterly hip, even the elevator swings to Thelonious Monk. *$$$; AE, DC, DIS, MC, V; checks OK; www.hoteltriton.com; at Bush St.* &

The Prescott Hotel / ★★★

545 POST ST; 415/563-0303 OR 800/283-7322 Opened in 1989 by the late San Francisco hotel magnate Bill Kimpton, the Prescott has put pressure on Union Square's neighboring luxury hotels by offering first-rate accommodations at a fairly reasonable price. This, combined with dining privileges at one of the city's most popular restaurants (the adjoining Postrio; see review, above), superlative service from an intelligent, youthful staff, and a prime location in the heart of San Francisco, places the Prescott at the top of the Union Square hotel list. The rooms, decorated with custom-made cherry-wood furnishings, black granite–topped nightstands and dressers, and silk wallpaper, have rich color schemes of hunter green, deep purple, cerise, taupe, and gold. The Prescott offers 166 rooms, including numerous suites and a wildly posh penthouse complete with a grand piano, a rooftop Jacuzzi, a formal dining room, and twin fireplaces. For a few additional fun-tickets you can gain "Club Concierge Level" status, which grants you access to a plush lounge (complete with a complimentary premium bar), an hors d'oeuvres reception, and a continental breakfast, as well as a host of other privileges—not a bad investment for 30 bones. Standard perks include limo service to the Financial District, overnight shoeshine, valet parking, laundry service, a daily newspaper delivered to your room, and access to the adjacent and newly renovated fitness facility. *$$$; AE, DC, DIS, MC, V; checks OK (for lodgings only); www.prescotthotel.com; between Mason and Taylor Sts.* &

Savoy Hotel / ★★

580 GEARY ST; 415/441-2700 OR 800/227-4223 Originally built in 1913 for the Panama-Pacific International Exposition, this seven-story hotel is a posh French country–style inn with a gorgeous facade of richly veined black marble, beveled glass, mahogany, and polished brass. It's ideally located in the center of the Theater District, just 2½ blocks from Union Square. The 83 guest rooms and suites are small but beautifully appointed, with reams of toile de Jouy fabrics, heavy French cotton bedspreads, imported Provençal furnishings, plump feather beds, goose-down pillows, two-line telephones with modem jacks, and minibars. A few of the suites come with Jacuzzi tubs. The most tranquil rooms are on the northeast corner (farthest from the traffic noise), facing a rear courtyard. Guests are nurtured with a continental breakfast and an afternoon tea and sherry; a full breakfast is also available. Additional amenities include an overnight shoeshine and room service from the hotel's popular Brasserie Savoy. This restaurant is a replica of an authentic French brasserie, right down to the zinc bar, black-and-white marble floors, comfy banquettes, woven-leather chairs, and a staff clad in long, starched white aprons. Its air of casual sophistication, reasonable prices, and generally very good food—foie gras, filet mignon with truffle sauce, crispy sweetbreads, duck confit—make it a reliable bet, especially for a meal before show time (ask about the well-priced three-course dinner special offered from 5pm to 8pm daily). *$$; AE, DC, DIS, MC, V; no checks; www.thesavoyhotel.com; between Taylor and Jones Sts.* &

Serrano Hotel / ★★★

405 TAYLOR ST; 415/885-2500 OR 877/294-9709 The staff at the Serrano Hotel like to play games. Literally. Guests arriving at this Theater District hotel sense the tongue-in-cheek fun immediately when invited to play "Check-in Challenge" and go up against the house in blackjack for free upgrades and other perks. This theme is carried throughout the hotel, from the residential-style lobby featuring ancient Egyptian games in front of the fireplace to the mini board games for sale in the honor bars. A 1999 restoration has completely transformed this 1920s historic landmark; the 236 guest rooms are decorated in a sophisticated yet whimsical style with an eclectic charm, including intricately painted ceiling beams and Moroccan-style carvings. If you're a theater buff, ask for the ACT Suite—the nearby American Conservatory Theater regularly updates its decor, and the headboard in the master suite is a replica of their stage. Guests are invited to an evening wine hour, and the hotel even brings in a chair masseuse and tarot card reader. The hotel restaurant, Ponzu, is a sexy, curvaceous velvet-draped space with huge glass aquariums and dazzling lighting. The menu is best described as Asian-fusion comfort food (think hoisin sauce sticky ribs), and the bar offers an exotic drink menu. The location is an easy 2½-block walk to Union Square and the Powell Street cable-car line. *$$$$; AE, DC, DIS, MC, V; no checks; www.serranohotel.com; at O'Farrell St.* &

Sir Francis Drake Hotel / ★★★

450 POWELL ST; 415/392-7755 OR 800/227-5480 While nowhere near as resplendent as the nearby Westin St. Francis (see review, below), the 21-story Sir Francis Drake gives us ordinary folks a reasonably priced opportunity to stay in one of San

Francisco's grande dames. A $5 million renovation in 1999 spruced up the 417 rooms a bit, but there's still a little wear around the edges. No matter—it's the experience of listening to the sounds of Union Square wafting through your window that makes staying here an enjoyable experience. Then there's Tom Sweeny, the legendary and ever-jovial Beefeater doorman who has graced more snapshots than any other San Franciscan; the top-floor Harry Denton's Starlight Room, one of the most fun and fashionable cocktail-dance lounges in the city; Scala's Bistro on the lower level, an upscale yet affordable restaurant we guarantee you'll enjoy; and all the requisite big-hotel services such as room service, newspaper delivery, business services, babysitting, in-room massage, and laundry service. So considering that you can get a standard room here for about half the price of rooms at the St. Francis—and with far better eating, drinking, and dancing—the Drake is definitely worth looking into. *$$$–$$$$; AE, DC, DIS, MC, V; no checks; www.sirfrancisdrake.com; at Sutter St.* &

Westin St. Francis / ★★★½

335 POWELL ST; 415/397-7000 OR 800/WESTIN-1 San Francisco's first world-class hotel still attracts a legion of admirers; most of them can't afford the steep room rates but are content with lounging in the lobby just to soak up the heady, majestic aura of this historic hotel. The who's who of the world have all checked in at one time or another, including Queen Elizabeth II, Mother Teresa, Emperor Hirohito, the Shah of Iran, King Juan Carlos of Spain, and all the U.S. presidents since Taft. Just strolling through the vast, ornate lobby with its century-old hand-carved redwood paneling is a treat in itself. To keep up with the times, the adjacent 32-story Tower was added in 1972, which doubled the capacity (1,194 guest rooms total) and provided the requisite banquet and conference centers. The older rooms of the main building vary in size, but have more Old World charm than the newer rooms. The newly renovated Tower rooms, however, have better views of the city from the 18th floor and above. In 1999 the Westin dumped a staggering $60 million into renovations, replacing the furniture, carpeting, and bedding in every guest room, as well as enhancing the lobby and restoring the facade. A $2 million fitness center has been added, too. And if there's one thing you must do while visiting San Francisco, it's high tea (3pm–5pm) at the hotel's Compass Rose cafe and lounge, one of San Francisco's most enduring and pleasurable traditions. *$$$$; AE, DC, DIS, JCB, MC, V; checks OK; www.westin.com; between Geary and Post Sts.* &

Nob Hill

The staggering wealth of railroad and silver barons had a significant impact on the history and development of San Francisco. The Big Four, as they were called, left their personal marks all over the city in the last half of the 1800s, particularly on the city peak called Nob Hill, where the city's first cable car started operating in 1873. Sacramento power brokers Leland Stanford, Collis Huntington, Charles Crocker, and Mark Hopkins joined forces to create the Central Pacific Railroad, which connected the rest of the country to California. These "nabobs" (Urdu for "very rich men") amassed an amazing fortune in the bustling days before the earthquake and fire, and they sank their money into ostentatious mansions high atop Nob Hill. Only the **FLOOD MANSION** (1000 California St at Mason St), now the exclusive Pacific

Union Club, remains. Although the original architecture was destroyed in 1906, the summit of Nob Hill still reflects that golden era of unbridled wealth. The Fairmont, Mark Hopkins, Stanford Court, and Huntington hotels are bastions of antique opulence. The manicured lawns, sandbox, swings, and central Tortoise Fountain attract tourists and locals alike to **HUNTINGTON PARK,** donated to the city in 1915 by the widow of Collis Huntington. **GRACE CATHEDRAL'S** 20th-century Gothic architecture creates an impressive profile on the corner of California and Taylor Streets. With its popular meditative labyrinth, stained-glass windows, and formidable bronze doors, this house of worship offers something for even the most ardent atheist.

RESTAURANTS

The Dining Room at the Ritz-Carlton / ★★★★

600 STOCKTON ST; 415/773-6198 For those special occasions (or when the other person is buying), few restaurants go the extra distance to spoil you rotten like the Dining Room at the Ritz-Carlton hotel. No less than five tuxedoed wait staff are at your beck and call, surreptitiously attending to your needs as you bask in your evening of opulence. The setting is, as one would expect, sumptuous and regal, dripping with Old World charm. Cushy high-backed chairs, rich brocade, crystal chandeliers, elegant table settings, and live harp music provide a definite air of formality (though the servers will lighten up if you prod them with humor). Chef Sylvain Portay (a Frenchman from the famed Le Cirque restaurant in New York) continues the Ritz-Carlton tradition of using only the finest, freshest ingredients from around the world, though he brings a more modern style of French cooking to the table than previous chefs. The seasonal menu is strictly prix fixe, offering a choice of three-, four-, or five-course dinners; optional wine pairings per course—chosen from one of most extensive wine lists in the country—are offered for a hefty additional fee. The menu changes seasonally, offering such decadent dishes as the frothy crayfish bisque, risotto with butternut squash and roasted squab, sweetbreads with scallions and bok choy, a juicy roasted rack of Colorado lamb, and grilled John Dory (a New Zealand fish) spiked with basil and olives. For the finale, indulge in the ultimate French dessert: dark chocolate soufflé with bitter almond ice cream. The Dining Room also features a unique rolling cheese cart, laden with at least two dozen individually ripened cheeses. *$$$–$$$$; AE, DC, DIS, MC, V; no checks; dinner Mon–Sat; full bar; reservations required; www.ritzcarlton.com; at California St.* &

Fleur de Lys / ★★★

777 SUTTER ST; 415/673-7779 Fleur de Lys is definitely a Grand Occasion restaurant, with fantastic food, formal service, breathtaking decor, and a superb wine list. Trained by such French superstars as Paul Bocuse and Roger Vergé, chef and co-owner Hubert Keller displays a formidable technique—beautifully prepared ingredients accompanied by surprising garnishes and subtle sauces—and many of his contemporary French dishes are near-miracles. And even though he was President Clinton's first guest chef at the White House, unlike a lot of celebrity chefs, Keller's probably in the kitchen preparing your meal (he's also a really nice guy). Standouts include the choucroute-crusted veal loin wrapped in applewood- smoked

A VIEW WORTH DRINKING TO

One big-city perk is riding one of those super-fast elevators to the top of a hotel sky-scraper and hanging out for a while in the bar. Sure, the drinks are overpriced, but for about $7 you get a million-dollar view of the city and the bay. Here's a list of our favorites; a few have a cover charge at night, but most are free during the day.

THE CARNELIAN ROOM (555 California St between Kearny and Montgomery Sts; 415/433-7500)

Located on the 52nd floor of the Bank of America Building, the Carnelian Room is a swanky reservations-only restaurant, but the adjoining cocktail lounge is open to everyone, and the view looking north toward the Golden Gate Bridge is phenomenal.

CITYSCAPE (333 O'Farrell St at Mason St; 415/923-5002)

OK, so it's a hokey Hilton hotel, but they can't corporatize the amazing views from high atop the 46th floor. Sit under the glass roof, knock down a few Long Islands, and ponder your existence among the stars.

CROWN ROOM (950 Mason St at California St; 415/772-5131)

Half the fun of getting here is riding in the glass elevator Willy Wonka–style. The panoramic 360-degree view from the 24th floor of the Fairmont Hotel—the highest observation point in the city—is well worth that $9 Manhattan you're carrying around; in fact, it's widely considered *the* best view in the city.

bacon, fresh Atlantic salmon baked in a tender corn pancake topped with imperial caviar and a watercress sauce, marinated loin of venison with a mustard seed sabayon, and his four-course vegetarian feast, which prompted a flurry of favorable press when it debuted several years ago. Critics sometimes sniff that particular dishes are too complex, portions small, and prices large, but these are small dents in Fleur de Lys's mighty armor. The restaurant's decor matches the splendor of its food step-for-step: the romantic dining area is draped in a luxurious tentlike fashion with 700 yards of rich, red-and-gold hand-painted floral fabrics, and in the center of the room sits a spectacular crown of fresh flowers on a pedestal. Mirrored walls double this visual spectacle while simultaneously allowing you to admire yourself and your glit-teringly attired companion. Strong wine list, but weak by the glass. Fleur de Lys isn't always crowded, but reservations are required; this is the sort of establishment that doesn't want to guess who's coming to dinner. *$$$–$$$$; AE, DC, MC, V; no checks; dinner Mon–Sat; full bar; reservations required; between Jones and Taylor Sts.* &

Masa's / ★★★★

648 BUSH ST; 415/989-7154 OR 800/258-7694 No one just drops in for dinner at Masa's. Not only do you have to make a reservation at least three weeks in advance, but also you may need that much time to arrange the financing: this is probably San Francisco's most expensive restaurant. That said, the

EQUINOX (5 Embarcadero Center off Market St; 415/788-1234)
The gimmick at this Hyatt Regency is the 17-story rooftop restaurant's revolving floor, which gives diners a 360-degree panoramic view of the city every 45 minutes. You'll never see a local there, but the tourists dig it.

HARRY DENTON'S STARLIGHT ROOM (450 Powell St at Sutter St; 415/395-8595)
On the 21st floor of the Sir Francis Drake Hotel is a 1930s-style club complete with chandeliers, red-velvet banquettes, and glittering views of the city streets far below. Afternoon tea runs from 3pm to 5pm Monday through Friday, but it's the nightly dig-me-and-dance scene that everyone shows up for.

TOP OF THE MARK (1 Nob Hill at California and Mason Sts; 415/616-6916)
"Meet me at the Mark" is the slogan of one of the most famous cocktail lounges in the world. During World War II, Pacific-bound servicemen toasted their good-byes to the States here, and you can kiss a $10 bill good-bye as you sip your cocktail and enjoy the magnificent 19th-floor view atop the Mark Hopkins Intercontinental.

THE VIEW LOUNGE (55 4th St between Market and Mission Sts; 415/442-6127)
The name says it all: this cocktail lounge on the top floor of the San Francisco Marriott hotel offers some of the best views in (and of) the city. Only thick glass windows separate you from one helluva first step. It's a very casual place where you can linger all day in your shorts and nobody will care.

prices accurately reflect the precious ingredients, generous portions, stunning presentations, and labor-intensive nature of the elegant French-California cuisine invented by the late Masataka Kobayashi (carried on flawlessly by Iron Chef winner Ron Siegel). Along with the new chef (lured from Charles on Nob Hill by a fat paycheck and a customized kitchen), Masa's also has a fresh, trendy look to go with its new $60 three-, $75 six-, and $105 nine-course tasting menus. By all accounts Masa's continues to impress its cultivated clientele with its inviting atmosphere (neither glitzy nor snobbish), professional service (never intimidating), and unremittingly stellar cuisine. To understand Masa's idea of indulgence, take a gander at the offerings from a typical *ménu dégustation:* sautéed Bellwether Farm baby lamb chops accompanied with potato gnocchi and spring onions; farm-raised Davenport abalone served with hand-cut linguine; lobster ravioli with fava beans and beech mushrooms in a lobster cream sauce; and potato-crusted Japanese halibut served with cinnamon cap mushrooms and baby leeks. The excellent wines are even more exorbitantly priced than the food; moreover, if you want to bring a special bottle of your own, you should know that the corkage fee is equal to the retail value of a top-flight chardonnay. *$$$; AE, DC, DIS, MC, V; checks OK; dinner Tues–Sat; full bar; reservations required; www.masas.citysearch.com; between Powell and Stockton Sts, in the Hotel Vintage Court.* &

Swan Oyster Depot / ★★

1517 POLK ST; 415/673-1101 You won't find white linen tablecloths at this oyster bar—in fact, you won't even find any tables. Since 1912, loyal patrons have balanced themselves on the 19 hard, rickety stools lining the long, narrow marble counter cluttered with bowls of oyster crackers, fresh-cut lemons, napkin holders, Tabasco sauce, and other seasonings. On the opposite side stands a quick-shucking team of some of the most congenial men in town, always ready and eager to serve. Lunch specialties include Boston clam chowder, sizable salads (crab, shrimp, prawn, or a combo), seafood cocktails, cracked Dungeness crab, Maine lobster, and smoked salmon and trout. If you want to take home some fish for supper, take a gander in the display case: fresh salmon, swordfish, delta crawfish, red snapper, trout, shrimp, lingcod, and whatever else the boat brought in that day. Truly, this is a classic San Francisco experience that you shouldn't miss, even if the line's long (it moves fast). *$$; no credit cards; checks OK; lunch Mon–Sat (open 8am–5:30pm); beer and wine; reservations not accepted; between California and Sacramento Sts.* &

LODGINGS

Fairmont Hotel & Tower / ★★★★½

950 MASON ST; 415/772-5000 OR 800/527-4727 The Fairmont is another one of San Francisco's grand old hotels that are part hotel, part tourist attraction. Few hotels in the world have such a fabulous entrance: massive Corinthian columns of solid marble, vaulted ceilings, velvet smoking chairs, enormous gilded mirrors, and a colossal wraparound staircase. Heck, they even have a harpist posted near the entrance. All that's lacking is your top hat and coattails. And thanks to a recent $85 million renovation, the impressive decor applies to the guest rooms as well, all of which are tastefully decorated with shiny new furnishings and oodles of luxury: goose-down pillows, large walk-in closets, multiline phones with private voice mail, and electric shoe buffers. Hefty room rates help pay for the 24-hour concierge and room service, complimentary morning limousine to the Financial District, free shoeshine, business center, and baby-sitting services. Within the hotel there's a beauty salon, a barbershop, a shopping arcade, and even a pharmacy (yes, this place is big). There are several restaurants and bars as well, including the famous Polynesian-style Tonga Room bar and restaurant, fine dining at Masons, and the top-floor Crown Room restaurant and bar, which has a spectacular panoramic view of the city. *$$$$; AE, CB, DC, DIS, MC, V; checks OK; www.fairmont.com; at California St.* &

Huntington Hotel / ★★★

1075 CALIFORNIA ST; 415/474-5400 OR 800/227-4683 The small, modest lobby of this imposing Nob Hill landmark belies its lavish interiors. The Huntington is graced with a remarkable array of antiques, plush sofas, and museum-quality objets d'art; the doorman is subdued and genteel but always seems delighted to see you; the staff maintains a professional attitude and at the same time treats you like a favored guest. These things—along with superb security—explain why the Huntington has long been a favorite of many visiting dignitaries and celebrities, from Archbishop

Desmond Tutu to Robert Redford. The 12-story hotel's 140 rooms are spacious and lavish, with imported silks, 17th-century paintings, and stunning views of the city and the bay. The rooms are individually decorated, and some are so handsome they have been featured in *Architectural Digest*. Several flaunt gold velvet sofas and fringed, tufted hassocks surrounded by antiques, while others boast modern leather couches, faux-leopard-skin hassocks, and marble bars. Guests are treated to a formal afternoon tea and complimentary sherry, a nightly turndown service, and a morning paper. Valet parking and room service are also available, along with a full range of business services and access to the Nob Hill Club, a top-of-the-line fitness center one block away. Yes, Virginia, it's expensive, but offers such as the Romance Package (including free champagne, sherry, and limousine service) make the Huntington worth considering for that special occasion. *$$$$; AE, DC, DIS, MC, V; checks OK; www.huntingtonhotel.com; between Mason and Taylor Sts.* &

The Ritz-Carlton, San Francisco / ★★★★
600 STOCKTON ST; 415/296-7465 OR 800/241-3333
In 1991, after a four-year, multimillion-dollar renovation, this 1909 17-columned neoclassical beauty—formerly the Metropolitan Life Insurance Company building—reopened as The Ritz-Carlton hotel. Since then, it's been stacking up heady accolades, including *Condé Nast Traveler's* "Gold List" for seven consecutive years. The hotel's lobby is breathtaking, with a series of enormous, high-ceilinged lounges, gigantic floral arrangements, an abundance of museum-quality paintings and antiques, and crystal chandeliers at every turn. The spectacular Lobby Lounge is the place to mingle over afternoon tea or sushi, and live piano performances perk up the scene every day. The 336 guest rooms are also luxury personified: sinfully plush and loaded with high-society amenities such as spiffy Italian-marble bathrooms, 300-thread-count sheets, fully stocked honor bars, thick terry-cloth robes, high-speed Internet access, and in-room safes. Some (though not many) have wonderful views of the city and the bay, but your best bets are the quieter rooms overlooking the landscaped courtyard. Business travelers should book one of the upper-floor club rooms, which come with a dedicated concierge, elevator-key access, and complimentary meals throughout the day. The hotel's ritzy fitness center has an indoor lap pool, a whirlpool, a sauna, a fully equipped training room, and massage services. Two restaurants are located in the hotel: the formal Dining Room at the Ritz-Carlton (see review, above), and the more casual Terrace, serving excellent Mediterranean fare and sensational desserts in a pleasant dining room adorned with handsome oil paintings. *$$$$; AE, DC, DIS, MC, V; no checks; www.ritzcarlton.com; between Pine and California Sts.* &

Russian Hill

Russian Hill earned its name from the Russian explorers and trappers who arrived in the early 1800s to trade with the Spanish and Native Americans in the San Francisco Bay area. The rough voyage from Fort Ross up north and exposure to the New World diseases proved too much for many sailors, who didn't live to make the journey home. They were buried high atop the hill that overlooked the harbor, the graves marked by black crosses with Russian inscriptions. For years the gravestones were all that distinguished this uninhabited hill. Today, graves are long covered over, and even the literati who once populated the summit of the hill—Mark Twain, Jack London, Ambrose Bierce, and Jack Kerouac among them—could barely afford an apartment in this high-rent district. Polk Street is the neighborhood commercial center, with shops, cafes, and restaurants that keep locals fat and happy, and draw those brave enough to try to find parking. Hyde Street has several excellent little restaurants tucked between apartment buildings and grocery stores. Oh, and if you're in search of that famous crooked street, it's here—on Lombard Street between Hyde and Leavenworth Streets.

RESTAURANTS

Antica Trattoria / ★★☆

2400 POLK ST; 415/928-5797 Soon after Antica Trattoria opened its doors in 1996, the surrounding Russian Hill neighborhood was abuzz with talk of how incredible the Italian fare is here. Occupying a moderately busy corner on Polk and Union Streets, this simply decorated restaurant with dark wood floors and cream-colored walls has developed a deserved reputation as one of the city's best Italian trattorias. Appetizers might include a purée of potato and vegetable soup seasoned with bacon, or delicate (and divine) slices of beef carpaccio enhanced with capers, arugula, mustard, and Parmesan shavings. A recent rendition of the creamy risotto was prepared with pears and Taleggio cheese, while a memorable chestnut-flavored *fedelini* (angel hair pasta) was dressed with leeks and a smoked-chicken cream sauce. Main dishes might include a savory monkfish wrapped in pancetta, potatoes, and wild mushrooms, or a tomato risotto spiced with fennel sausage. It's not the most surprising Italian fare in the city, but it's some of the best prepared and reasonably priced. Top it off with the terrific tiramisu. *$$; AE, DC, MC, V; no checks; dinner Tues–Sun; beer and wine; reservations recommended; at Union St.* ♿

Gary Danko / ★★★★

800 NORTH POINT; 415/749-2060 Call them the dynamic duo if you will—the culinary team of award-winning chef Gary Danko (of San Francisco's Ritz-Carlton fame) and well-connected maître d' Nick Peyton created quite a stir in San Francisco when they opened this highly anticipated restaurant. The concept sounds simple, but is surprisingly difficult to achieve: fine French–New American cuisine combined with impeccable service. At Gary Danko, it seems to be working like a well-oiled machine, so much so that it was rated the #1 restaurant in *San Francisco* magazine's readers' poll when it opened in 2001. The namesake chef fashions a seasonally changing menu rooted in the classical school. His signature dishes include glazed oysters; seared foie gras with peaches, caramelized onions, and verjuice sauce; roast lobster with chanterelle mushrooms; and an amazing herb-crusted lamb loin. Dinners are served in three tasting-menu formats: you choose either the three-, four-, or five-course meal. Sommelier Renee-Nicole Kubin shows a deft touch with her recommended pairings. Everything seems well thought out, including the understated elegance of the 75-seat room and the art collection curated by a local gallery owner. *$$$; AE, DC, MC, V; no checks; dinner every day; full bar; reservations recommended; www.garydanko.com; at Hyde St.*

Harris' / ★★

2100 VAN NESS AVE; 415/673-1888 Not just another steak house, Harris' is a living monument to the not-quite-bygone joys of guiltless beef-eating. You can even get a sneak preview of your meal by peering at the deep-pink slabs in the showcase window facing the street. The hushed, formal club setting boasts dark wood paneling, plush carpets, large brown tufted booths, well-spaced white-draped tables, and chairs roomy enough to accommodate the most bullish build. Jackets are appreciated (though no longer required). Harris's choice Midwestern beef, impeccably dry-aged for three weeks on the premises, bears the same relation to supermarket beef as foie gras bears to chicken liver; the tender steaks, grilled to order, can even be chosen by cut and by size. The larger bone-in cuts (such as the Harris Steak and the T-bone) have the finest flavor, but the pepper steak and the rare prime rib are great, too. Those who prefer calf brains to these sanguine beauties will find a flawless version here. You might want to skip the usual steak-house appetizers in favor of Harris's excellent Caesar salad. For true-blue traditionalists, the exemplary martini—served in a carafe placed in a bucket of shaved ice—makes an excellent starter course. *$$$; AE, DC, DIS, MC, V; no checks; dinner every day; full bar; reservations recommended; at Pacific Ave.* ⅙

La Folie / ★★★⯪

2316 POLK ST; 415/776-5577 After a stingy San Francisco restaurateur fired him for spending too much on ingredients and serving overly generous portions, French-born chef Roland Passot decided to open his own restaurant where he could spend as much as he liked to make the food perfect. The paradisiacal result is the charming, small, family-run La Folie. The intimate, whimsical, theatrical dining room with white puffy clouds painted on the sky-blue ceiling has red-patterned carpeting, a colorful stained-glass entryway, and even marionettes from Lyon dangling from the wall—an appropriate stage for Passot's creative, exuberant, but disciplined menu. His Roquefort soufflé with grapes, herbs, and walnut bread alone is worthy of four stars. Other memorable starters are the wonderful foie gras dishes; the potato blinis with golden osetra caviar, salmon, asparagus, and crème fraîche; the rabbit loin stuffed with exquisitely fresh vegetables and roasted garlic; the velvety corn-and-leek soup; the parsley and garlic soup with snails and shiitake mushrooms; and the lobster consommé. For an entree, choose whatever meat or fish suits your fancy, for it surely will be exquisitely prepared. To accommodate vegetarians, Passot has thoughtfully included a separate Vegetable Lovers' menu. And for those who can't make up their minds, there's the Discovery menu, which allows you to choose five courses à la carte (though it's pricey). For dessert, indulge in clafouti with chocolate sauce or croquettes of chocolate with orange zest sauce. The wine list is extensive, but the prices are steep. *$$$–$$$$; AE, DC, DIS, MC, V; no checks; dinner Mon–Sat; full bar; reservations recommended; near Union St.* ⅙

Marina/Cow Hollow

With spectacular views of the Golden Gate Bridge, Alcatraz, and the bay, the Marina is desirable real estate for the young and affluent. A middle-class Italian neighborhood until the 1960s, the Marina now houses some of that community's wealthiest families, who live in the elegant homes that line the waterfront. Cozy art deco flats and stucco houses with Mediterranean-tiled roofs sit on quiet streets only steps away from waterfront activities. At the turn of the century, the Marina was virtually under water. The marshland was filled in when it was chosen as the site of the 1915 Panama-Pacific International Exposition, which celebrated the opening of the Panama Canal. Today, the Palace of Fine Arts building, located at Baker and Beach Streets, serves as a beautiful reminder of that festive event. Within a few blocks of home, Marina residents often spend their weekends at the **EXPLORATORIUM** and **PALACE OF FINE ARTS**, the historic Presidio (now a national park featuring attractions like Crissy Field, a former airfield turned wetland and bird refuge), and the Marina Green, popular with joggers, in-line skaters, sunbathers, kite flyers, and outdoor sports enthusiasts of all kinds. The heart of the Marina is **CHESTNUT STREET** between Fillmore and Divisadero Streets. Once a quaint shopping district, Chestnut was permanently altered by the 1989 earthquake. Extensive damage forced a number of small businesses to close. It was only a matter of months before big-name chains and high-end boutiques set up shop (an unwelcome citywide trend that sticks in the gullet of most every San Franciscan). Today, it's a yuppie shopping haven, complete with Gap Kids, Pottery Barn, and Williams-Sonoma.

RESTAURANTS

Betelnut / ★★

2030 UNION ST; 415/929-8855 A member of the Real Restaurants company (which includes such successes as Tra Vigne and Bix), this sumptuously decorated Asian "beerhouse" has the ever-so-slightly-tarty feel of an exotic 1930s Shanghai brothel. Named after a popular seed that is chewed throughout Asia for its intoxicating side effects, Betelnut became a huge success in a short time, and it's still on everyone's list of places to try (though, alas, the namesake nut is not offered here). Tall glass doors facing Union Street are opened on warm evenings to provide alfresco dining, and mechanized bamboo fans sway languorously above the busy bar. The mixed menu is pan-Asian, with an array of authentic dishes from Vietnam, Singapore, China, Thailand, Indonesia, and Japan. While the unusual concept entices diners, the reality is not always up to par. With more than a dozen cooks in the kitchen on busy nights, results can vary. Some dishes consistently get raves, including the spicy coconut chicken with eggplant, lemongrass, and basil; the crunchy tea-smoked duck; the succulent short ribs; and the sun-dried anchovies with peanuts, chilies, and garlic. But the green papaya salad gets mixed reviews, and Betelnut's dumplings can be downright disappointing. For dessert try the dreamy coconut tapioca. *$$; DC, DIS, MC, V; no checks; lunch, dinner every day; full bar; reservations recommended; between Buchanan and Webster Sts.* &

Cafe Marimba / ★★☆

2317 CHESTNUT ST; 415/776-1506 This exuberant little restaurant sandwiched between shops in the Marina District is easy to miss, despite its vibrant sunset-purple facade and the seemingly endless stream of people who squeeze through its lime-green doors every evening. Step inside and you'll be bowled over by a profusion of more screaming colors—pink, turquoise, green, orange—not to mention a fiery-red, 10-foot-tall papier-mâché diablo towering above the room. The secret to eating at Marimba, which packs more people into a small space than a yuppie-express MUNI bus, is to make a reservation early in the evening so you won't have to wait long for a table. San Francisco chef Reed Hearon, famous for his Black Cat and Rose Pistola restaurants, pioneered this festive place, and although he has since moved on to other projects, Marimba has retained a huge following. The quite reasonably priced fare here is Oaxacan—not an overpriced upscale version of Taco Bell. Once you're seated, immediately order the wonderful guacamole and chips. The restaurant has a changing repertoire of more than 50 salsas; the nightly selections might include roasted corn, avocado-tomatillo, or tomato with smoked chilies. Have a margarita to douse the flames, or sip a delicious fresh-fruit juice. Then move on to the sublime shrimp *mojo de ajo,* drenched in garlic, chilies, and lime; spicy snapper tacos with pineapple salsa; or grilled chicken spiced with mild, smoky achiote seed. Even the more common fare has a twist: the seafood comes with a choice of five sauces, including garlic, caramelized onions, and fresh jalapeño sauces, or a combination of capers, olives, tomatoes, and jalapeños. Top it all off with the fantastic flan. *$$; AE, MC, V; no checks; lunch Wed–Sun, dinner every day; full bar; reservations recommended; between Scott and Divisadero Sts.* ♿

Greens / ★★☆

FORT MASON CENTER, BLDG A; 415/771-6222 As Le Tour d'Argent in Paris is to the dedicated duck fancier and the Savoy Grill in London is to the roast beef connoisseur, so is Greens at Fort Mason to the vegetarian aesthete. Not only is the food politically correct here, it's also often so good that even carnivores find it irresistible. Part of the Greens treat is visual: located in a converted barracks in the historic Fort Mason Center, the enormous, airy dining room is surrounded by huge windows with a spectacular view of the bay and the Golden Gate Bridge, and a gigantic sculpted redwood burl is a Buddhist-inspired centerpiece in the waiting area. Yes, Greens is owned and operated by the Zen Center—but this is a restaurant, not a monastery. The menu changes daily: expect to see such dishes as mesquite-grilled polenta; filo turnovers filled with mushrooms, spinach, and Parmesan; pizza sprinkled with onion confit, goat cheese, and basil; and fettuccine with mushrooms, peas, goat cheese, and crème fraîche. Greens to Go, a takeout counter inside the restaurant, also sells baked goods, savory soups, sandwiches, and black-bean chili. An à la carte dinner menu is offered Monday through Friday; guests may order from the $45 prix-fixe five-course dinner menu only on Saturday. *$$–$$$; DIS, MC, V; local checks only; lunch Tues–Sat, dinner Mon–Sat, brunch Sun; beer and wine; reservations recommended; www.greensrestaurant.com; off Marina Blvd at Buchanan St.* ♿

Isa / ★★★

3324 STEINER ST; 415/567-9588 This modest Marina restaurant has the locals raving about the tapas-style French dishes emanating from the tiny kitchen. At this family-run affair (the owners, Luke and Kitty Sung, live upstairs—well, sleep upstairs, live downstairs), the staff puts heart and soul into both the service and the à la carte–sized dishes. Typical of Marina restaurants, the long, narrow building has a few tables up front, but most everyone requests a table in the tent-covered and heated outdoor patio in back (très romantique). The menu offers only about 10 selections, all of which are enticing and carefully crafted using fresh, seasonal ingredients (and would cost twice as much at a fancy French restaurant). Try the potato-wrapped sea bass in a caper, pepper, olive, and brown butter sauce (a mere $10); or the roasted rack of lamb with ratatouille niçoise ($16); or the baked Laura Chenel goat cheese salad with fresh tomatoes, pine nuts, and basil ($6). Other dishes range from leek and potato soup with roasted scallops and white truffle oil ($5) to a ragout of veal sweetbreads and mushrooms ($14). The impressive wine list features numerous European wines, including a few paired selections such as muscadet with the Miyagi oysters or the sauternes matched with the seared Hudson Valley foie gras. Really, you'll love this place. *$$; AE, DC, MC, V; no checks; dinner every day; full bar; reservations recommended; between Chestnut and Lombard Sts.* &

Pane e Vino / ★★★

3011 STEINER ST; 415/346-2111 Well hidden on the outskirts of posh Pacific Heights, this dark-wood-trimmed trattoria framed by a cream-colored awning is a local favorite. The two tiny, simply furnished dining rooms with small white-clothed tables fill up fast, and as waiters spouting rapid-fire Italian dart back and forth between the kitchen and their customers, folks waiting for a table are often left frantically searching for a place to stand out of the way. It's all enchantingly reminiscent of the real ristorante scene in Italy, which is perhaps one of the reasons people keep coming back. Newcomers unaccustomed to the hustle and bustle may be a bit disconcerted at first, but after a sip or two of wine and a bite of rustic Italian fare, everything becomes rather entertaining. Do yourself a favor and indulge in the amazing chilled artichoke appetizer, stuffed with bread and tomatoes and served with a vinaigrette—it's divine! Follow that lead with one of the perfectly prepared pastas, ranging from the simple but savory capellini tossed with fresh tomatoes, basil, garlic, and extra-virgin olive oil to the zesty bucatini (hollow straw pasta) smothered with pancetta, hot peppers, and tomato sauce. The excellent entrees vary from rack of lamb marinated in sage and rosemary to the whole roasted fresh fish of the day. Before you raise your napkin to your lips for the last time, dive into the delightful dolci: a luscious crème caramel, assorted gelati, and a terrific tiramisu are the standouts. *$$; AE, MC, V; no checks; lunch Mon–Sat, dinner every day; beer and wine; reservations recommended; at Union St.* &

PlumpJack Cafe / ★★★

3127 FILLMORE ST; 415/563-4755 Co-owned by Bill Getty (son of billionaire Gordon Getty) and wine-connoisseur-cum-mayor Gavin Newsom, this exotic California–Mediterranean bistro is one of San Francisco's leading restaurants, with consistently excellent food and (thanks to its companion wine store a few doors away) a surprisingly extensive wine list featuring fine bottles offered at near-retail prices. The appetizers are often the highlight of the menu, particularly the bruschetta, topped with roasted beets, goat cheese, and garlic one night, and eggplant, sweet peppers, and chèvre the next. Don't miss the remarkable risottos, richly flavored with artichokes, applewood-smoked bacon, and goat cheese, or perhaps smoked salmon and shiitake mushrooms. Other recommended dishes include the superbly executed roast herb chicken breast with foie gras, hedgehog mushrooms and spinach, and the roast duck breast and leg confit with French green lentils, barley, parsnip chips, and a sour cherry jus. While the restaurant's highly stylized, hand-crafted interior design is unique—gold-leafed lights, chairs with medieval shield–shaped backs, curved metal screens at the windows—the unpretentious taupe and olive color scheme ensures that what really stands out is the food. *$$$; AE, MC, V; no checks; lunch Mon–Fri, dinner Mon–Sat; full bar; reservations recommended; www.plumpjack.com; between Filbert and Greenwich Sts.* &

LODGINGS

Marina Inn / ★★☆

3110 OCTAVIA ST; 415/928-1000 OR 800/274-1420 If you don't really care where you stay in San Francisco and you want the most for your money, book a room here; we checked out all the inexpensive lodgings in the city and none have come close to offering as good a deal. The building, located on busy Lombard Street (the only caveat), is a handsome 1924 four-story Victorian, and the guest rooms are equally impressive: two-poster beds with cozy comforters and mattresses, rustic pine-wood furnishings, attractive wallpaper, and a pleasant color scheme of rose, hunter green, and pale yellow. You'll especially appreciate the high-class touches that many of the city's expensive hotels don't include, such as full bathtubs with showers, remote-control televisions discreetly hidden in pine cabinetry, and nightly turndown service à la chocolates on your pillow. How much for all these creature comforts? As little as $65 a night, and that includes complimentary continental breakfast and after-noon sherry. It's in a good location as well—within easy walking distance of the shops and restaurants along Chestnut and Union Streets, and right on the bus route to downtown. *$–$$; AE, MC, V; no checks; www.marinainn.com; at Lombard St.* &

Pacific Heights

Pacific Heights is one of San Francisco's most exclusive neighborhoods. When trans-portation extended to the outer districts of the city, the elite moved west away from the noise of downtown, seeking quieter streets and bigger lots on which to build their grand mansions. Whether your architectural tastes lean toward Victorians, over-the-top neoclassical manors, or something elegantly in between, there are jaw-dropping buildings for you to admire and many to tour. The views from the higher intersec-tions are stunning, particularly at sunset. Two beautiful parks offer greenery in this otherwise cramped neighborhood. Landscape architect John McLaren, who designed Golden Gate Park, also left his mark on **ALTA PLAZA PARK,** a small patch of land bordered by Clay, Steiner, Jackson, and Scott Streets. The park's terraced landscape was modeled after the Grand Casino in Monte Carlo. The uppermost level affords spectacular vistas in all directions. A few blocks to the east, **LAFAYETTE PARK** sits at the corner of Laguna and Sacramento Streets. The four square blocks of open space offer views of Twin Peaks and the bay to the north.

RESTAURANTS

Cafe Kati / ★★★

1963 SUTTER ST; 415/775-7313 Cafe Kati may not have the elbow room of some of San Francisco's other top restaurants, but there are few chefs on the West Coast who can match Kirk Webber—a California Culinary Academy graduate—when it comes to culinary artistry. Obscurely located on a residential block off Fillmore Street, this tiny, modest, 60-seat cafe has garnered a monsoon of kudos for Webber's weird and wonderful arrangements of numerous cuisines. Even something as mundane as a Caesar salad is transformed into a towering monument of lovely romaine arranged upright on the plate and held in place by a ribbon of thinly sliced cucumber. Fortunately, it tastes as good as it looks. Though the menu changes monthly, it always spans the globe: miso-marinated Chilean sea bass topped with tempura kabocha squash; pancetta-wrapped pork tenderloin bathed in a ragout of baby artichokes and chanterelle mushrooms; walnut-crusted chicken with Gorgonzola; and crispy duck confit with sweet potato polenta and wild mushrooms. Complete the gustatory experience with the to-die-for butterscotch pudding. When making a reservation, request a table in the front room—and don't make any plans after dinner, because the kitchen takes its sweet time preparing your objet d'art. *$$; AE, MC, V; no checks; dinner Tues–Sun; beer and wine; reservations recommended; katikwok@aol.com; www.cafekati.com; between Fillmore and Webster Sts.*

Chez Nous / ★★☆

1911 FILLMORE ST; 415/441-8044 Yes, it's a bit cramped, and yes, you'll probably have to wait for a table since they don't take reservations, but these are minor inconveniences for the opportunity to dine at Chez Nous, one of our favorite places to have a casual meal in the city. We like everything about this restaurant: the friendly staff, the erudite patrons, the energetic European ambiance, the love-of-good-food esprit de corps, and particularly the tapas-style Mediterranean dishes. If you're a meat-'n'-puhtatoes kinda guy, this isn't for you, but if you enjoy a multicourse sampling of light, clean, fresh dishes such as grilled asparagus, smoked squid with olives and frisée, potato gnocchi flavored with bits of prosciutto and mint, and lamb chops sprinkled with lavender salt, you'll become yet another Chez Nous repeat customer. The menu also offers a modest wine list and dessert selection (the lemon cake wins), and excellent bread from nearby Boulangerie Bay Bread, whose owners run this place as well. *$$; MC, V; no checks; lunch Wed–Sun, dinner Tues–Sun; beer and wine; no reservations; between Pine and Bush Sts.* ♿

Eliza's / ★★★

2877 CALIFORNIA ST; 415/621-4819 Eliza's is not only one of our favorite Chinese restaurants in San Francisco, it's also one of our favorite San Francisco restaurants, period. Where else can you get such fresh, high-quality cuisine in an artistic setting for less than $7 a dish? You'll either love or be confused by the decidedly anti-typical-Chinese-restaurant decor—oodles of gorgeous hand-blown glassware, orchids, and modern accents create a rather curious ambiance that works for some and appalls others, but it's neither here nor there once the food arrives at your table. The menu offers a large array of classic Hunan and Mandarin dishes, all served on beautiful Italian plates. Start with the assorted appetizer dish, which is practically a meal in itself for les than $10. Three other recommended dishes are the *kung pao* chicken (a marvelous mixture of tender chicken, peanuts, chile peppers, hot sauce, and fresh vegetables), the sea bass in black bean sauce, and the vegetable moo-shu (with sweet plum sauce). Regardless of what you order you're likely to be impressed, and the lunch specials are a steal. The only drawback is the line out the door that often forms around 7pm (they don't take reservations). *$; MC, V; no checks; lunch, dinner every day; beer and wine; reservations not accepted; at Broderick St.* &

Garibaldi's / ★★☆

347 PRESIDIO AVE; 415/563-8841 Evocative of the great neighborhood-type restaurants in New York's Greenwich Village and SoHo, Garibaldi's seems like a place where every diner has just walked over from his or her home around the corner. The restaurant is small and the tables are jammed so close together that at times you feel like reaching over and trying something from your neighbor's plate. So it's a good thing the atmosphere is friendly and lively, if at times decidedly loud. The staff, polished yet down-to-earth, makes everyone feel like a regular. In fact, many people become regulars because the Italian-Mediterranean food is so good. The dishes are sophisticated without being highfalutin. The risottos (there are usually two on the menu, and sometimes one nightly special) are quite good. If you are looking to eat light but don't want to forsake robust flavor, try one of the entree salads, such as the grilled prawns marinated in charmoula. Among the entree highlights are a Mediterranean lamb dish and a generous cut of tender filet mignon. And don't miss the rich desserts: the signature sweet is a white-chocolate cheesecake with a crunchy cookie crust. *$$; AE, MC, V; local checks only; lunch Mon–Fri, dinner every day; full bar; reservations recommended; between Sacramento and Clay Sts.* &

LODGINGS

Hotel Drisco / ★★★

2901 PACIFIC AVE; 415/346-2880 OR 800/634-7277 If you're a fan of San Francisco's Ritz-Carlton, you'll adore Hotel Drisco. The five-story structure, perched on one of the most coveted blocks in the city, was built in 1903 as a boardinghouse for neighborhood servants. After surviving the great fire of 1906, it was converted into a hotel in the mid-'20s but eventually fell into major disrepair. Combining the financial might of hotelier Tom Callinan (Meadowood, the Inn at Southbridge) and the interior design skills of Glenn Texeira (Ritz-Carlton, Manila), Hotel Drisco's proprietors transformed years of blood, sweat, and greenbacks into one of the finest small hotels in the city. The 24 rooms and 19 suites are bathed in soothing shades of alabaster, celadon, and buttercup yellow and feature rich fabrics, quality antiques, and superior mattresses. Standard amenities include a two-line phone with a modem hookup, a CD player, a discreetly hidden TV with a VCR, and a minibar; each suite includes a handsome sofa bed, an additional phone and TV, and a terrific view. Each spacious marble-clad bathroom is equipped with a hair dryer, plush robes, and (in most units) a bathtub. Room 404A—a corner suite with an extraordinary view of Pacific Heights mansions and the surrounding neighborhood—is a favorite. An extended continental breakfast is served in one of the three quiet, comfortable common rooms. *$$$; AE, DC, DIS, MC, V; no checks; www.hoteldrisco.com; at Broderick St.* &

Civic Center

Politics, highbrow culture, and homelessness all mingle at the Civic Center. The mayor's office and the board of supervisors' chambers are housed in the beautiful Beaux Arts **CITY HALL** designed in 1916 by Arthur Brown. Its magnificent dome measures 308 feet tall, a full 16 feet higher than the Capitol dome in Washington, D.C., and is a visible landmark from many points in the city. The **WAR MEMORIAL OPERA HOUSE**—another Arthur Brown design—stretches along Van Ness Avenue, the city's widest thoroughfare. **LOUISE M. DAVIES SYMPHONY HALL,** built in 1981 on the corner of Van Ness Avenue and Gough Street, houses the largest concert-hall organ in North America—so massive that the instrument's 9,235 pipes are played with the aid of a computer. The **SAN FRANCISCO PUBLIC LIBRARY** (100 Larkin St at Grove St; 415/557-4257) opened in 1996 to mostly rave reviews and more than a few boos for its less-than-inviting exterior. On Grove Street across from the Main Library, the **BILL GRAHAM CIVIC AUDITORIUM,** named after the late rock impresario, is used as a convention hall and music venue. The Civic Center borders the city's infamous red-light district, the **TENDERLOIN,** where many homeless live on the streets. While this has long been a neighborhood to avoid, an influx of Vietnamese, Laotian, and Cambodian families has changed the neighborhood over the years. And while it's still not for the faint-hearted, it now has a number of good ethnic markets and many excellent—though bare-bones—eateries. If you're looking for Kaffir lime leaves or galangal (and who isn't?), this is the place to come.

RESTAURANTS

Absinthe Brasserie and Bar / ★★

398 HAYES ST; 415/551-1590 Stylish Absinthe, named for the green herbal liqueur so potent it was banned in turn-of-the-century France, re-creates the romance and mystery of the bygone Belle Epoque. The sumptuous decor begins at the entry with French rattan cafe chairs, copper-topped tables, and a mosaic checkerboard floor. The brasserie-style French and Italian menu offers such starters as veal sweetbreads sautéed in a sweet marsala sauce, a delicious version of the classic pissaladière, and fluffy ricotta dumplings. A generous seafood platter loaded with Dungeness crab, shrimp, and mussels is a highlight. Entrees change daily and vary in consistency (much like, alas, the service). You'll find everything from roasted veal chops and seasonal risottos to inventive vegetarian creations. Desserts are more dependable: a Scharffen Berger chocolate pot de crème is sublime, as is the lavender crème brûlée. And while you won't find actual absinthe on the menu, professional bartenders mix a range of amusingly named cocktails, including one named after Ernest Hemingway's Death in the Afternoon—an unusual combination of Pernod and champagne. *$$; AE, DC, DIS, MC, V; no checks; lunch Tues–Fri, dinner Tues–Sun, brunch Sat–Sun; full bar; reservations recommended; at Gough St.* ♿

Jardinière / ★★★☆

300 GROVE ST; 415/861-5555 A native Californian, chef Traci Des Jardins worked in many notable restaurants in France, New York, and Los Angeles before co-opening Rubicon in San Francisco, which launched her culinary reputation nationwide. She won the prestigious James Beard Rising Star Chef of the Year award and was named one of the best new chefs in America by *Food & Wine* magazine With those kudos, it's no wonder that her own restaurant, Jardinière (pronounced zhar-dee-NAIR), was a smashing success as soon as the highly stylized glass doors swung open in September 1997. With award-winning designer-restaurateur Pat Kuleto as her business partner, Des Jardins was assured of an impressive setting for her French-California cuisine. Formerly home to a jazz club, the two-story interior is elegantly framed with violet velvet drapes, and the focal point is the central oval mahogany and marble bar, frequently mobbed with local politicos and patrons of the arts (the symphony hall and opera house are across the street). Appetizers are Des Jardins's strong point, especially the flavor-packed lobster, leek, and chanterelle strudel and the delicate kabocha squash ravioli with chestnuts and sage brown butter. Some of her best entrees thus far have included the crisp chicken with chanterelles and applewood-smoked bacon; herbed lamb loin with cranberry beans and tomato confit; and pan-roasted salmon with lentils, celery root salad, and red-wine sauce. After your meal, consider the chef's selection of domestic and imported cheeses, which are visible in the temperature-controlled cheese room on the main floor. The live entertainment makes this restaurant ideal for a special night on the town. *$$$; AE, DC, DIS, MC, V; no checks; lunch Mon–Fri, dinner, late-night menu every day; full bar; reservations recommended; at Franklin St.* ♿

Zuni Cafe / ★★★

1658 MARKET ST; 415/552-2522 Before it got famous, Zuni was a tiny Southwestern-style lunch spot in a low-class neighborhood. When Chez Panisse alumna Judy Rodgers came on board as chef and co-owner, the cafe became so popular it had to more than double its size. Today, with its roaring copper-topped bar, grand piano, and exposed-brick dining room, it's nearly as quintessential a San Francisco institution as Dungeness crab and sourdough bread (though many loyal patrons miss the days when it was little more than a hole-in-the-wall). It wouldn't be stretching the truth to say that one reason the neighborhood started improving was Zuni's Mediterranean-influenced upscale food, as divinely simple as only the supremely sophisticated can be. Picture a plate of mild, house-cured anchovies sprinkled with olives, celery, and Parmesan cheese; polenta with delicate mascarpone; a

CHINA CAMP STATE PARK

China Camp State Park, featuring 1,640 acres of natural watershed, is one of Marin's best-kept secrets. Only 4 miles east of downtown San Rafael, a hundred years ago a quaint fishing village thrived on its quiet shores. Most of the residents came from the Kwangtung province of China and brought with them a heritage of fishing methods dating back thousands of years. Their first stop was San Francisco. Good fortune smiled on these hardworking immigrants, who carved out a new life doing what they knew best. Business flourished, thanks in part to the Gold Rush frenzy and bounty from the bay (daily catches were as much as 3,000 pounds). By 1852 the enterprising immigrants were peddling fresh fish door to door, but times were changing. Some resented the success of these first commercial fishermen. In 1860 the state legislature placed a heavy tax on commercial Chinese fishing. The Chinese, eager to avoid the tax collector and discrimination, relocated to Marin. Fishing camps, where residents lived and worked in isolation, soon dotted the shoreline along San Pablo Bay.

By 1887 China Camp had become a prosperous shrimp fishing village. Shrimp caught in the bay were dried and then exported to Hawaii, Japan, and China, where

terrific Caesar salad; a small, perfectly roasted chicken for two on a delicious bed of Tuscan bread salad (perhaps the best chicken you've ever tasted); and a grilled rib-eye steak accompanied by sweet white corn seasoned with fresh basil. At lunchtime and after 10pm, you can get some of the best burgers in town here, too, served on focaccia with aioli and house pickles (and be sure to order a side of the great shoe-string potatoes). Service is first-rate for regulars and those who resemble them. Tip: Dinner is served until midnight Tuesday through Saturday. *$$$; AE, MC, V; no checks; lunch, dinner Tues–Sun; full bar; reservations recommended; at Franklin St.* &

LODGINGS

The Archbishop's Mansion / ★★★

1000 FULTON ST; 415/563-7872 OR 800/543-5820 This stately Belle Epoque mansion, built in 1904 for San Francisco's archbishop, is an exercise in Victorian splendor and excess: a three-story staircase winds beneath a gorgeous, 16-foot-tall stained-glass dome, and the surrounding redwood Corinthian columns, crystal chandeliers, Oriental carpets, and gorgeous antiques create an aura of almost papal splendor. The 15 large rooms and suites, each named after a famous opera, are decorated with lush fabrics, embroidered linens, and 19th-century antiques. All have partial canopied beds and private baths with stacks of plush towels and French-milled soaps. Many rooms have a fireplace, a Jacuzzi tub, and a view of Alamo Square Park, and some have a parlor and sitting area. The posh, rose-colored Carmen Suite has a claw-footed bathtub in front of a fireplace, a comfortable sitting room with yet another fireplace, and another pretty park view. The ultra-luxurious they were used to flavor and garnish traditional Asian dishes. Discarded shells were sold as fertilizer and feed for farm animals. The lucrative shrimp industry supported the community of 3,000 until 1910, when the State of California introduced sea bass into San Pablo Bay. New regulations forced the Chinese to abandon their trap-nets. The village population dwindled. Finally, only the well-known Quan family remained at China Camp.

Leave it to Hollywood to capture the lovely cove setting and lasting impressions of China Camp on celluloid. *Blood Alley*, starring Lauren Bacall and John Wayne, was filmed there in 1955. Like a deserted movie set, remnants of the past greet visitors today. The old fan mill formerly used to winnow shrimp is displayed in a wooden building, along with a replica of a sampan used by Chinese fishermen, and haunting photographs of early settlers.

China Camp State Park also features extensive intertidal, salt marsh, meadow, and oak habitats that are home to a variety of wildlife, including deer and red-tailed hawks. Visitors enjoy camping, hiking, swimming, boating, and windsurfing. Call for additional information (415/388-2070).

Don Giovanni Suite boasts a cherub-encrusted antique four-poster bed imported from a French castle, as well as a parlor with a palatial fireplace and a lavish seven-head shower in the bathroom. You may breakfast in bed on scones and croissants; then, after spending the day strolling through the park admiring the neighborhood's cherished Victorian homes, return in the afternoon for wine in the French parlor, which is graced by a grand piano that once belonged to Noël Coward. *$$$; AE, DC, MC, V; checks OK; www.archbishopsmansion.com; at Steiner St.*

The Richmond District

The Richmond District neighborhood, which sits at the western end of the city and stretches from Arguello Boulevard out to the ocean, is known as "the avenues" (as opposed to SoMa and the Mission District, which are referred to as "the streets"). This area first became popular at the end of the last century when Adolph Sutro created two crowd-pleasing attractions in the city's western reaches. The first and foremost in the city's memory was the seven-story Victorian masterpiece called the **CLIFF HOUSE** (Sutro was responsible for its second and most splendid incarnation). The second was the ambitious **SUTRO BATHS,** a compilation of a half-dozen indoor ocean-water swimming pools. Sadly, neither attraction remains standing today—at least not as conceived by Sutro—but in their heyday they helped to bring the growing city out west.

Many present-day landmarks still draw tourists and San Franciscans alike to the Richmond District. Perhaps the most dramatic are the rocky cliffs that loom over the pounding surf at Land's End. At the end of Clement Street and 34th Avenue,

Lincoln Park is home to the **CALIFORNIA PALACE OF THE LEGION OF HONOR** art museum. In recent decades, thousands of Russian, Irish, and Chinese immigrants have landed in the Richmond District. They've settled in the bland stucco-covered houses that stretch from just past Pacific Heights to the Pacific Ocean, making this one of the most international neighborhoods in the city.

RESTAURANTS

Khan Toke Thai House / ★★☆

5937 GEARY BLVD; 415/668-6654 If you're in the mood for an exotic dining experience (or you just want to impress the heck out of your date), dine at the Khan Toke Thai House, the loveliest Thai restaurant in San Francisco. Following Thai tradition, you'll be asked to remove your shoes at the entrance, so be sure to wear clean (and hole-free) socks. You'll then be escorted through the lavishly decorated dining room—replete with carved teak, Thai statues, and hand-woven Thai tapestries—and seated on large pillows at one of the many sunken tables (or, if you prefer, at a table in the garden out back). Start with the appetizing *tom yam gong*, lemongrass shrimp with mushroom, tomato, and cilantro soup. Other delicious dishes include the prawns with hot chilies, mint leaves, lime juice, lemongrass, and onions; the chicken with cashew nuts, crispy chilies, and onions; and the ground pork with fresh ginger, green onion, peanuts, and lemon juice. For those dining family style, be sure to order the exquisite deep-fried pompano topped with sautéed ginger, onions, peppers, pickled garlic, and yellow-bean sauce. If the vast menu has you bewildered, opt for the multicourse dinner: appetizer, soup, salad, two main courses, dessert, and coffee. And if you're feeling frivolous after sipping a Singha beer or two, you might want to engage your table-mate in a game of shoeless footsie—after all, how often do you get a chance to do that in public? $$; AE, MC, V; no checks; dinner every day; beer and wine; reservations recommended; between 23rd and 24th Aves.

Ton Kiang / ★★☆

5821 GEARY BLVD; 415/387-8273 Ton Kiang has established a solid reputation as one of the best Chinese restaurants in the city, particularly when it comes to dim sum and Hakka cuisine (a mixture of Chinese cuisines sometimes referred to as "China's soul food," developed by a nomadic Chinese tribe). Ton Kiang's dim sum is phenomenal—fresh, flavorful, and not the least bit greasy. (Tip: On weekends, ask for a table by the kitchen door to get first dibs from the dim sum carts.) Other proven dishes on the regular menu are the ethereal steamed dumplings, chicken wonton soup, house special beef and fish-ball soup (better than it sounds), fried spring rolls, steamed salt-baked chicken with a scallion and ginger sauce (a famous though quite salty Hakka dish), and any of the stuffed tofu or clay pot dishes (a.k.a. Hakka casseroles). Seriously, this place is worth the drive and the wait. *$$; AE, DC, DIS, MC, V; no checks; lunch, dinner every day; beer and wine; reservations recommended; between 22nd and 23rd Aves.* &

Haight-Ashbury

The Summer of Love lasted a mere 3 months, but 30 years later tourists and nostalgic San Franciscans still flock to the Haight to experience the flavor of the late '60s. Once home to Janis Joplin, the Grateful Dead, and myriad hippies, Haight-Ashbury has long since lost the uplifting spirit of that infamous summer, but drugs, alcohol, and tie-dye remain. A new generation of street urchins zones out along the storefronts of the neighborhood, playing guitars, stringing beads, or mumbling "Kind bud" (translation: "Want to buy some pot?") to random passersby. Economically, Haight-Ashbury, or the Upper Haight as it is also known, has cashed in on its illustrious past: stores dedicated to the hippie legacy sell tie-dyed shirts, psychedelic posters, incense, pot paraphernalia, and used records. The **RED VICTORIAN BED, BREAKFAST & ART** (see review, below) dedicates its entire lower level to '60s and '70s memorabilia. Tattoo parlors and pipe shops draw alternative crowds, but the majority of people parading down Haight Street are tourists. Hundreds flock here each day to witness the nonstop freak show this street has become. When Jerry Garcia died in 1995, the neighborhood became a meeting place for the bereaved. His former home at 710 Ashbury (at Waller St) has long been part of the Haight pilgrimage. As a sign of the times, the Gap now holds down the fort at the infamous corner of Haight and Ashbury; across the street is the hippie-capitalist bastion Ben & Jerry's.

RESTAURANTS

Cha Cha Cha / ★★☆

1801 HAIGHT ST; 415/386-5758 2327 / MISSION ST; 415/648-0504 When we're asked which San Francisco restaurants are our favorites (and we're asked all the time), one of the first we mention is Cha Cha Cha. It's fun, it's festive, the Caribbean food is very good, the prices are reasonable, the sangría is addictive, and every meal ends with a free Tootsie Roll. What's not to like? The cafe is wildly decorated with Santeria altars and such, which blend in perfectly with the varied mix of pumped-up patrons quaffing pitchers of sangría while waiting for a table (which often takes up to an hour on weekends, but nobody seems to mind). We always start with these tapas-style dishes: sautéed mushrooms, fried calamari, fried new potatoes (dig the spicy sauce), Cajun shrimp, mussels in saffron (order more bread for the sauce), and plantains with black-bean sauce. Check the specials board for outstanding seafood dishes, but skip the so-so steak. There's also a second branch in the Mission District, which serves exactly the same food in a much larger space; not only is the wait shorter (or nonexistent), but there's also a full bar. Still, the original is our favorite simply for its only-in-SF ambiance. *$; MC, V; no checks; lunch, dinner every day; beer and wine; no reservations; Haight St location at Shrader St; Mission St location between 19th and 20th Sts.* ♿

Eos Restaurant & Wine Bar / ★★★

901 COLE ST; 415/566-3063 One of the most-talked-about restaurants in the city, Eos has the tourists asking, "Where is Cole Valley?" It's not so much the menu—the Euro-Asian fusion theme is hardly original—as it is the portions (generous) and presentations (brilliant) that have brought throngs of visitors and residents to this once-little-known San Francisco neighborhood nestled near the southeast corner of Golden Gate Park. Owner-chef Arnold Wong, a California Culinary Academy graduate and a former architecture student, has taken the art of arrangement to a whole new level: every dish is masterfully crafted to take full advantage of the shape, color, and texture of each ingredient. And—egad!—it's a desecration simply to dig in to such culinary artwork, though one's guilt is soon assuaged after the assault begins, particularly when it's upon the tender breast of Peking duck, smoked in ginger-peach tea leaves and served with a plum-kumquat chutney. Other notable dishes are the almond-encrusted soft-shell crab appetizer dipped in spicy plum ponzu sauce; shiitake mushroom dumplings; blackened Asian catfish atop a bed of lemongrass risotto; five-pepper calamari; and the red curry–marinated rack of lamb. Desserts are as fetching as the entrees, particularly the Bananamisu (akin to tiramisu) with caramelized bananas and the warm bittersweet chocolate soufflé cake. Unfortunately, a quiet, romantic dinner is out of the question here, since the stark deco-industrial decor merely amplifies the nightly cacophony. After dinner, adjourn to the restaurant's popular wine bar around the corner, which stocks more than 400 bottles—many at reasonable prices—from around the globe. Nearly 50 red and white wines are available by the glass, too. *$$$; AE, MC, V; no checks; dinner every day; beer and wine; reservations recommended; at Carl St.* &

Kan Zaman / ★★

1793 HAIGHT ST; 415/751-9656 Glass-beaded curtains lead into Kan Zaman, a favorite destination for grunge types who populate the Haight. Shed your shoes and gather around knee-high tables under a canopy tent—or snag the premier window seat—and recline on pillows while sampling the tasty, inexpensive hot and cold Middle Eastern meze (appetizers). Before long, you'll think you've been transported to (as Kan Zaman literally translates) "a long time ago." Traditional menu items include hummus, *baba ghanouj, kibbee* (cracked wheat with spiced lamb) meat pies, and various kebabs. Sample platters offering tastes of a little bit of everything are ideal for large parties. For a novel and truly exotic finish, puff on an *argeeleh* (hookah pipe) filled with fruity honey or apricot tobacco. Wine, beer, and spiced wine round out the beverage offerings. Another plus: Kan Zaman serves till midnight—a real find in this town. *$; MC, V; no checks; lunch Sat–Sun, dinner every day; beer and wine; reservations recommended; at Shrader St.* &

Thep Phanom / ★★★

400 WALLER ST; 415/431-2526 Thailand's complex, spicy, cosmopolitan cuisine has always been adaptive, incorporating flavors from India, China, Burma, Malaysia, and, more recently, the West. San Francisco boasts dozens of Thai restaurants; virtually all of them are good, and many (including Khan Toke Thai House and Manora's Thai Cuisine) are excellent. Why, then, has Thep Phanom alone had a permanent line out its front door for the last 14 years even though it takes reservations? At this restaurant, housed in a grand Victorian, a creative touch of California enters the cultural mix, resulting in sophisticated preparations that have a special sparkle. The signature dish, *ped swan,* is a boneless duck in a light honey sauce served on a bed of spinach—and it ranks with the city's greatest entrees. Tart, minty, spicy *yum plamuk* (calamari salad), *larb ped* (minced duck salad), coconut chicken soup, and the velvety basil-spiked seafood curry served on banana leaves (available Wednesday and Thursday only) are superb choices, too. Service is charming and efficient; the tasteful decor, informal atmosphere, eclectic crowd, and discerning wine list are all very San Francisco. *$$; AE, DC, DIS, MC, V; no checks; dinner every day; beer and wine; reservations recommended; www.thaitaste.com/thepphanom; at Fillmore St.* &

LODGINGS

Red Victorian Bed, Breakfast & Art / ★☆

1665 HAIGHT ST; 415/864-1978 The Red Vic, located smack-dab on an exciting stretch of Haight Street, is one of the most eclectic and groovy lodgings in the city. You'll have the quintessential Haight-Ashbury experience staying in any of the 18 colorfully decorated rooms, each with its own '60s Summer of Love heritage theme. For example, the luxury Peacock Suite features stained-glass windows, a canopied king bed, and a bathtub in a mirrored window alcove looking into the sitting room. Economy double rooms include the Earth Charter Room and Summer of Love Room. Eight of the guest rooms have private baths, while the remaining rooms share four "theme" bathrooms down the hall. In fact, owner Sami Sunchild will *suggest* that you take the time to explore the shared Aquarium Bathroom (where goldfish swim in the toilet tank), the Starlight Bathroom, the Love Bathroom, and the Infinity Bathroom. (How could one resist such an offer?) A complimentary breakfast is served family-style in the breakfast salon at 9am each morning, offering an opportunity to meet the other guests (and what an interesting lot they are) and discuss the social and environmental needs of the planet. Sami (also known as founder and artist-in-residence) runs this one-of-a-kind tribute to the '60s, and you couldn't dream up a more dedicated, gracious host. So c'mon, inject a little peace, love, and happiness into your travels and give Ms. Sunchild a call. *$–$$$; AE, DIS, MC, V; checks OK; www.redvic.com; between Clayton and Cole Sts.*

SoMa (South of Market Street)

The area south of Market Street, known by the acronym SoMa, is many things to many people: cutting-edge arts mecca, club-hopping heaven, and—as of recently—overdevelopment hell. The multiple-personality syndrome is not surprising, considering that SoMa encompasses a huge amount of real estate that continues to increase in value even though the Internet economy hasn't.

Until recently, much of SoMa had long been a bastion of affordable—albeit ramshackle—housing; even in the early days of the Gold Rush, it was home to a tent city for newly arrived immigrant forty-niners. As San Franciscans prospered on Gold Rush fever, the area around South Park—once the heart of Multimedia Gulch—evolved into a gated community surrounded by opulent mansions. The mansions have since vanished, but a bit of Old World charm remains: at 615 Third Street, a plaque marks the site where Jack London was born in 1876 (the original structure was destroyed in the 1906 quake). Though the **MOSCONE CONVENTION CENTER**—completed in 1981 and named after the mayor who was slain in 1978—

was the first major development to inject tourist money into the area, it was the 1995 unveiling of Swiss architect Mario Botta's **SAN FRANCISCO MUSEUM OF MODERN ART** that solidified SoMa's reputation as the artistic heart of the city, attracting visitors from all over the world. On the heels of the museum's completion came the **YERBA BUENA CENTER FOR THE ARTS,** which hosts exhibitions ranging from avant-garde video and installation art to the more conventional "Impressionists in Winter." Surrounding the center is **YERBA BUENA GARDEN,** a 5-acre public oasis that includes a Martin Luther King Jr. memorial—etched glass panels displayed behind a long, shimmering cascade of water—and other sculptures.

RESTAURANTS

Azie / ★★★

826 FOLSOM ST; 415/538-0918 Chef-restaurateur Jody Denton wants to corner the culinary market in the up-and-coming scene on Folsom Street. By the looks of Azie, wedged in next door to his wildly popular Restaurant LuLu, he's well on his way. This stylish restaurant bears its South of Market surroundings in mind, with 22-foot ceilings vaulted by four huge columns. The dining room is split-level; in the booths on the main level, you can draw a set of curtains for a truly exclusive feel. The main level is also home to the exhibition kitchen, where Asian-inspired French cuisine such as roulade of monkfish, grilled veal medallions with sea urchin–wasabi butter, and aromatic oxtail bundles are beautifully arranged. Some of the most popular dishes are the boneless short ribs, roasted lobster in scallion-ginger cream, braised duck in red curry, and the Nine Bites appetizer; if you have trouble making a decision, opt for the nightly tasting menu. Dining is also available at the bar, where a DJ plays oh-so-cool music nightly. *$$$; AE, DC, MC, V; no checks; dinner every day; full bar; reservations recommended; at 4th St.*

bacar / ★★★

448 BRANNAN ST; 415/904-4100 You don't even want to know how much money was poured into this three-decker restaurant, the latest venture of Eos (see review, above) owner-chef Arnold Eric Wong and wine director Debbie Zachareas. The exposed-brick-and-timber, warehouse-size restaurant consists of a lower-level wine salon filled with couches, armchairs, and pretty people acting oh-so-cool, a high-energy (and loud) mezzanine bar, and somewhat quieter seating upstairs. Dishes like wild boar osso buco, duck and vegetable pot pie, salt-cod cakes, and crispy thin-crust pizzas are expertly paired with Zachareas's mind-melting 1,000-bottle-long wine list, including 100 selections by the glass, as a 2-ounce sampler, or via a decanter. In fact, no other restaurant in the city pays such careful attention to pairing wines with each dish, and Zachareas is almost always on the floor to offer suggestions and answer questions. Whether bacar can survive the neighborhood's dot-com demise is the $64K question, but for now it's the scene for being seen. Tip: bacar offers live jazz nightly after 10pm, and the kitchen stays open until 1pm. *$$$; AE, MC, V; no checks; dinner every day; full bar; reservations recommended; between 3rd and 4th Sts.* ✦

BLACKIE'S PASTURE

In an urbanized area, it isn't often that a patch of land becomes so well known that locals give directions with it as a landmark—but for that we have Blackie himself to thank. Blackie, a sweet-natured sway-backed horse, lived 28 of his 40 years in Tiburon, standing in a pasture off Tiburon Boulevard. A woman who grew up in Tiburon said that many local children stopped by the pasture on the way to school to offer apples and carrots to the old fellow; when he died in 1968, the nearby elementary school proclaimed a half-day of mourning. Blackie still stands in his pasture, in the form of a life-size bronze statue by sculptor Albert Guibara. As you drive along Tiburon Boulevard toward Tiburon, look to your right—you can't miss him.

Bizou / ★★★

598 4TH ST; 415/543-2222 Bizou means "a little kiss" in French, but San Francisco foodies seem to have planted a big fat wet one on this lively bistro with the rustic Mediterranean menu. Since 1993, chef-owner Loretta Keller (formerly of Stars) has seduced even normally conservative diners into eating such exotica as braised beef cheeks, parsnip chips, cod ravioli, and house-cured anchovies (with the heads on, no less), winning them over with her deceptively simple, flavorful preparations. There are plenty of less adventurous items, to be sure, including a wonderful salad of pear, Gorgonzola, radicchio, frisée, and toasted walnuts; day-boat scallops with wild mushrooms, endive, and balsamic vinegar; stuffed young chicken with celeriac, grilled apples, and goat cheese; and desserts like French cream with persimmon and fig sauces and a Seville orange and Meyer lemon–curd cake. Housed in a 1906 building, the corner storefront restaurant has an updated bistro feel, with window boxes, vintage light fixtures, weathered mustard-colored walls, large windows, and an oak bar. A few caveats, though: The tables are packed tightly together, the place can get very noisy, and the service can range from boffo to beastly. *$$; AE, MC, V; no checks; lunch Mon–Fri, dinner Mon–Sat; full bar; reservations recommended; at Brannan St.* &

Fringale / ★★★★

570 4TH ST; 415/543-0573 Chef/co-owner Gerald Hirigoyen, named one of the 10 best chefs in the nation by *Food & Wine* magazine, draws crowds to his tiny, boisterous 50-seat French restaurant tucked away in a charmless section of the city. Behind this restaurant's cheery yellow facade, however, there's plenty of charm emanating from the casual, blond-wood-trimmed interior, petite curved bar, and friendly, largely French wait staff. Hirigoyen was born and raised in the Basque country of southwest France, and his origins serve as the abiding inspiration for his gutsy, flavor-packed—and reasonably priced—fare. Outstanding dishes include the frisée salad topped with a poached egg and warm bacon dressing, steamed mussels sprinkled with garlic and parsley, wild mushroom ravioli, rack of lamb, and his signature (and meltingly tender) pork tenderloin confit with onion and apple marmalade. Hirigoyen was originally a pastry chef, and he flaunts his talents with his incredible crème brûlée and rich chocolate Basque cake topped with chocolate mousse. Fringale (French for "a sudden pang of hunger") is perpetually packed with famished folks at dinnertime, so expect a noisy crowd and a wait for a table, even if you've made a reservation. *$$; AE, MC, V; no checks; lunch Mon–Fri, dinner Mon–Sat; full bar; reservations recommended; bistro@aol.com; www.fringale.city search.com; between Brannan and Bryant Sts.* &

Hawthorne Lane / ★★★⯪

22 HAWTHORNE LN; 415/777-9779 When Hillary Rodham Clinton was in town to promote her book *It Takes a Village,* she ate a late dinner at Hawthorne Lane. Probably learned about it from hubby Bill, who supped here the year before and might have raved about the miso-glazed black cod with sesame spinach rolls, the special lobster tempura, the roasted Sonoma lamb with butternut squash and Parmesan risotto, or the house-made fettuccine with chanterelle mushrooms. Ever since it opened in 1995, Hawthorne Lane has been one of the city's hottest restaurants, its popularity fueled by its lovely design, its proximity to the happening SoMa scene, and the pedigree of chef-owners David and Anne Gingrass (formerly of Spago and Postrio fame), who meld the cuisines of Italy, France, and Asia using the finest California foods. The dining room is a refined, beguiling space, with wrought-iron cherry blossoms, a massive skylight, giant urns with dazzling fresh floral displays, and light-colored woods creating an air of perennial spring. Hawthorne also wins raves for its varied selection of wonderful breads and desserts. If you can't get a reservation, snag one of the seats at the long, oval bar, where you can order from the dining room menu, or sign up for one of the many tables set aside for walk-ins. *$$$; DC, DIS, MC, V; checks OK; lunch Mon–Fri, dinner every day; full bar; reservations recommended; dcg@hawthornelane.com; www.hawthornelane.com; off Howard St between 2nd and 3rd Sts.* &

Restaurant Lulu / ★★

816 FOLSOM ST; 415/495-5775 Restaurant LuLu may not enjoy the legendary status it once commanded, but it's still one of the most energetic and popular restaurants in San Francisco and yet another feather in the chef's cap of Reed Hearon (who has since gone on to fry bigger fish). It's easy to see why LuLu was and *is* a hit. As soon as you enter, you're pleasantly assaulted with divine aromas emanating from the massive open kitchen, which overlooks the cavernous-yet-stylish dining room where a hundred or more diners are feasting family-style and creating such a din that the kitchen staff has to wear two-way headsets (it's quite a scene). The sine qua non starter is the sputtering iron-skillet-roasted mussels served with drawn butter. Essentially everything that comes from the twin wood-burning ovens is superb, particularly the pork loin rubbed with fennel, garlic, and olive oil and served with mashed potatoes; the rosemary-infused chicken served with warm potato salad; and the thin, crisp pizzas topped with first-rate prosciutto, pancetta, and other savory toppings. Everything is served on a large platter to facilitate sharing. For dessert, go for the gooey chocolate cake served with a scoop of gourmet ice cream. *$$; AE, DC, MC,*

V; no checks; lunch, dinner every day; full bar; reservations recommended; www.restaurantlulu.com; at 4th St. &

LODGINGS

Harbor Court Hotel / ★★★

165 STEUART ST; 415/882-1300 OR 800/346-0555 On the southwest edge of the Financial District, this low-key, high-style hotel caters mainly to business travelers, but will equally impress the weekend vacationer. It was once a YMCA, but don't let that dissuade you: the high-quality accommodations, gorgeous views of the bay, and complimentary use of the adjoining fitness club—complete with indoor Olympic-size swimming pool—add up to one sweet deal. Each of the 131 guest rooms is nicely equipped with soundproof windows, a half-canopy bed, a large armoire, and a writing desk. Amenities range from limited room service to secretarial services, laundry and dry cleaning, evening wine reception, newspaper delivery, valet service, and car service to the Financial District. When the sun drops, slip on down to the bar at Boulevard and mingle with the swinging yuppie singles (see review, above). *$$$–$$$$; AE, DC, MC, V; no checks; www.harborcourthotel.com; between Mission and Howard Sts.* &

W Hotel / ★★★

181 3RD ST; 415/777-5300 OR 877/W-HOTELS Hip hotels are all the rage now, and the Starwood Hotels & Resorts corporation has capitalized on the craze with a San Francisco version of the popular W hotel in New York. Art, technology, service, and sex appeal are all applied in force from the moment you walk into the lobby. In fact, you don't even know you're in a 31-story hotel at first, because the first person to greet you is the bartender (brilliant). To your right is a gaggle of hip, young, beautiful people lounging in the ever-so-chic lobby, and to the left is XYZ, a popular SoMa restaurant. The decor of each guest room mimics the overall theme—bold colors, soft fabrics, sensual curves—almost enough to make you *not* notice how small the rooms are. No matter: Dive onto the thick, luscious goose-down comforter and you won't ever want to leave. High-tech toys include a 27-inch TV with Internet service, CD player, and modem jacks for your laptop. The location is fantastic as well, smack-dab in the smoking-hot SoMa district and literally sharing real estate with the beautiful San Francisco Museum of Modern Art and Yerba Buena Gardens. The verdict? If you want to play with San Francisco's in-crowd, W is the place to be (at least for now). *$$$$; AE, DC, JCB, MC, V; checks OK; www.whotelscom; between Mission and Howard Sts.* &

Potrero Hill

Sitting between two freeways and on a rise directly south of downtown, Potrero Hill flutters between industrial chic and leafy residential. Sometimes the lines cross, and the results are brightly hued, high-tech abodes in the middle of sleepy old streets. Once called Goat Hill, this former home to ungulates is now an up-and-coming residential area, shedding its former incarnation as a site for affordable housing "projects." Interior design heaven (furniture and antique shops as well as design studios) lies at its base, in the area between 16th and Division Streets. Climb the hill, and the views of downtown and the bay are expansive. On 18th Street, a little commercial area (between Arkansas and Texas Sts) features several charming restaurants.

RESTAURANTS

42 Degrees / ★★★

499 ILLINOIS ST; 415/777-5558 42 Degrees, popular with a relentlessly hip crowd of young professionals, boasts a spare, high-tech warehouse look, with a soaring ceiling and lots of concrete, metal, and glass. As night falls, however, candlelight, table linens, and strains of live jazz soften the effect, transforming the stark 100-seat space into an appealing supper club. The name refers to the latitude of Provence and the Mediterranean Sea, and chef-owner James Moffat's ever-changing menu reflects this sun-splashed influence with starters like watercress salad with duck confit, walnuts, and pomegranates; Medjool dates with Parmesan and celery; and grilled artichokes with Meyer lemons. Entrees might include risotto with shaved truffles and mushrooms, pan-roasted chicken with lemon and black olive sauce, or grilled pancetta-wrapped salmon. Lighter eaters can look to the chalkboard for small plates such as pizzettas, Iberian blood sausage, and herb-roasted potatoes with aioli. Desserts include a sublime chocolate pot de crème, milk chocolate crème brûlée, and a warm apple Napoleon with vanilla ice cream and huckleberry sauce. The service is courteous and professional, the mezzanine-level windows afford a view of the bay, and the pleasant courtyard patio is perfect for dining alfresco on warm days. *$$–$$$; MC, V; no checks; dinner Wed–Sat; full bar; reservations recommended; one block off 3rd St at 16th St.* &

Mission District

The site of San Francisco's original Spanish settlement, Mission Dolores, the Mission District owes much to the Mexican ranchers who bought up large tracts of land during the pre–Gold Rush days when Alta California belonged to Mexico. During the early 1900s, a large number of immigrants settled here. But the Mission isn't merely a home to recent arrivals. For decades artists, students, and blue-collar workers of all stripes have flocked here for sunshine and affordable housing. The heart and namesake of the neighborhood, **MISSION DOLORES**, sits on Dolores Street at 16th Street. The newer basilica's spires tower above the much-smaller mission next door, which was dedicated in 1791 and still has original adobe walls and roof tiles. Cruise Valencia and 16th Streets for interesting shopping and good restaurants, 24th Street between Guerrero and South Van Ness for the epicenter of the Mission's Latino culture, and the entire neighborhood for ethnic markets, inexpensive taquerias, and vibrant murals.

RESTAURANTS

Blowfish Sushi to Die For / ★★

2170 BRYANT ST; 415/285-3848 Japanese animation films play on two suspended television sets for the young and the hip who pack this place, lounging against a backdrop of velvet walls, techno dance music, and acid jazz. Clearly, Blowfish caters to a crowd that wants more than just good sushi. Located in the industrial northeast Mission District, the restaurant offers a combination of traditional and more adventurous sushi. For example, if you're intent on trying the infamously deadly blowfish, the Japanese delicacy otherwise known as puffer fish, expect to fork over about $30 if it's in season, and be prepared for a letdown: it's fairly bland. Move on to the mavericks: Maui Maki (tuna, mango, and macadamia nuts); double crab salad with soft-shell crab; tempura-battered asparagus maki wrapped in rice; and the restaurant's namesake, Blowfish Maki (a roll of yellowtail, scallions, and tobiko, draped with salmon—but, ironically, no blowfish). Non-fish-eaters also have choices: filet mignon with rosemary garlic butter, chicken pot stickers, or asparagus spring rolls with duck. Chef Ritsuo Tsuchida likes to tempt his regular customers with some of his more unusual creations: seared ostrich on portobello-mushroom tempura, anyone? Service is friendly and efficient. *$$–$$$; AE, DC, DIS, MC, V; no checks; lunch Mon–Fri, dinner every day; full bar; reservations recommended; between 19th and 20th Sts.* &

Delfina / ★★★

3621 18TH ST; 415/552-4055 Opening to rave reviews in 1998, this tiny Mission District neighborhood restaurant with a clean, modern design and pea-green walls has been packed ever since. Partners Anne and Craig Stoll have extensive pedigrees at other Bay Area restaurants, and chef Stoll's daily-changing creations showcase his skills for cooking Italian regional cuisine. Top-notch starters have included nettles-and-ricotta ravioli; a salad studded with fresh cracked crab, fennel, and grapefruit segments; and the far-from-ordinary fried Ribollita da Delfina minestrone. Entrees are hearty and include rich, braised meat dishes, excellent pastas, and fish. Pancetta-wrapped rabbit loin bursts with flavor, as do the buttermilk-battered fried onions with polenta served on the side. A textbook spaghetti with tomatoes, garlic, olive oil, and chili flakes has a little heat to warm the throat. The swordfish rests on a bed of soft leeks, a salmon may be served with fresh vegetables and a tangy citrus dressing, and the salt cod is outstanding. Desserts are simply delicious: profiteroles stuffed with coffee ice cream, creamy buttermilk panna cotta (baked custard), and Gorgonzola with chestnut honey. Delfina's wine list is a well-edited one, with many moderately priced bottles among the offerings. *$$; MC, V; no checks; dinner every day; beer and wine; reservations recommended; between Dolores and Guerrero Sts.* &

Foreign Cinema / ★★

2534 MISSION ST; 415/648-7600 Like a Steven Spielberg movie, the opening of this Mission District restaurant was anticipated at least a year in advance. The hype reached such a fevered pitch, locals were half expecting to see a line of product tie-ins in local stores. When the place finally opened, in the summer of 1999, it was quickly apparent the throngs hadn't waited in vain. The concept behind this contemporary French restaurant is to combine dinner and a movie in a single location. Accessed through an unassuming door along Mission Street, the restaurant has an industrial-chic appearance, with deliberately unfinished walls, exposed mechanics in the ceiling, a stark open kitchen, and hard surfaces throughout. On one wall in a center courtyard, classic foreign films are projected in all their grainy black-and-white glory (early features included Fellini's *La Dolce Vita* and Bergman's *Seventh Seal).* Drive-in-movie–type speaker boxes are placed at each table so you can listen along as you dine—sort of like a movie-and-dinner-date all rolled into one. But mostly the films are just an imaginative distraction from the main attraction: the food. The lobster and monkfish bouillabaisse is rich and decadent, the roasted Sonoma duck breast is tender and bursting with flavor, the rosemary-marinated lamb melts in your mouth, and for dessert it's the chocolate pot de crème. It's all quite a production, enough so that you may not even notice that some of the dishes seem a bit rushed and decidedly sub-par (read: go with the wait staff's suggestions). *$$–$$$; MC, V; no checks; dinner every day; full bar; reservations recommended; www.foreigncinema.com; between 21st and 22nd Sts.* &

La Taqueria / ★★

2889 MISSION ST; 415/285-7117 Among the colorful fruit stands, thrift shops, and greasy panhandlers lining bustling Mission Street sits La Taqueria, the Bay Area's best burrito factory. Its lackluster interior is brightened only by a vibrant mural depicting south-of-the-border scenes and a shiny CD jukebox pumping out merry Mexican music, all of which could mean only one thing: people come here for the food. Don't expect a wide variety, for the folks behind the counter just churn out what they do best: burritos, tacos, and quesadillas. It's all fresh, delicious, and guaranteed to fill you up—for little more than pocket change. The moist, meaty fillings include excellent *carnitas* (braised pork), grilled beef, sausage, beef tongue, and chicken (you won't find any rice in these burritos); and the *bebidas* vary from beer and soda to cantaloupe juice and even *horchata* (a sweet rice drink). Stand in line to place your order and pay, then take a seat at one of the shared, long wooden tables and wait for someone to bellow out your number (somehow they just know whether to say it in Spanish or English). *$; no credit cards; local checks only; lunch, dinner every day; beer only; reservations not accepted; between 24th and 25th Sts.* &

Ti Couz / ★★★☆

3108 16TH ST; 415/252-7373 Other restaurants offer crepes, but none compare to what this popular Mission District establishment does with the beloved French pancake. Ti Couz—French for "The Old House" and pronounced "tee cooz"—serves delectable, Brittany-style sweet and savory crepes in a homey setting that feels very much like an old French inn. Don't be overwhelmed by the menu: though countless ingredients are listed so you can create your own *crêpe bretonne*, the menu (in French and English) lists several suggestions. Entree recommendations include ham and cheese, mushroom-almond, and fresh tomato. A ratatouille-and-cheese creation bursts with flavor, and a hearty sausage-filled pancake won't disappoint. But be forewarned: the large buckwheat crepes are très énormes! And you must leave room for dessert. The sweet wheat-flour crepes, fluffier than the savory buckwheat versions, are ideal for luscious fillings such as apple, ice cream, and caramel, or fresh berries à la mode. Complete the meal with a choice of several hard ciders served in bowls— the fruity flavors complement this unique and tasty fare like nothing else. You can also choose from a list of French wines or Celtic beers, as well as French-style coffees and cocktails. Open until midnight Friday and Saturday. *$; MC, V; no checks; lunch, dinner every day; full bar; reservations not accepted; at Valencia St.* &

The Castro

Once part of the 4,000-acre ranch belonging to Jose de Jesus Noe, former alcalde of Mexican San Francisco, the Castro area underwent a huge transformation when the Yankees moved into town. The 1920s were boom years for the newly developed neighborhood. Built in 1922, the Castro Theatre stood as the elegant centerpiece of this growing community (and still does). In the 1970s, a large number of gay men moved into the area, renovated weathered Victorians, and gave the neighborhood a general face-lift. The Castro came alive again, this time as the epicenter of gay pride. The neighborhood rejoiced in 1977 when local camera-store owner Harvey Milk was elected to the city council, becoming the nation's first openly gay elected city official. A year later, the community suffered a devastating blow when Supervisor Milk and Mayor George Moscone were gunned down in City Hall by former supervisor Dan White. Today, **HARVEY MILK PLAZA** at Castro and Market Streets is a popular gathering place for marches and political rallies. The Spanish Renaissance–style **CASTRO THEATRE** (429 Castro St near Market St; 415/621-6120) draws crowds for its innovative and retro movie offerings as well as its landmark architecture. Another added plus is the restored Wurlitzer on which an organist plays "San Francisco, Open Your Golden Gate" before each show (it then sinks into the floor by way of a hydraulic lift—very cool). Market, Castro, and 18th Streets are lined with eclectic purveyors of clothing and housewares, bookstores, gift shops, and cafes such as the **METRO** (3600 16th St at Market St; 415/703-9750), a great place to sit on the balcony and watch the locals stroll by.

RESTAURANTS

Mecca / ★★☆

2029 MARKET ST; 415/621-7000 Mecca is a magnet for those who want sexy atmosphere with hearty American bistro fare—and this sexy, silver supper club lined with chocolate-brown velvet drapes delivers. Start with one of the sassy cocktails (how about She's-a-Bad-Girl—a Mecca-rita with Cuervo, Cointreau, and lime?) at the slick, zinc-topped bar inset with multicolored fiber-optic lights, and enjoy the moody music, which is often provided by live jazz and R&B ensembles on the small stage. The restaurant specializes in contemporary American cuisine with an emphasis on influences from Asia and the American Southwest. Signature dishes are the oysters on the half shell with red chilie ponzu sauce, the barbecued oysters with crispy pancetta, and the ahi tuna spring rolls with balsamic and soy vinaigrette. The kitchen also excels in pastas and meats: a Sicilian sausage penne in a rosemary cream sauce spiked with tomatoes and fava beans; a thick-cut Jamaican jerked grilled pork chop with a side of potato and sweet onion hash; and a tamarind-glazed Muscovy duck breast served with mustard-braised French fingerling potatoes, red onion, and snow peas. Yes, it's as good as it reads. Unlike most San Francisco restaurants, the glamorous Mecca serves dinner until midnight Thursday through Saturday, making it the perfect stop during those late-night benders. *$$$; AE, DC, MC, V; no checks; dinner every day; full bar; reservations recommended; www.sfmecca.com; between Dolores and Church Sts.* &

2223 Restaurant & Bar / ★★★

2223 MARKET ST; 415/431-0692 Also known as the No Name, this popular Castro District spot has been packing in the crowds because it's one of the first upscale restaurants in the area that offers serious food, friendly and professional service, and a terrific bar scene. You'll see only the restaurant's address on the outside of the building, so look for a red exterior and a lively crowd visible through large storefront windows. A long bar flanked by a mural dominates one side of the restaurant. You'll probably end up waiting there for a table, which will give you time to enjoy the great cosmopolitans and martinis. Across the room, the narrow dining area has wood tables, bistro chairs, and cushioned banquettes. The menu is as eclectic as the crowd—mostly American-Mediterranean, with Southwestern and Southeast Asian touches. The romaine salad is a great Caesar variation, with capers, thinly sliced cornichons, and smoky onions. Try one of the pizzas, such as the pancetta, onion confit, Teleme cheese, marjoram, and sun-dried tomato pesto version. For entrees, the kitchen serves generous portions of comfort food: juicy pan-roasted chicken with garlic mashed potatoes, a double-cut pork chop served with a side of chayote squash, grilled salmon with lemon-caviar fondue, and sliced lamb sirloin fanned on a ragout of fava beans and fresh artichoke hearts. Indulge in the Louisiana crème brûlée with pecan pralines for dessert. Despite the noise from the bar, 2223 Market is a terrific neighborhood spot—especially if you can find a nearby parking place. *$$; AE, DC, MC, V; local checks OK; dinner every day, brunch Sun; full bar; reservations recommended; www.2223restaurant.com; between Sanchez and Noe Sts.* ᕁ

LODGINGS

Inn on Castro / ★★

321 CASTRO ST; 415/861-0321 This convivial bed-and-breakfast, catering to the gay and lesbian community for nearly two decades, has developed an ardent following—hence the intriguing collection of more than 100 heart-shaped boxes on the sideboard in the hallway, trinkets left behind by a legion of wistful patrons who can say they left their hearts in San Francisco. The restored Edwardian exterior is painted in a pleasing medley of blue, rose, and green, with gilded details and dentils. The interior is equally festive, with contemporary furnishings, original modern art, exotic plants, and elaborate flower arrangements. There are eight individually decorated guest rooms ranging from a small single to a suite with a deck; each room has a private bath, a cable TV, and a direct-dial phone. Avoid the sunny but noisy rooms facing Castro Street. An elaborate breakfast, served in the dining room, may feature a fresh fruit salad, house-made muffins, fruit juice, and scrambled eggs, French toast, or pancakes. After your repast, relax in the cozy living room with its fireplace and deeply tufted Italian couches, or head out for a stroll in the colorful, ever-bustling Castro. Note: For longer stays, the inn also rents three corporate apartments. *$$; MC, V; checks OK; www.innoncastro2.com; at Market St.*

Noe Valley

Sunny Noe Valley sits west of wide, palm-lined Dolores Street and below Twin Peaks. Twenty-fourth Street is the bustling commercial center for this mostly resi-

A ROOM WITH A VIEW AT THE "Q"

San Quentin State Prison (a.k.a. "Q"), considered functionally obsolete by 1972, was scheduled to be torn down, but it lives on. Prisoners play a variety of sports, are allowed conjugal visits, produce a newspaper—the *San Quentin News*—and attend school inside the walls. They also produce items for the San Quentin Handicraft Shop: leather goods, candles, jewelry, T-shirts, and other gift items that are available to the public. San Quentin's main gate is accessed via the last off-ramp before the Richmond–San Rafael Bridge. You'll pass through a small town of pretty cottages with one of the best views in the area before reaching the parking lot and main gate. If San Quentin is ever decommissioned, the real estate feeding frenzy will be astounding. The prison museum, which details the history of Q, is an on-again, off-again affair due to the vagaries of volunteer labor. The Handicraft Shop is open Wed–Sun, 8:30am–2pm. Call the prison at 415/454-1460 for more information.

dential neighborhood, with plenty of places to grab a bagel or ice cream, as well as some great restaurants. The street's shops reflect the surrounding demographics (largely young families and couples): organic produce and groceries, children's clothing and supplies, shoes, and body and bath sundries. Primarily residential Church Street has restaurants for every palate—from American to German to Japanese to Thai to vegetarian—in the stretch between 24th and 30th Streets.

RESTAURANTS

Firefly / ★★☆

4288 24TH ST; 415/821-7652 Hidden in a cluster of homes on the west end of 24th Street is Noe Valley's best restaurant—just look for a giant metal sculpture of its namesake nocturnal insect perched above a lime green and sizzling yellow door. Inside, an eclectic array of modern art surrounds small tables laden with an equally eclectic display of food, which might include steaming bowls of bouillabaisse de Marseilles bubbling over with monkfish, prawns, scallops, and bass; shrimp-and-scallop pot stickers served with a spicy sesame-soy dipping sauce (Firefly's signature appetizer); and a portobello mushroom Wellington served with linguine that's swirled with fresh vegetables. Chef/co-owner Brad Levy and co-owner Veva Edelson, both formerly of Embarko, dub it "home cooking with few ethnic boundaries." They also proudly announce on every menu that their meat comes from the well-known Niman Ranch, home of "happy, drug-free animals with an ocean view," which leaves politically correct Noe Valley carnivores smiling as they savor the spicy pork stew. The changing roster of desserts is as good as it looks, especially the not-too-sweet strawberry shortcake and the banana bread pudding with caramel anglaise. *$$–$$$; AE, MC, V; checks OK; dinner every day; beer and wine; reservations recommended; at Douglas St.*

Marin County

When you consider that the San Francisco Bay Area has more people than the entire state of Oregon, and that Marin County has the highest per-capita income in the nation, you would expect Marin to be brimming with four-star resorts and restaurants. Well, that's not the case. The third-smallest county in California, this little package is full of natural wonders, picturesque towns, and attractions, but nary a Spago or megaresort. It's no wonder that weary urbanites seeking respite and recreation stream across the Golden Gate Bridge to visit Marin's secluded beaches, pristine mountain lakes, and virgin redwood forests. In fact, the Marin coast is just short of Eden for the outdoor adventurer, a veritable organic playground for nature lovers in search of a patch of green or a square of sand to call their own for a day.

ACCESS AND INFORMATION

Two major airports provide access to Marin County. **SAN FRANCISCO INTERNATIONAL AIRPORT (SFO;** 650/821-8211; www.flysfo.com) is 34 miles away, and **OAKLAND INTERNATIONAL AIRPORT (OAK;** 510/563-3300; www.oaklandairport.com) is 19 miles from Marin. **SHUTTLE SERVICE** to and from SFO is provided throughout the day by two carriers: **MARIN AIRPORTER** (415/461-4222; www.marinairporter.com) and **MARIN DOOR TO DOOR** (415/457-2717; www.marindoortodoor.com) pick up and deliver in Marin. Marin Door to Door also offers service to Oakland International Airport. **RADIO CAB** (415/485-1234) services all of Marin County. Marin Door to Door is the only company that provides daily 24-hour service to San Francisco, Oakland, and San Jose airports.

BUS and **FERRY SERVICE** is offered by the **GOLDEN GATE TRANSIT SYSTEM** (415/455-2000; www.goldengate.org). Ferries run daily between the Larkspur Landing Terminal and Sausalito to San Francisco's Ferry Building and Fisherman's Wharf. The **BLUE & GOLD FLEET** (Pier 41, Fisherman's Wharf; 415/705-5555; www.blueandgoldfleet.com) runs to and from Sausalito and Tiburon. The **ANGEL ISLAND–TIBURON FERRY** (415/435-2131; www.angelislandferry.com) provides service between downtown Tiburon and Angel Island.

Buses connect to the terminals and run daily throughout the county. However, it is generally not convenient to get around Marin on the bus. Schedules are focused on the commute to and from San Francisco. The service to West Marin is infrequent.

Two major bridges connect Marin to the greater Bay Area. The **GOLDEN GATE BRIDGE** provides access to and from San Francisco (pedestrians and bicyclists can use bridge sidewalks); the southbound toll is $5. The **RICHMOND–SAN RAFAEL BRIDGE** connects the county to the East Bay; the westbound toll is $2. Most Marin visitors travel north to south using Highway 101 (the central artery) or coastal Highway 1, with its near-legendary grades, narrow winding roads, and gorgeous views. Sir Francis Drake Boulevard, the longest east-west artery in the county, extends from Interstate 580 (Richmond–San Rafael Bridge) to the Point Reyes Lighthouse. This route runs through the heart of scenic West Marin; it features pastoral settings and rolling hills. Highway 1 and Sir Francis Drake intersect at Olema.

Although Marin enjoys a temperate climate all year round, the **WEATHER** changes quickly from one location to the next. Expect cool, foggy mornings close to

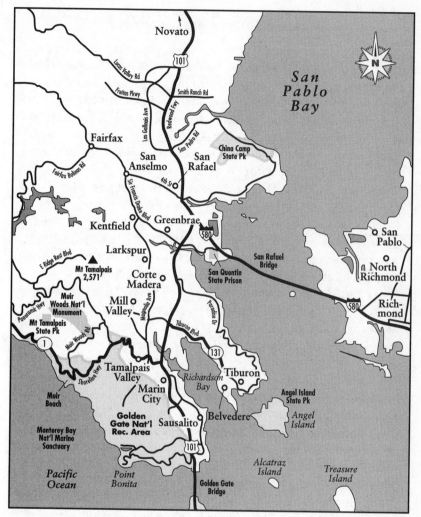

the bay and the ocean. The central part of the county is located in a sun belt. Spring and fall can be the best seasons of the year along the coast: southern Marin can be socked in with fog, but the sun will be shining brightly over West Marin beaches. Layers of clothing are recommended, along with comfortable walking shoes.

The **MARIN COUNTY CONVENTION & VISITORS BUREAU** (1013 Larkspur Landing Circle, Larkspur, CA 94939; 415/499-5000; www.visitmarin.org) is an excellent county resource.

MARIN COUNTY THREE-DAY TOUR

DAY ONE: Indulge yourself. Start the day in **SAN ANSELMO** with a down-home breakfast at **BUBBA'S DINER**. Browse the shops along San Anselmo Avenue. You'll find antiques and collectibles, vintage clothing, home and gardening delights, new and used books, and upscale attire. Stock up with picnic fixings at **COMFORT'S** (335 San Anselmo Ave; 415/454/9840). Head for the hills and points west via Sir Francis Drake Boulevard. You'll know the season by the ever-changing colors in the pastoral land-scape—lush greens come with a rainy winter and spring; golden browns appear in the dry summer and fall. Make **SAMUEL P. TAYLOR STATE PARK** (off Sir Francis Drake Blvd; 415/488-9897) your next stop. Picnic under a canopy of giant redwoods, and stretch your legs on the 1¼-mile self-guiding Pioneer Trail before heading back to San Rafael. It'll take about 30 minutes to reach the inviting **GERSTLE PARK INN**. Check in and enjoy a late-afternoon refreshment. How about dinner? Sausalito here we come, because the best sushi in the entire Bay Area is at **SUSHI RAN**. Toast the end of a per-fect day with a cocktail while admiring the city view from **HORIZONS**.

DAY TWO: Past perfect. Linger over breakfast on the inn's sun porch, anticipating the discovery of nearby hidden places. Step into the past at **MISSION SAN RAFAEL ARCANGEL** (1104 5th Ave, San Rafael; 415/457-4879), Marin's oldest historic site. Your next destination is North San Pedro Road and a beautiful loop drive around San Pablo Bay. Stop at the Frank Lloyd Wright–designed **MARIN CIVIC CENTER** (3501 Civic Center Dr, San Rafael; 415/499-6646) and stroll around the peaceful lagoon. Next, head for lunch at the **BUCKEYE ROADHOUSE,** then drive south to the **SAN FRANCISCO BAY–DELTA MODEL** (2100 Bridgeway Blvd, Sausalito; 415/332-3870). In addition to the amazing ½-acre scale model operated by the U.S. Army Corps of Engineers, you'll enjoy exploring the world-class visitor center and *Marinship*, an exhibit on a World War II shipbuilding facility. Relax back at the Gerstle Park Inn and top off the evening with dinner at **INSALATA'S** or **LEFT BANK**.

DAY THREE: Lazy does it. Be sure to take a peek at neighboring **GERSTLE PARK** before leaving. Make your way to Tiburon and **BLACKIE'S PASTURE** park (located off Tiburon Blvd), where you'll access the popular multiuse path that traces the former railroad right-of-way. Join the local runners, bikers, walkers, and rollerbladers headed for downtown (it'll take about an hour to walk there). You'll think this waterfront setting is postcard-perfect, but wait until you arrive at **SAM'S ANCHOR CAFE**. Head for the deck and order a margarita and bowl of spicy cioppino. Time permitting, you might want to visit **MILL VALLEY**. Tool around the plaza for a while, then have an early dinner at **PIAZZA D'ANGELO** to complete your Mill Valley experience.

Sausalito

Nestled on the east side of Marin County is the pretty little Mediterranean-style town of Sausalito, a former Portuguese fishing village that's now home to about 7,500 residents, including several well-heeled owners of spectacular hillside mansions. It's hard to imagine Rosie the Riveter here, much less victory ships rolling off assembly lines, but Sausalito was a major shipbuilding site during World War II. Today most folks are browsing the upscale boutiques or popular art galleries between gourmet dining and wine tasting. If you're driving to Sausalito from the city, immediately after crossing the Golden Gate Bridge, turn right on Alexander Avenue, which after about a mile turns into Bridgeway, the main drag through the center of town. Pricey boutiques and waterfront restaurants line this street, and a paved promenade offers a truly breathtaking, unobstructed view of Angel Island, Alcatraz, and the San Francisco skyline. For more information contact the Sausalito Visitor Center (415/332-0505; www.sausalito.org).

RESTAURANTS

Guernica / ★★

2009 BRIDGEWAY, SAUSALITO; 415/332-1512 Guernica is named after a town in northern Spain—the site of an infamous battle of the Spanish Civil War and the subject of one of Picasso's most famous paintings—and serves well-prepared dishes in the Basque tradition. An oak-paneled, candlelit hideaway, this small restaurant features a menu that includes sweetbreads, pâtés, fresh seafood, and excellent paella. Seating is either at small tables or at booths, and service is quiet and efficient. The space works well for both boisterous holiday parties and intimate, romantic evenings (often happening at the same time). The warmly decorated wine bar, illuminated by a stained glass window, is a welcome stop for an aperitif. *$–$$; MC, V; no checks; dinner every day; beer and wine; reservations recommended; at the intersection of Marinship Wy.*

Hamburgers / ★

737 BRIDGEWAY, SAUSALITO; 415/332-9471 One of the best places to eat in Sausalito also happens to be one of the cheapest: a narrow little hamburger stand with a sign outside that says simply "Hamburgers." Look for the flat rotating grill in the window off Bridgeway, then stand in line. For $5 and some change, you'll get a burger made with human hands, just like the ones Dad used to flip off the grill. Order a side of crispy fries, grab a bunch of napkins, and then head over to the park down the street. Hot dogs, meatball sandwiches, and steak sandwiches are also served here. *$; cash only; lunch every day; no alcohol; no reservations; downtown Sausalito, north of Princess St.*

Horizons / ★★

558 BRIDGEWAY, SAUSALITO; 415/331-3232 To see the all-time best view of San Francisco, walk through this venerable restaurant and grab a seat on the wind-sheltered deck in back, where you can sip the spirit of your choice and wave at the yachters sailing just a few feet under your nose. This building was the home of the San Francisco Yacht Club until 1925. Later, the site was bought by the popular folk group the Kingston Trio and renamed the Trident. Psychedelic menus from the Trident days are behind glass just inside the polished custom-wood foyer; the restaurant was also the setting for a scene in Woody Allen's film *Play It Again, Sam*. Horizons is a great place to stop for a Bloody Mary and snack and is an easy and casual place to find a seat for lunch during the week. The servings are bountiful and the menu is typical American—shrimp or crab salads, hamburgers, broiled steaks, roast chicken, or grilled or sautéed fish entrees. *$–$$; AE, DC, DIS, MC, V; no checks; lunch, dinner every day, brunch Sun; full bar; reservations recommended;ww.horizonssausalito.com; on the strand 1 block south of the intersection of Bridgeway and Princess St.*

Sushi Ran / ★★★⯪

107 CALEDONIA, SAUSALITO; 415/332-3620 To the loyal patrons of this southern Marin culinary landmark, sushi is not just food—it's a way of life (and we couldn't agree more). Hanging on the wall near the cash register is the smiling image of a portly gentleman who patronized the establishment more than 400 times in one year. (Folks, that's more than once a day.) The sushi served here is impeccable, prepared with aplomb and served with a flourish by highly trained sushi chefs and an amiable wait staff. The fish is glisteningly fresh, and the daily specials are invariably fantastic. Be sure to start off with the miso-marinated cod or sea bass, along with a seaweed salad and miso soup. The kamikaze roll is stuffed with yellowfin tuna, bright flying-fish roe, and crunchy green onions; the spider roll enfolds a delicate tempura-fried soft-shell crab. Rice-wine lovers can choose from 17 sakes, including two from nearby Napa County, and surprisingly, for such a little restaurant, there is a mighty fine wine list offering 100 bottles. If you can't wait for a table in the main restaurant, the adjoining wine and sake bar serves a wide variety of appetizers. *$$$; AE, DIS, MC, V; no checks; lunch Mon–Fri, dinner every day; beer, wine, and sake; reservations recommended; managementoffice@sushiran.com; www.sushiran.com; next to the Marin Theater.* &

LODGINGS

Casa Madrona Hotel & Spa / ★★★★

801 BRIDGEWAY, SAUSALITO; 415/332-0502 OR 800/567-9524 There are two Sausalitos—the tourist-trampled waterfront area and the exclusive residential region in the hills—and the Casa Madrona is where they meet. The entrance to this unique hotel complex is on boutique-lined Bridgeway, where natives never venture and visitors love to shop. Step onto the Madrona property and you'll quickly be transported into Sausalito's enclave of multimillion-dollar mansions and panoramic bay views. The hotel offers everything you could possibly desire: sweeping bay vistas, an outdoor Jacuzzi, a full-service spa, a fine restaurant, and all the amenities of a citified hotel. Casa Madrona's 63 rooms are spread throughout the landscaped hillside. A major renovation in 2002 added a new wing of 31 contemporary guest rooms and suites, all with with sunken tubs and most with private balconies overlooking the Sausalito waterfront. The rates depend on the view: the garden and courtyard rooms are the least expensive, followed by the bayview rooms and the one-bedroom suites. For greater privacy, choose one of the charming Victorian cottages. If an extraordinary view is what you're after, reserve one of the newer bayview rooms (worth the higher rate). Perched on the side of a terraced hill with glimmering views of Belvedere and Angel Island, the hotel's romantic and engaging restauant, Mikayla, specializes in seafood. *$$$$; AE, DC, DIS, MC, V; no checks; 2-night minimum stay Nov–Apr, 3-night minimum May–Oct; casa@casamadrona. com; www.casamadrona.com; located downtown.* &

The Inn Above Tide / ★★★☆

30 EL PORTAL, SAUSALITO; 415/332-9535 OR 800/893-8433 The soothing ebb and flow of gentle tides is a natural attraction at this idyllic hideaway, the only hotel in the Bay Area built over the water. Every room faces the bay, and 24 of the 30 rooms have balconies that you could literally drop a line and fish from. Airy and spacious interiors, awash with soft aquatic blues and misty greens, enhance the sense of serenity. Check out the Vista Suite, a private world of luxury featuring a romantic king-size canopied bed, wet bar, wood-burning fireplace, and spa tub (for a mere $655 a night). Water and views, the best that Sausalito has to offer, are always beckoning. Grab the binoculars found in each room and head for a balcony; relax and enjoy the comings and goings of ferries, sleek sailboats, and oceangoing vessels. There's plenty to look forward to at this comfortably elegant inn: complimentary wine and cheese at sunset, evening turndown service, overnight shoeshine, morning newspaper delivery, and an elaborate continental breakfast, which may be delivered to your room on request. *$$$$; AE, DC, MC, V; no checks; 2-night minimum stay on weekends May–Nov; stay@innabovetide.com; www.innabovetide.com; Portal is off Bridgeway, turn toward the water at downtown plaza.* &

Tiburon and Belvedere

Priceless views, waterfront dining, and interesting shops make Tiburon a popular destination for explorers arriving by ferry, car, or tour bus. Formerly a railroad town—until 1963 it was the terminus of the Northwestern Pacific Railroad—Tiburon (Spanish for "shark") is now a quaint New England–style coastal village. Its short Main Street is packed with expensive antique and specialty shops, as well as restaurants with incredible bay views. You can leave your car on the outskirts and walk to the village, or park in the large pay lot off Main Street. An even better way to get here is by bicycle or by ferry from San Francisco; it drops off passengers at the edge of town.

Past the Yacht Club, the road continues around the protected bay—this is where Tiburon blends into Belvedere (Italian for "beautiful view"), an ultra-exclusive community. The entire city consists of only half a square mile of land, but this is one tony piece of real estate. To get a better view of Belvedere, reclaim your car and drive up the tiny town's steep, narrow roads for a glimpse of the highly protected, well-shielded multimillion-dollar homes where international celebrities such as Elton John have been known to hide out.

RESTAURANTS

Guaymas / ★★

5 MAIN ST, TIBURON; 415/436-6300 Mexican food is as elaborate and nuanced as any of the world's great cuisines, with its mixture of indigenous, Spanish, and French flavors (French soldiers occupied Mexico from 1852 to 1857, and the only good that came of it was some new recipes). Guaymas's kitchen offers superb versions of Mexican classics such as posole, a hearty stew from Jalisco, as well as California-inspired variations like the *sopes con pato*—crisp, deep-fried corn shells filled with braised duck, pasilla peppers, onions, and garlic. The piping-hot white-corn tortillas are served with three sauces: a tangy salsa verde; a sweet and tantalizing salsa chipotle with smoked jalapeños, pineapples, and carrots; and a more pedestrian salsa cruda with tomatoes, onions, cilantro, and garlic. For an appetizer, try the tender marinated slices of nopales (cactus) with onion and Mexican cheese or the pico de gallo, a large plate of fresh fruit served with wedges of lime and a dish of hot red pepper and other seasonings. Once your palate is warmed up, move on to the spicy tamales, the marinated shrimp, or the seafood platter of grilled octopus, squid, shrimp, and salmon. When the weather is favorable, dine on the deck and take in the incredible view of the bay, Angel Island, and the San Francisco skyline as you sip one of the mighty margaritas. *$$$; AE, DC, MC, V; no checks; lunch, dinner every day; full bar; reservations recommended; on Tiburon Harbor at the ferry landing.* ⅃

Sam's Anchor Cafe / ★★

27 MAIN ST, TIBURON; 415/435-4527 It's another marvelous day in Marin. You want to relax with friends on a sun-drenched deck, enjoy a burger and fries, and relish views of neighboring San Francisco—so it's time to rally the troops and head for Sam's and a quintessential Marin experience. This is probably the only restaurant in the Bay Area that promises a refund if a marauding seagull spoils a meal. There's also lots of indoor space if you're looking for peace and quiet. The classic bar is a great spot to eavesdrop, spin your own tale, or ask about Sam, a bootlegger and colorful character. Seafood is a popular choice; try the house specialty, cioppino, or stay with the tried-and-true oysters on the half shell. Or how about cracked Dungeness crab or a grilled halibut sandwich with pesto on focaccia? Weekend brunches feature eggs Benedict and a longtime favorite, Ramos gin fizzes. Unless you're arriving by boat or bike, keep an eye on that alcohol intake—it catches up with you here. Also, bring a hat and plenty of sunscreen. *$$; AE, DC, DIS, MC, V; no checks; lunch, dinner every day, brunch Sat–Sun; full bar; no reservations for outside seating (reservations recommended for inside dining Sat–Sun); sam@samscafe.com; www.samscafe.com; downtown.* ⅃

Mill Valley

Everything in Mill Valley is either on or near Mount Tamalpais, the focal point of Marin County. Today's residents, including a bevy of famous musicians, writers, and actors, wouldn't dream of living anywhere else. The **MILL VALLEY BOOK DEPOT AND CAFE** (87 Throckmorton Ave; 415/383-2665), site of the town's last railway depot, is a favorite spot for locals to meet and greet. Brightly garbed bikers, hikers, and runners headed for the mountain add pops of color. Annual claims to fame include the **DIPSEA**, the oldest cross-country foot race on the West Coast, in June, and the **MILL VALLEY FILM FESTIVAL** in the fall. Seasoned shoppers will be happy to learn that the original Banana Republic still calls Mill Valley home. You never know who will be jamming at **SWEETWATER** (153 Throckmorton Ave; 415/388-2820; www.sweetwatersaloon.com) or enjoying a soothing massage at **TEA GARDEN SPRINGS** (38 Miller Ave; 415/389-7123; www.teagardensprings.com). For more information, contact the Mill Valley Chamber of Commerce (85 Throckmorton Ave, Mill Valley, CA 94941; 415/388-9700; www.millvalley.org).

RESTAURANTS

Buckeye Roadhouse / ★★★

15 SHORELINE HWY, MILL VALLEY; 415/331-2600 The decor at the Buckeye Roadhouse combines a reserved elegance with over-the-top Marin kitsch—lofty ceilings, mahogany beams, glass chandeliers and sconces, a massive stone fireplace, a huge stuffed yellowfin tuna, and a moose head. The cuisine, likewise, is both classic and eclectic. For an appetizer, try local oysters on the half shell; Buckeye's memorable Caesar salad; a tangled mound of thin, sweet onion rings cooked in a feathery batter and served with house-made ketchup; or the house-smoked Atlantic salmon. The most popular entrees are the barbecued baby back ribs served with coleslaw, smoked Sonoma duck with wild rice and huckleberry sauce, and a sweet, tender, marinated grilled pork chop with to-die-for garlic mashed potatoes. Top off your meal with one of the old-time desserts such as warm gingerbread cake with Meyer lemon curd and whipped cream. *$$$; DC, DIS, MC, V; no checks; lunch Mon–Sat, dinner every day, brunch Sun; full bar; reservations recommended; www.buckeyeroadhouse.com; from Hwy 101 take the Stinson Beach–Mill Valley exit.* &

Dipsea Cafe / ★★

200 SHORELINE HWY/HWY 1, MILL VALLEY; 415/381-0298 / 2200 4TH STREET, SAN RAFAEL; 415/456-9950 At the Dipsea—a local favorite for big breakfasts—the cooks flip huge, delicious buttermilk and whole-wheat blueberry pancakes every day of the week. Other well-loved standbys include an eggs Benedict big enough for two, an eggless tofu-vegetable scramble, and excellent house-made corned beef hash. The lunch plates, especially the salade niçoise and special pasta entrees (chorizo sausage in a thick tomato base over fettuccine, for example), are equally hearty. Expect a wait on weekends for both breakfast and lunch as the locals and tourists fuel up for a day of hiking around Mount Tam. There's also a new Dipsea Cafe at the west end of San Rafael. *$; MC, V; no checks; breakfast, lunch every day; beer and wine; no reservations; 200 yards south of Tam Junction (where Shoreline Hwy/Hwy 1 meets Almonte Blvd on the S side of town).* &

Joe's Taco Lounge / ★

382 MILLER AVE, MILL VALLEY; 415/383-8164 This exuberant Mill Valley hole-in-the-wall taqueria with cherry-red counters and festive decor is where the locals go to feast on gordo soft tacos as big as your forearm. Joe's specialty is grilled Pacific snapper tacos with salsa fresca and habanero mayonnaise; a close second are the *carnitas*—shredded pork braised in orange juice and molasses, served with *cebolla* (onion) salsa. A painted penguin on the window proclaims "Cool Inside," and we couldn't agree more. *$; MC, V; no checks; lunch, dinner every day; beer and wine; no reservations; at Montford and La Goma Sts.* &

Piazza D'Angelo / ★★

22 MILLER AVE, MILL VALLEY; 415/388-2000 When owners Paolo and Domenico Petrone renovated this restaurant in 1990, Piazza D'Angelo became one of Mill Valley's most popular restaurants—and it still is, with large (often noisy) crowds of Marinites packing the pleasant, airy bar. They don't necessarily come for the food, mind you, but for the charged atmosphere. D'Angelo's Italian menu abounds with familiar though not always well-executed fare, including numerous pasta plates—spaghetti sautéed with kalamata olives, chile pepper, baby spinach, onions, sun-dried tomatoes, white wine, and pecorino cheese is one of the better choices—and several juicy meat dishes from the rotisserie. The calzone, stuffed with fresh ingredients like ricotta, spinach, caramelized onions, mozzarella, and sausage, comes out of the pizza oven puffy and light. Desserts are made fresh daily, and if there's a crème brûlée on the tray, oh yeah. The extensive wine list features a respectable selection of California and Italian labels (about 150 bottles), including 10 wines poured by the glass. *$$; AE, DC, MC, V; no checks; lunch Mon–Fri, dinner every day, brunch Sat–Sun; full bar; reservations recommended; located on the downtown square.* &

LODGINGS

Mill Valley Inn / ★★★

165 THROCKMORTON AVE, MILL VALLEY; 415/389-6608 OR 800/595-2100 Smack in the heart of trendy Mill Valley, you'll discover towering redwoods and a babbling creek just beyond the small reception area at this European-style inn. Accommodations, all designed with convenience, comfort, and California charm in mind, are secluded and quiet. There are 25 rooms, including one Executive Suite and two cottages, each with a private bath, king- or queen-size bed, and French doors that open onto views of redwood trees or downtown Mill Valley. Room service is available from Piazza D'Angelo (see review, above). A complimentary continental breakfast, along with the morning paper, is served on the flower-filled Sun Terrace. Would you like a double latte with low-fat milk and a sprinkling of chocolate to go with your assortment of pastries, breads, cereals, and fresh fruits? Make your request at the espresso bar before you head for the east peak of Mount Tam, test your lung capacity on the famous Dipsea Trail, or enjoy a picnic at Muir Beach. *$$$; AE, DC, MC, V; no checks; 2-night minimum stay on weekends; mgr@millvalleyinn.com; www.millvalleyinn.com; downtown.* &

Mountain Home Inn / ★★

810 PANORAMIC HWY, MILL VALLEY; 415/381-9000 Much has changed at the remote Mountain Home Inn since it opened in 1912 as a Bavarian restaurant, but what has stayed constant through the years is the stunning view. On clear days you can see the Marin hills, San Francisco Bay, the East Bay hills, and even Mount Diablo at the edge of the Central Valley. Perched high above Mill Valley on the side of Mount Tamalpais, the inn now has 10 guest rooms decorated in what might best be described as Marin modern, with plush carpeting and wood-paneled walls. All of the rooms have private baths. The TV-less guest rooms come with a wide variety of amenties—the most deluxe rooms have wood-burning fireplaces, decks, king-size beds, and oversize tubs with Jacuzzi jets. The New American cuisine served for lunch and dinner (Wed–Sun) in the dining room is adequate, but you'd be better off bringing a picnic or making the winding 15-minute drive down the mountain to a restaurant in one of the neighboring towns. Mountain Home Inn becomes a madhouse on sunny weekends, when hikers and mountain bikers descend for après-trek drinks and snacks or a late brunch on the deck. A full breakfast is included with your stay. $$$–$$$; AE, MC, V; *no checks;* 2-night minimum stay on Sats May–Oct; *info@mtnhomeinn.com; www.mtnhomeinn.com.* &

Larkspur

Larkspur got its name from the blue flowers that grew on nearby hillsides in the late 1800s. Today white larkspurs are found in the historic downtown village, adorning the blue banners that hang from the old-fashioned lampposts lining Magnolia Avenue. There's lots to discover within four short blocks: boutiques, restaurants, and splashes of European influence.

RESTAURANTS

Lark Creek Inn / ★★★

234 MAGNOLIA AVE, LARKSPUR; 415/924-7766 When famed Bay Area chef Bradley Ogden took over the Lark Creek Inn in 1989, he faced the unique task of creating a restaurant around a well-established local landmark. This beautiful century-old two-story Victorian inn, nestled in a stately redwood grove along Lark Creek, demanded a strong presence—and Ogden, fresh from worldwide acclaim at San Francisco's Campton Place, met the challenge. He soon opened what many have considered for years the best restaurant in Marin County; now that he has launched several other Bay Area restaurants, however, Lark Creek has been suffering from his absence and food critics have been stripping the inn of its once-untouchable four-star status. Yet when things are going well in the kitchen, the dishes can still be wildly imaginative and successful, and they are always rooted in Ogden's superb mastery of basic American cooking. For instance, he marries a tender Yankee pot roast with roasted vegetables and horseradish mashed potatoes; he roasts a free-range chicken with a tang of lemon and herbs and serves it with mashed red potatoes; and he grills the thickest, most perfect pork chop and enhances it with sweet braised red cabbage.

I ONLY HAVE EYES FOR YOU

In north San Rafael, Guide Dogs for the Blind has been breeding and training Labrador retrievers, German shepherds, and golden retrievers to act as eyes for the blind since 1942. At that time, founder Lois Mayhew realized a dream and became the first female guide dog trainer in the United States, creating the school that would move permanently to San Rafael in 1947. After the dogs go through a rigorous four- to five-month training (you'll often see them on the streets of San Rafael with their trainers), they're introduced to their new owners, who then go through another few weeks of training with their new canine companions. The dogs are provided free of charge. Visitors may watch a graduation ceremony (one takes place every four to five weeks), tour the kennels, and see a demonstration of the dogs' skills. (350 Los Ranchitos Rd; 415/499-4000; www.guidedogs.com; drop-in tours of the campus Mon–Sat 10:30am and 2:00pm).

Instead of potatoes au gratin, you might find root vegetables au gratin. For dessert, a devil's food cake is blessed with chocolate malt ice cream, and the classic strawberry shortcake gets a scoop of cheesecake ice cream for a kick. $$$$; AE, DC, MC, V; no checks; lunch Mon–Fri, dinner every day, brunch Sun; full bar; reservations recommended; on the N edge of downtown. &

Left Bank / ★★★

507 MAGNOLIA AVE, LARKSPUR; 415/927-3331 Roland Passot, chef-owner of La Folie (long regarded as one of San Francisco's best restaurants), has transformed Larkspur's historic Blue Rock Inn into a fun, vibrant restaurant with a phenomenal French bistro–style menu. Sink your teeth into his leek and onion tart studded with applewood-smoked bacon or the roasted duck breast garnished with a sour cherry sauce, and *la Tour Eiffel* looms. The menu changes seasonally, prompting Passot's fans to return again and again for the latest rendition of his wonderful, traditionally prepared Gallic fare. And you'll love the mood as much as the food. Dine on the covered L-shaped veranda hugging the front of the restaurant and you just might believe you've been transported to Paris (especially if you've given the terrific fruit-infused vodkas a generous taste test). For the grand finale, indulge in the warm tarte Tatin topped with thick caramelized apple slices and a scoop of vanilla-bean ice cream. $$$; AE, MC, V; no checks; lunch, dinner every day; full bar; reservations required Fri–Sat; www.leftbank.com; at Ward St. &

Marin Brewing Company / ★

1809 LARKSPUR LANDING CIRCLE, LARKSPUR; 415/461-4677 Noisy, fun, and crowded, this brewery produces excellent ales and beers—Mount Tam Pale Ale and the unfiltered-wheat Hefeweizen are favorites—and hearty pub food (the Mount Tam burger with a side of onion rings is the bomb). Specials include Monday night's $1.50 tacos, Tuesday's $2.50 pints (always fills the place), and summer oyster barbecues. This is a good place to meet and greet, too; the crowd often has quite a few brew-and-pizza lovers from the nearby gym, and seating outside during warm days is a real pleasure. *$; AE, MC, V; no checks; lunch, dinner every day; beer and wine; no reservations; www.marinbrewing.com; in Larkspur Landing Circle shopping center off Sir Francis Drake Blvd, across from the ferry landing.* &

Kentfield

RESTAURANTS

Half Day Cafe / ★★

848 COLLEGE AVE, KENTFIELD; 415/459-0291 Breakfast in this beautifully renovated, plant-filled mechanic's garage features a number of first-rate dishes, including fluffy omelets stuffed with a variety of fresh fillings, jumbo orange-currant scones, and fine, dark espresso. The only complaint is that you may have to wait a stomach-growling hour for a table on a busy weekend morning, and even longer if you have your eye on the sunny patio. At lunchtime, the College of Marin's ravenous crowds pack the place for fresh salads, hearty sandwiches, and grilled specials. *$; MC, V; local checks only; breakfast, lunch every day; beer and wine; no reservations; across from the College of Marin.* &

San Anselmo

Most people don't set out for San Anselmo; they pass through it on their way to West Marin, via Sir Francis Drake Boulevard. The smart rows of **ANTIQUE STORES** situated along the boulevard are eye-catching enough, but they're only a preview of downtown attractions. You'll discover a diminutive version of a sophisticated city, a blending of old and new, on **SAN ANSELMO AVENUE.**

RESTAURANTS

Bistro 330 / ★★

330 SAN ANSELMO AVE, SAN ANSELMO; 415/460-6330 The fresh French dishes here are delicious, and the origins of the ingredients couldn't be better: local ranch-raised beef, lamb, and chicken (no antibiotics or hormones), produce from local farmers, and farmed seafood. The restaurant uses organic and humane resources, and the French-inspired menu—including such dishes as *coquelet rôti au balsam* (pan-roasted young chicken in rosemary balsamic reduction) and *côtes d'agneau grillées provençale* (grilled Atkins Ranch lamb chops with Provençal sauce)—is consistently a winner. The sleek, modern interior is made user-friendly by the judicious use of warm reds and golds in the decor. This is a true bistro—patrons don't have to wrestle with floor-length tablecloths or pretentious waiters; the service is efficient and friendly. *$$; MC, V; no checks; dinner Tues–Sun; beer and wine; reservations recommended; www.eatdish.com; downtown San Anselmo.* &

Bubba's Diner / ★★

566 SAN ANSELMO AVE, SAN ANSELMO; 415/459-6862 There's probably nothing on the menu at Bubba's that you couldn't make at home, but chances are you just couldn't make it as well. Bubba's offers classic diner food with decor to match: red naugahyde booths, a black-and-white tile floor, a big Bubba's clock, and a daily special board. People stand in line for the hearty breakfast offerings, including chunky corned beef hash, honey whole-wheat flapjacks, and eggs prepared however you like 'em with home fries and a big, delicious, freshly baked biscuit. For lunch or dinner choose from a selection of salads, or order from an equally delicious, if slightly less health-conscious, list of sandwiches, such as the burger slathered with Swiss cheese or the terrific meat-loaf sandwich smothered in barbecue sauce. After 5:30pm you can indulge in chicken-fried steak with red-eye gravy, pot roast and mashed potatoes, crisp fried chicken, and similar fare. And since you've totally blown your diet by now, celebrate your newfound freedom with a real milk shake or malt, tapioca pudding, or a slice of banana-butterscotch pie. *$$; MC, V; no checks; breakfast, lunch, dinner Wed–Sun; beer and wine; reservations recommended for 6 or more; downtown.* &

Insalata's / ★★★½

120 SIR FRANCIS DRAKE BLVD, SAN ANSELMO; 415/457-7700 In a handsome, mustard-colored building large enough to be a car showroom, chef-owner Heidi "Her Lusciousness" Insalata Krahling (formerly of Square One in San Francisco and Butler's in Mill Valley) has chosen to showcase her dazzling Mediterranean fare behind her restaurant's floor-to-ceiling windows. At tables cloaked in white linen, diners bask in the spaciousness while noshing on the seven-vegetable Tunisian *tagine* served on a bed of fluffy couscous, or the savory Genovese fish and shellfish stew simmering in a prosciutto broth seasoned with sage. You'll have no problem finding the perfect wine to accompany your meal from Insalata's good list, and don't hesitate to ask the staff for suggestions. Service is quite friendly and attentive, and once you've paid your bill, head to the back of the restaurant, where goodies-to-go are sold (Mon–Sat 11am–7:30pm) and pick up a little bag of biscotti studded with plump golden raisins—a great treat for the drive home. *$$$; MC, V; no checks; lunch, dinner every day; beer and wine; reservations recommended; insalatas@comcast.net; www.insalatas.com; at Barber St.* &

Fairfax

Hippiedom gone glossy—that's Fairfax. Once an enclave of refugees from the '60s, the town has kept a lot of that friendly open feel, even though housing prices have soared and many of the artists, musicians, and writers who called Fairfax home have been forced to move elsewhere. Fairfax has an active nightlife scene, with several bars and music-and-food venues. If it seems like everyone knows each other here, they do: residents sometimes refer to their town as Fairfax, Center of the Universe.

RESTAURANTS

Ross Valley Brewing Company / ★★★

765 CENTER BLVD, FAIRFAX; 415/485-1005 Innovative and sophisticated food (no pub grub at *this* brewery), handcrafted beers, a light-filled natural wood and burnished aluminum interior, and friendly service add up to one of the best brew pubs in the county. The clientele changes with the time of day: the pub attracts hikers and bikers in the late afternoon, families at dinnertime, and a late-night crowd that sticks around until closing time. The garlic fries are generously sprinkled with chunks of garlic and parsley—good stuff unless you're on a first date. Start with an organic D'Anjou pear salad with mizuna, Bolinas frisée, spicy pecans, Shaft blue cheese, and vanilla-bean vinaigrette, followed by corn meal–fried Monterey calamari with tomatillo sauce, Meyer lemon aioli, and organic frisée. Entrees run the gamut: Southern-style jambalaya with andouille sausage, red prawns, roasted chicken, Cajun mirepoix, and dirty rice; penne pasta with artichokes, roasted sweet pepper, and ricotta; and Moroccan couscous with roasted vegetables and goat yogurt. Even the burgers are extra-ordinary—half-pound Black Angus beauties on a sesame-seed bun with balsamic roasted onions, French fries, and house-made pickles. *$–$$; MC, V; no checks; lunch Sat–Sun, dinner every day (bar opens at 4pm, dinner service begins at 5:30pm); beer and wine; reservations recommended; www.rossvalley brewing.com; on the north end of town across from Safeway.* &

San Rafael

San Rafael wins the prize for being the oldest, largest, and most culturally diverse city in Marin. **SAN RAFAEL ARCANGEL** (415/454-8141), the second-to-last in the California mission chain, was founded here in 1817. Masses in Haitian and Vietnamese are offered regularly at the mission chapel. Every second weekend in June, the **ITALIAN STREET PAINTING FESTIVAL** (415/457-4879; www.youthinarts.org) takes place on Fifth Avenue and A Street in front of the mission. Scores of professional and student artists create chalk reproductions of old masterpieces or vivid original works.

The **MARIN COUNTY CIVIC CENTER** (415/499-6646; www.marincenter.org) was the last design on **FRANK LLOYD WRIGHT**'s famous drawing board. Completed in 1969, the center is the seat of county government and has been designated a state and national historic landmark. Its 74-foot golden spire, rising above the azure roof, is a familiar beacon for those traveling north on Highway 101.

Fourth Street coffeehouses, trendy microbreweries, and restaurants with international cuisine offer popular choices night and day. Movie buffs will enjoy the **SAN RAFAEL FILM CENTER** (1118 4th St; 415/454-1222), a vintage art deco theater restored to perfection in 1998. Independent and art films from all over the world are showcased year-round.

RESTAURANTS

The Rice Table / ★★★

1617 4TH ST, SAN RAFAEL; 415/456-1808 Decorated with rattan screens and bright batik tablecloths, this small, popular, dimly lit restaurant offers dozens of wonderfully aromatic Indonesian dishes that are a treat for the soul as well as the palate. The menu here is deliberately simple: there are only 11 entrees. For a real Indonesian feast, order the Rice Table Dinner or the Rice Table Special. All meals begin with shrimp chips served with a trio of distinctly spiced sauces, followed by mint-tinged coleslaw, a raw vegetable salad, and *lumpia* (deep-fried Indonesian spring rolls stuffed with shrimp and pork). Favorite entrees include savory satays cooked with peanut sauce and an assortment of fork-tender curried meats in coconut milk. If you like your fare fiery hot, dip into the wonderful *sambals* (a paste of hot chile peppers mixed with various spices and lime juice), then cool the flames with an icy cold beer. For dessert, treat yourself to deep-fried bananas, accompanied by an Indonesian coffee or the floral jasmine tea. *$$; AE, MC, V; no checks; dinner Wed–Sun; beer and wine; reservations recommended; 4th and G Sts.* &

Royal Thai / ★★

610 3RD ST, SAN RAFAEL; 415/485-1074 Now that Thai restaurants have sprouted up all over the Bay Area, it takes something special to lure people away from their neighborhood favorites. Royal Thai, housed in a restored Victorian frame house underneath Highway 101, brings in Thai aficionados from far and wide with an array of classics and innovative variations. Chef-owner Jamie and co-owner Pat Disyamonthon's dishes are expertly prepared and beautifully presented, but what really distinguishes this restaurant is its range. In addition to thick coconut-milk curries and perfect pad thai, it turns out a kaleidoscope of beef and chicken satays sparkling with ginger paste, chili oil, nuts, fresh mint, basil, and garlic. Roll up the *miang kham* (dried shrimp, peanuts, small chunks of fresh lime, red onion, baked coconut, ginger, and chile) in butter lettuce leaves and dip it in a sweet tamarind sauce, or explore the somun salad, a wonderfully textured combination of shredded green papaya mixed with carrots, green beans, tomatoes, and ground peanuts. Other favorites are the salmon in red curry sauce and the barbecued squid. *$; AE, DIS, MC, V; no checks; lunch Mon–Fri, dinner every day; beer and wine; reservations recommended on weekends; in the little French Quarter shopping area under Hwy 101 between 3rd and 4th Sts.*

Yet Wah / ★★

1238 4TH ST, SAN RAFAEL; 415/460-9883 There are many Yet Wahs—the restaurant started in San Francisco in 1969 and has replicated itself throughout the Bay Area since then, for good reason. The menu is classic Chinese—glazed walnut prawns, Mandarin beef, barbecued spareribs—and the food is always plentiful, beautifully presented, and reliably good. The spring rolls are crunchy and the hot-and-sour soup is both. The Marin branch of Yet Wah began life as a classic Mandarin-style restaurant near Larkspur Landing and has been reborn downtown, warmly decorated in a modern theme—think upscale Hong Kong: a cross between elegant and trendy. The service is quick and quiet. Yet Wah offers lunch specials during the week and is often crowded. If you're in the mood for Chinese food, you can't go wrong here. *$; AE, MC, V; no checks; lunch, dinner every day; full bar; reservations recommended; downtown.* &

LODGINGS

Gerstle Park Inn / ★★★

34 GROVE ST, SAN RAFAEL; 415/721-7611 OR 800/726-7611 One step onto the grounds of this inviting inn and you'll want to stay, return often, and share the experience with family and friends. Tucked away on a quiet street in the charming old Gerstle Park neighborhood in San Rafael, it's like no other place in Marin—or almost anywhere. The owners recognized the hidden possibilities when they purchased the run-down property in 1995. It feels as though each lovingly restored room, nook, and cranny was created to complement an eclectic collection of family heirlooms, Asian treasures, and European antiques. The bold patterned fabrics, worn polished wood, and sparkling glass all blend to please the eye and reflect elegant comfort. Each of the unique suites in the wood-shingled main house has a private bath and an individual patio or deck; four suites have Jacuzzi tubs. The Lodge, or "Honeymoon Suite," comes with a separate parlor, private outside entrance, and double-size Jacuzzi tub with shower. Families and long-term guests might prefer one of the two separate cottages, complete with living room, bedroom, and kitchen. Business travelers especially appreciate the high-tech amenities and the comfortable balance between a full-service hotel and a homelike environment. All guests enjoy the idyllic 1½-acre setting and proximity to beautiful Gerstle Park. A full breakfast is served either in the glassed-in sunporch, outside on the terrace, or in suites. The kitchen, offering snacks and beverages, is open to guests at all hours. *$$$–$$$$; AE, DIS, MC, V; checks OK; innkeeper@gerstleparkinn.com; www.gerstleparkinn.com; off San Rafael Ave.* &

EAST BAY, SOUTH BAY, AND THE PENINSULA

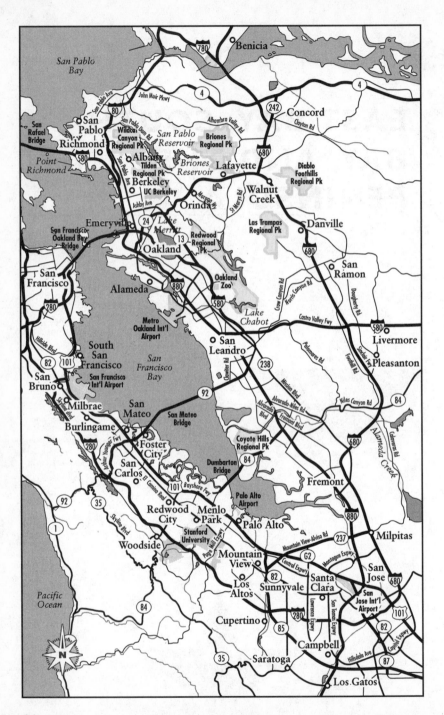

EAST BAY, SOUTH BAY, AND THE PENINSULA

It's been a long time coming, but the Bay Area is finally growing out of the restrictive name "the San Francisco Bay Area." It's as if the once lesser-known municipalities of the Bay Area, like younger siblings paying due respect to an older one, are saying to San Francisco, "Thank you very much for all you've done for us, but we've got our own identities now and would prefer to be called by our own names."

To the south of San Francisco on a verdant stretch of land referred to as the Peninsula, with the Pacific Ocean on one side and a grand bay on the other, lie the posh communities of Burlingame, Redwood City, Woodside, and San Carlos. Posher still, if that's even possible, is Atherton, as well as Menlo Park and most of Palo Alto, situated farther south.

Beyond the Peninsula, capping the bottom tip of the bay, is that massive and sometimes ambiguous stretch of land known as Silicon Valley—perhaps the only instance on earth in which a business moniker has redefined geography. Silicon Valley is a valley, true, but where it stops and starts is difficult to track. It includes, at present, Santa Clara, Sunnyvale, Mountain View, and even Saratoga and Los Gatos, but keep an eye on it as it inches its way toward Morgan Hill to the south.

Working your way up the eastern side of the bay, banked by rolling hills, you'll find Milpitas—once the butt of Bay Area jokes because its only claim to fame was a sprawling dump site, but now a blossoming residential city rising from the compost of its former reputation. North of Milpitas are Fremont, Newark, Hayward, and San Leandro. Across the bay from San Francisco is Oakland; once considered the bad stepchild of the Bay Area, it's now in the throes of a renaissance. Baby boomers will remember Berkeley, to the north of Oakland, for its legacy of '60s radicalism. Farther north still are Albany, Richmond, Pinole, and the charming Benicia.

East Bay

You've heard the comments about Californians: "Oh, those Californians are weird," or "Oh, those sprout-eating, tree-hugging Californians." When tightly wound outsiders refer to Californians as too "granola" or "woo-woo" or just plain old "touchy-feely," they don't realize they are unwittingly complimenting the East Bay, from whence the perception came. There are good reasons for the perception.

First of all, the East Bay is cradled by the San Francisco Bay on one side and a range of beautifully undulating hills on the other—an enviable location for any segment of civilization. Who wouldn't feel a little "organic" living in such surroundings? The East Bay is also home to the largest regional park system in the United States. Founded in the 1930s, the system boasts 59 exquisitely maintained parks and untamed sanctuaries—each a haven for indigenous wildlife and plants as well as the East Bayers who cherish them.

Aside from being a topographical paradise, the region is also known for representing just about every ethnicity and major religion in the world. It's a place where

Chinese, Ethiopian, Cambodian, and Brazilian cuisine is readily available; where a mosque and a church can be happy neighbors; where you can hear the exuberant harmonies of a gospel choir on one corner, then cross the street and be mesmerized by chanting coming from an ashram. And, not to refute the rumors, it's a place where words like *karma, chakras, channeling, aromatherapy, reiki,* and *feng shui* are part of everyday mainstream vocabulary.

ACCESS AND INFORMATION

Not all that long ago, Northern Californians would scoff haughtily at the traffic and smog problems that plagued their Southern California neighbors. That is no longer the case. The influx of people into the Bay Area has turned its freeway and bridge system into a baywide web. On these highways, there are only a few precious hours on a weekday—sometimes even on a weekend—when you actually get up to the speed limit. So if your destination is the East Bay, it's advisable to fly directly into **OAKLAND INTERNATIONAL AIRPORT (OAK)** rather than its San Francisco or San Jose counterparts. **SHUTTLE SERVICES** such as Door to Door (888/806-8463) or Bayporter Express (510/864-4000 or 877/467-1800) abound. Taxis are available, though not in unending streams, and charge a flat rate of $30 from the airport to downtown Oakland.

The Bay Area's public transit crown jewel is still Bay Area Rapid Transit, or **BART** (510/465-2278), but even though locals would agree it's in the Bay Area and it's transit, they'd likely take issue with the "rapid" part. Consider yourself warned. Occasional delays aside, it's still a relatively stress-free, quiet way to travel the greater part of the Bay Area. BART now has six lines, including a newly completed and eagerly awaited San Francisco International Airport line. Hours of operation are weekdays 4am–midnight, Saturday 6am–midnight, and Sunday 8am–midnight. **AC TRANSIT** (Alameda/Contra Costa Transit; 510/817-1717 or 800/448-9790) is the bus system covering Alameda and western Contra Costa counties and also provides trans-bay service from those areas to San Francisco. If your travels take you into San Francisco from the East Bay, try slicing the waters of the bay via ferry; it's the most scenic and enjoyable way to get there. Just make sure you wear a jacket, as it's always several degrees colder than on land. The **OAKLAND/ALAMEDA FERRY** (510/522-3300) runs between Alameda, Oakland, and San Francisco on a daily basis, and the **HARBOR BAY MARITIME** (510/769-5500) provides commuter service from Harbor Bay Isle in Alameda to San Francisco.

Unlike its politics, the Bay Area's **WEATHER** is moderate most of the year, but there are several microclimates that vary by a few degrees. The Peninsula, like San Francisco, is generally the coolest because it's closest to the ocean; the East Bay is often two to four degrees warmer; and San Jose can run a couple of degrees warmer still. Savvy residents whose agendas will take them to more than one locale in the course of a day will not leave the house unlayered—ready to strip or cloak themselves at a moment's notice. Of course, the *El Niño* and *La Niña* cycles have made the weather a bit unpredictable over the past few years, but it's still safe to say that in winter and spring you can expect some rain, and summer will be temperate. The real treat comes in early fall, and it goes by the name Indian summer. Then you can expect temperatures to rise as if summer is offering everyone one last hurrah before disappearing into a mellow autumn.

The staff at the office of the **OAKLAND CONVENTION AND VISITORS BUREAU** (475 14th St, Ste 120, near Broadway; 510/839-9000; www.oaklandcvb.com) is cordial and helpful. The **BERKELEY CONVENTION AND VISITORS BUREAU AND FILM COMMISSION** (510/549-7040) is at 2015 Center Street, between Shattuck and Milvia (www.visitberkeley.com).

Benicia

RESTAURANTS

Camellia Tea Room / ★★

828 1ST ST, BENICIA; 707/746-5293 If you've fallen under the spell of the ubiquitous tea trend, but are put off by the formality of the English ritual, you'll appreciate the Camellia Tea Room. Located in historic Benicia in a sunflower-yellow Victorian storefront, this minute establishment pays homage to the afternoon tea tradition with a decidedly California-esque nod. The decor is spare in comparison to tearooms in Great Britain but not without beautiful antiques, like the long bar that lines the left side of the room. The ceiling is the eye-catcher—a masterpiece of molding and wallpaper in burgundy, pistachio green, and cream. Even if you didn't tilt your head back to admire it, the sugar rush from the chocolate cookies would induce the movement anyway. At once subtle and shocking, they're part of the lineup called "Traditional Tea," which includes finger sandwiches, scones, wickedly rich Devon cream, and sweets. But of course, the featured act is tea, and the 42-tea menu doesn't disappoint. Aside from the expected Earl Grey and English Breakfast offerings, selections include teas with exotic names like Niligri, Russian Caravan, Gunpowder, and Haiku. If the three-tiered sandwich and cake presentations aren't your cup of tea, consider the reasonably priced, though minimal, lunch menu and follow with a decadent dessert like chocolate orange cloud cake. *$$; DC, MC, V; checks OK; lunch, tea service Tues–Sun; champagne only; reservations recommended; www.camelliatearoom.com; near the corner of 1st and Military Sts.* ⅙

Walnut Creek

RESTAURANTS

Lark Creek Cafe / ★★

1360 LOCUST ST, WALNUT CREEK; 925/256-1234 The Walnut Creek branch of the popular Lark Creek Cafe serves the same updated versions of American classics as the San Mateo branch. For a full review, see the Restaurants section of San Mateo. *$$; AE, DIS, MC, V; no checks; lunch Mon–Sat, dinner every day, brunch Sun; full bar; reservations recommended; near Mount Diablo.*

Le Virage / ★★★

2211 N MAIN ST, WALNUT CREEK; 925/933-8484 Eating at Le Virage is just like dining at a bistro in Paris. Truly. Yes, the exterior is adorned with Lautrec-inspired murals—not especially Walnut Creek in sensibility—but it's the ambiance inside that lulls you into believing you're in the City of Lights. From the hearty handshake—or the kiss on the hand if you're female—you receive from the owner, Lolek Jasinski, to the warm wooden walls carved with Lautrec-ish images, the place exudes the charm of an authentic French restaurant. Jasinski's long and illustrious history as a restaurateur is evident in the classic menu. His executive chef, Rick Delamain, has delivered consistently for more than 15 years with appetizers like petite ragout of foie gras and sweetbreads, served with sautéed mushrooms and a marsala veal demi-glace, and the ever-popular escargot bourguignon, baked in plenty of garlic and shallot butter with Pernod. Some of the fantastic entrees you can expect are the canard à l'orange, roasted duck breast with an orange and anise glaze; and steak au poivre flambé, a New York steak with black peppercorns flamed with brandy at your table. The desserts are equally sumptuous and include strawberries flambé and, of course, crème brûlée. To complement your dinner, an extensive wine list captures the best of Europe and America. The only disappointment you'll experience is when the spell is broken as you leave the restaurant to find yourself on a busy intersection in Walnut Creek, a little too close to a freeway off-ramp, rather than the Boulevard Saint-Germain in Paris. *$$$$; AE, DIS, MC, V; no checks; dinner Tues–Sat; full bar; reservations recommended; www.levirage.com; near Pine St.* &

Prima / ★★

1522 N MAIN ST, WALNUT CREEK; 925/935-7780 When Italophiles Michael and Janet Verlander first offered sidewalk dining outside their restaurant on Walnut Creek's tree-lined Main Street, the city had laws against it. City politicos soon wised up, however, so now you can people-watch to your heart's content while savoring chef Peter Chastain's fine repertoire of northern Italian specialties. If you've opted for dining alfresco, start off with a refreshing watermelon cocktail of mint, chives, and aged balsamico. Then try a perfectly al dente tagliolini with fresh seafood and house-dried organic tomatoes sautéed in a white wine sauce, or sample the risotto of the day. The roasted loin of rabbit wrapped in pancetta with fresh morels and mashed potatoes or the grilled pork rib chop smothered with braised fennel are just a couple of the well-executed entrees prepared nightly. The wine list is encyclopedic—more than 1,500 California, Italian, and French bottles, with several available by the taste or the glass. Some can even be purchased in the adjacent wine shop. In addition to the high-quality, freshly made meals, Prima's patrons are treated to live jazz on the grand piano starting at 7pm Thursday through Saturday. *$$; AE, DIS, MC, V; no checks; lunch Mon–Sat, dinner every day; full bar; reservations recommended; www.primaristorante.com; downtown, near Lincoln St.* &

Lafayette

RESTAURANTS

Miraku / ★★

3740 MOUNT DIABLO BLVD, LAFAYETTE; 925/284-5700 Don't let the drab blue-and-white exterior of this Japanese restaurant perched high on a hill fool you: inside there's an elegant, airy dining room lined with sea-blue padded booths and a sushi bar brightened by several large Oriental good-luck statues. The sushi and other traditional Japanese dishes are top-notch—whether you indulge in the teriyakis, tempuras, or such specialties as the beef shabu shabu, thinly sliced prime beef that's cooked tableside with fresh napa cabbage, spinach, bamboo shoots, mushrooms, green onions, tofu, and yam noodles and served with a pair of dipping sauces. A generous selection of combination plates is offered, too. And you can rest assured that no MSG enters any of the authentic cuisine at Miraku (Japanese for "joy of the taste"). *$$; AE, DC, DIS, MC, V; no checks; lunch Mon–Fri, dinner every day; full bar; reservations recommended; next to the Hillside Inn & Suites on the W side of town.*

LODGINGS

Lafayette Park Hotel / ★★

3287 MOUNT DIABLO BLVD, LAFAYETTE; 925/283-3700 Set at the end of a cobblestone drive on a hill on the east side of town, this golden ersatz French château is a briskly efficient operation catering to the booming Contra Costa corporate scene. In keeping with its upscale image, rates are steep for this part of the Bay Area (about $175 to $400). But the 139 rooms—all of which are designated nonsmoking—are suitably commodious. Wood-burning fireplaces and vaulted ceilings adorn the more luxurious rooms and suites. Bathrooms are equipped with Italian granite counters, hair dryers, ironing boards, and telephones (three in every room). An inviting 50-foot heated lap pool, a Jacuzzi, a redwood sauna, and a fitness center are also available to guests 24 hours a day. The hotel's cushy Duck Club Restaurant overlooks the pretty fountain courtyard and offers a small, pricey menu featuring filet mignon, fresh fish, pasta, and, of course, plenty of duck, including a light crepe topped with crème fraîche and a succulent roasted duckling with orange-raspberry sauce. A prix-fixe menu with well-selected, mostly California wine pairings is worth the splurge ($75 per person). The hotel's Bistro at the Park—reminiscent of an erudite men's club lounge—is a great place for a drink, especially when the weather is cool and you can cozy up to the roaring fireplace. *$$$; AE, DC, DIS, MC, V; checks OK; www.lafayetteparkhotel.com; from Hwy 24, take Pleasant Hill Rd S exit and turn right on Mount Diablo Blvd.*

Danville

RESTAURANTS

Blackhawk Grille / ★★

3540 BLACKHAWK PLAZA CIRCLE, DANVILLE; 925/736-4295 In the exclusive community of Blackhawk, this glamorous, offbeat 7,000-square-foot restaurant is a testament to California's adoration of the automobile. The Grille's exotic interior glows with brushed stainless steel, copper, and verdigris. Lighting fixtures are stylized hubcap sconces, and the bar is topped with etched glass. There's an eclectic but down-to-earth menu of wood-fired pizzas and satisfying and competently prepared entrees, including the pan-seared Alaskan halibut with golden tomato gazpacho, bay shrimp, and sweet peppers. The wine list is vast and focuses on California vintners. Desserts, like everything else about this place, are excessive and fluctuate in quality: try the decadent Blackhawk peanut butter cup with roasted peanut fudge gelato and chocolate ganache or the blackberry-cassis granita with macerated berries and vanilla tuile. *$$$; AE, DC, DIS, MC, V; no checks; lunch Mon–Sat, dinner every day, brunch Sun; full bar; reservations recommended; www.calcafe.com; from I-680, take Crow Canyon exit, head E on Crow Canyon, drive 7 miles to Camino Tassajara, and bear right to Blackhawk Plaza.* &

Bridges / ★★★

44 CHURCH ST, DANVILLE; 925/820-7200 Japanese businessman Kazuo Sugitani was so happy with the education his son received at Danville's famed Athenian prep school that he wanted to give something back to the town. Blending the best of East and West cuisine, Bridges is a pretty nifty gift. Beautifully landscaped grounds and an inviting outdoor terrace encircle a building that mingles the brown-shingled architectural influence of Morgan and Maybeck with soaring angles and interior spaces reminiscent of 17th-century Kyoto. The senior Sugitani eventually passed the restaurant on to his well-educated son, Ryoto, who wisely recruited executive chef Allen Vitti, previously of Fringale in San Francisco. With a stronger nod to the French than in previous years, Vitti has created a pared-down selection of superbly well-crafted dishes. The menu includes a delicate three-fish tartare of ahi, yellowfin tuna, and salmon with diced mango, tomatoes, and avocados; a seared lemongrass-rosemary marinated rack of lamb served with mashed sweet potatoes and a cherry port wine sauce; a melt-in-your-mouth spinach and mushroom ravioli; and spicy pan-seared sea scallops and prawns with a roasted pepper curry sauce. The respectable wine list includes an extensive collection of dessert wines to match such sweet delights as the Tahitian vanilla-bean crème brûlée, a berry pudding topped with lychee gelée, or the popular go-ahead-and-splurge dessert sampler for two. Single-malt scotch lovers are in for a treat too—more than 15 carefully selected offerings round out the impressive list. For those on a budget, step across the street to Bridges' latest offspring, Zensai, for a slightly more Pacific Rim experience at much slighter prices. *$$$; AE, DC, MC, V; no checks; dinner Tues–Sat; full bar; reservations recommended; www.bridgesrestaurant-bar.com; from I-680, take Diablo Rd exit, go W to Hartz Ave, turn left on Hartz, and drive 2 blocks to Church St.*

San Ramon

RESTAURANTS

Bighorn Grill / ★★

2410 SAN RAMON VALLEY BLVD, SAN RAMON; 925/838-5678 As the name suggests, this pleasant Western-themed restaurant attracts big beef eaters. They come for baby back pork ribs slathered with a watermelon barbecue sauce, meat loaf topped with country gravy and mashed sweet potatoes, and a 14-ounce garlic-roasted Black Angus New York steak, to name just a few of the meaty entrees. Freshly tossed salads and pasta and fish dishes are also on the menu. Designed by popular San Francisco Bay Area restaurateur Pat Kuleto (think Farallon, Kuleto's, and Boulevard), the Bighorn's large, airy, lodgelike dining room has antler chandeliers and horn-shaped hooks on the walls. A bronze bighorn sheep's head hangs over the long bar, where urban cowboys and business execs sip frosty beers or very large martinis. Families love the Bighorn, too, and a Just for Kids menu caters to the young buckaroo wannabes. *$$; AE, MC, V; no checks; lunch Mon–Fri, dinner every day; full bar; reservations recommended; www.bighorngrill.com; near Crow Canyon Rd.* &

Cafe Esin / ★★

2416 SAN RAMON VALLEY BLVD, SAN RAMON; 925/314-0974 At first glance this nondescript little place in a suburban strip mall appears to be little more than a generic, run-of-the-mill restaurant. But looks can be deceiving and when it comes to the food, Cafe Esin is neither generic nor run-of-the-mill. Husband-and-wife team Curtis and Esin DeCarion, who have cooked in restaurants throughout the Bay Area, are now behind their own stoves cooking up simple, exceptionally well-prepared food for lucky Contra Costa residents. Look for Mediterranean-inspired dishes like creamy zucchini fritters with a tangy yogurt-dill sauce and grilled chicken breast salad with toasted pecans, blue cheese, and raisins. Nourishing entrees include a couple of fresh pastas daily (like fettuccine with rock shrimp and mushrooms in a light cream sauce); Niman Ranch pot roast with garlic mashed potatoes; and grilled pork tenderloin served with fruit chutney and fingerling potatoes. The exquisite dessert list might include up to 10 choices, including seasonal fruit tarts with winning combinations of raspberries and figs dabbed with whipped cream, classic crème brûlée, and the signature Esin's baklava. A substantial wine list features a range of mostly California wines, with several good choices available by the glass. *$$; AE, DC, MC, V; no checks; lunch Tues–Fri, dinner Tues–Sat; full bar; reservations recommended; www.cafeesin.com; near Crown Canyon Rd.* &

Mudd's Restaurant / ★★

10 BOARDWALK, SAN RAMON; 925/837-9387 Mudd's is about more than just food. The Mudd's experience conveys a sense of community from the minute you arrive. The wooden building exudes a sense of homey warmth, and a cat named Flower often sleeps in a planter box by the front door on a cluster of colorful rugs provided by the staff. Beyond the restaurant spread 10 acres of municipal gardens, creeks, and open space. It's from the lush garden, used as an

EAST BAY AREA THREE-DAY TOUR

DAY ONE: The historic hills of the East Bay. Check into your room at **LORD BRADLEY'S INN,** in Fremont at the foot of Mission Peak, and start your day with a large continental breakfast. From there, it's just a few feet to Mission San Jose, 14th of the 21 world-famous Spanish missions in California. If you're feeling energetic, you can pack a picnic lunch, hike to the top of Mission Peak, and enjoy a breathtaking view of the Bay Area. If, however, the mission has whetted your appetite for more history, including the kind you can purchase, drive down Mission Boulevard to Niles. Originally intended to be the moviemaking capital of the world—where Charlie Chaplin was filmed in his early movies— it's now a charming, refurbished enclave of antique shops and restaurants. Stop by the **NILE FOUNTAIN AND COFFEE HOUSE** (121 I St, Niles; 510/791-6049), a hip and artsy establishment for refreshments, or **TYME FOR TEA & CO.** (37501 Niles Blvd; 510/790-0944) for a light lunch and tea. After you've returned to your room and freshened up, walk across the street to **OLIVE HYDE ART GALLERY** (123 Washington Blvd, Fremont; 510/791-4357) and enjoy one of the many rotating exhibits featuring the first-rate work of local artists. For dinner, the best and only choice is **PEARL'S CAFE** in Fremont.

DAY TWO: Shop-till-you-drop day. After breakfast at the inn, put on comfortable shoes and drive up to Berkeley's famous **FOURTH STREET**. There you'll find an array of stores including the Gardener, which features the finest in ethnic antiques, contemporary home decor, and an olfactory delight of a bed-and-bath department. Other gorgeous boutiques dot the narrow street, including Summer House, Sur La Table, Garden Home, and Miki's Paper for beautiful handmade papers. There's even an exotic pet store on **FIFTH STREET**, Vivarium—almost as educational as a trip to the zoo. If you really must buy an iguana, have it shipped. Enjoy lunch at **BETTE'S OCEANVIEW DINER**, but expect a wait and don't expect an ocean view because you won't be anywhere near the ocean. However, if you want to see the bay and distant San Francisco, go to the nearby **BERKELEY MARINA** for an after-lunch walk. Then, assuming you haven't had your fill of shopping, wander through **IKEA** (4400 Shellmound St; 510/420-4532),

educational tool for children, that Mudd's draws a third or so of its fruits, vegetables, and herbs. What it doesn't retrieve from the garden, it purchases from local farms. (Chef Ron Ottobre is committed to supporting local sustainable food production.) Chef de cuisine Josephine Segrave creates preserves, pickles, and relishes from her own organic garden as well as the restaurant's garden. Though the offering changes monthly, some dependable items include the wine barrel–smoked pork located in Emeryville. The Swedish home store opened in April 2000 to a crowd of approximately 15,000 and still attracts throngs of people on a daily basis. Be ready to drag your bag-laden self to your luxurious room at the **CLAREMONT RESORT AND SPA**. Collapse poolside or schedule an afternoon massage to loosen your limbs. Then, having already made dinner reservations in advance, head over to **CHEZ PANISSE**, the most notoriously divine restaurant in Northern California, for a meal you'll never forget.

DAY THREE: This is park-yourself-someplace day. After a luxurious breakfast and equally luxurious view at **JORDAN'S**, located in the Claremont Resort, you're pretty much on your own. The only requirement is that you choose one of the East Bay's 59 regional parks to visit—one cannot visit the East Bay without enjoying the natural beauty that comprises over 91,000 acres of its total mass. **LAKE CHABOT** is nestled in the hills and features boating and incredibly scenic walks. **MOUNT DIABLO** is one of the most bucolic spots and, with its spectacular views, one of the most awe-inspiring. This, after all, is the point from which much of the Bay Area's early survey work was done because it was and is the highest peak for miles. **DIABLO FOOTHILLS PARK**, entree to Mount Diablo, has no developed facilities but is perfect for hiking and wildlife watching. If you decide on Diablo, leave for the mountain early.

TILDEN PARK is thought of as the jewel of the East Bay park system. Some of its many attractions are the Botanic Garden, Lake Anza, and the Herschell Spillman merry-go-round, complete with intricately carved antique horses. Before you head out, pack a picnic lunch of delectables from **WHOLE FOODS MARKET** (3000 Telegraph Ave; 510/649-1333) in Berkeley on Telegraph Avenue. You might also want to pick up a book to read in the sun. To that end, there's no better place to go than **CODY'S BOOKS**. After communing with nature, end the day by indulging in a romantic dinner at **BAY WOLF RESTAURANT** in Oakland. Before you settle in for a night at the Claremont Resort, stop by the famous **FENTON'S CREAMERY** (4226 Piedmont Ave, Oakland; 510/658-7000) for some memorable homemade ice cream—or, better yet, pick up a pint to go.

chop, buttermilk Oregon russet mashed potatoes with house-canned spiced apples and sun-dried cranberries, and the grilled vegetable and portobello mushroom spinach lasagne. Portions are extremely generous, even by country cooking standards. $$$; AE, DC, MC, V; no checks; lunch Mon–Fri, dinner every day, brunch Sun; full bar; reservations recommended; www.muddsrestaurant.com; just off Crow Canyon Rd and Park Pl, 1 mile W of I-680. &

Livermore

RESTAURANTS

Wente Vineyards Restaurant / ★★★

5050 ARROYO RD, LIVERMORE; 925/456-2450 The Wente family couldn't have devised a better way to showcase its wines than with this exquisite neo-Spanish colonial restaurant set among the vineyards and rolling hills of the 1,200-acre Wente estate. Chef Kimball Jones's daily-changing menu is a pleasant blend of traditional and experimental, showcasing fresh Hog Island oysters on the half shell served with a sparkling wine mignonette and roasted butternut squash soup with crème fraîche and sage. House-smoked meats and fresh fish are presented with intriguing, tangy sauces and exotic chutneys, and Wente's trademark beef dishes, such as rib-eye steak with a fire-roasted onion and portobello mushroom relish, are delicious. While it's unfortunate that the Wente wines don't usually measure up to the food, the good news is that the restaurant sells other wines, too. *$$$; AE, DC, MC, V; checks OK; lunch Mon–Sat, dinner every day, brunch Sun; wine and wine-based spirits; reservations recommended; www.wentevineyards.com; follow L St until it turns into Arroyo Rd, about 4 miles S of town.* &

Pleasanton

LODGINGS

Evergreen / ★★

9104 LONGVIEW DR, PLEASANTON; 925/426-0901 High in the emerald hills of Pleasanton stands the grand, flower-rimmed Evergreen. A contemporary bed-and-breakfast, this two-story cedar house is lined with windows, decks, and skylights so you can see the sky and treetops at nearly every turn. Evergreen offers four comfortable, pretty guest rooms, including the coveted Grand View, with a private outdoor deck overlooking the garden and valley, a huge white-tiled bathroom with a Jacuzzi tub for two, a fireplace, and an antique king-size sleigh bed that overlooks the trees. Breakfast is served on bistro tables in the sunroom or on the deck, and after the morning repast guests can walk right out the door for a great hike through neighboring Augustin Bernal Park and along panoramic Pleasanton Ridge. *$$; AE, MC, V; checks OK; www.evergreen-inn.com; from Hwy 680, take the Bernal Ave exit, turn left on Foothill Rd and drive ¼ mile, then turn right on Longview Dr.*

Point Richmond

LODGINGS

Hotel Mac / ★★

10 COTTAGE AVE, POINT RICHMOND; 510/235-0010 Who would have thought there'd be a handsome hotel nestled in the quaint village of Point Richmond, a remote hamlet straddling the edge of the city of Richmond? Built in 1911, this imposing three-story, red-brick edifice on the National Register of Historic Places was remodeled in 1995 and now offers 10 lovely guest rooms (including two deluxe suites) that cost half as much as a similar room in San Francisco. Each unit is individually decorated with rich, colorful fabrics and brass light fixtures, and the windows are framed with handsome white plantation shutters. Every room also has a queen- or king-size bed, cable TV with a VCR, a small refrigerator, terry-cloth robes, and a safe for storing valuables; four rooms have gas fireplaces that you can turn on with the flick of a light switch. Colorful stained-glass windows line the Hotel Mac's dining room, where a respectable mix of cuisine—ranging from risotto with Florida rock shrimp to rack of lamb and chicken cordon bleu—is served. But the hotel's highlight is the spacious, high-ceilinged oak and mahogany bar, an ideal place for an apéritif. A continental breakfast is included in the room rate. *$$; AE, MC, V; checks OK; at Washington Ave.*

Albany

RESTAURANTS

Britt-Marie's / ★★

1369 SOLANO AVE, ALBANY; 510/527-1314 As inviting as a pair of favorite slippers, Britt-Marie's offers comfort food from many corners of the globe. Partisans of the Portuguese sandwich—garlic-rubbed toast topped with salt cod and potatoes—would revolt if it were to disappear from the menu, as would avid fans of the cucumbers in garlicky sour cream, the roast chicken with herbs, and the pork schnitzel with buttered noodles. Two Greek restaurateurs took over Britt-Marie's in 1987, six years after its founding, and enhanced a good thing by adding a few native dishes, including an incredible spanakopita as well as a California-style menu to supplement the roster of European classics (the fresh fish and risotto items are especially good). Sweet-toothed patrons can top off their meal with desserts like bourbon-pecan tart or chocolate cake with a thin layer of marzipan tucked under the chocolate frosting. *$$; no credit cards; checks OK; lunch Tues–Sat, dinner Tues–Sun; beer and wine; no reservations; between Ramona and Carmel Sts.* &

Fonda / ★★

1501 SOLANO AVE, ALBANY; 510/559-9006 The team behind longtime favorite Lalime's in Berkeley has jumped on the tapas bandwagon to bring *antojitos*, or little Latin American plates, to Albany. Chef David Rosales, who won the *San Francisco*

Chronicle's rising star of the year award, creates delicious flavor-packed dishes at this lively corner hot spot. If you want to be part of the action, opt for a seat at the bar or any of the downstairs tables that overlook the bustling kitchen for a more intimate meal, head upstairs to the mezzanine. The menu features about 13 little plates, including a popular Veracruz-style cocktail brimming with scallops, sea bass, and crab; succulent duck tacos with sweet and smoky arbol salsa; unusual deep-fried quesadillas with mushrooms, epazote, and cream; and a grilled skirt steak with *nopales* (cactus), chayote, and an avocado salad. Be sure to try one of the specialty drinks like the eponymous Fonda—an exotic concoction of tequila and hibiscus infusion—or the fresh cucumber and vodka martini. With the tasty eats and a fun bar scene, this warehouselike space with exposed brick walls and sparse lighting has quickly become a favorite among locals and out-of-towners alike. *$$; AE, DC, MC, V; no checks; dinner every day; full bar; no reservations; at Curtis St.* &

Berkeley

The minds of Berkeley's residents are almost audible. Try walking down Telegraph Avenue and looking into the faces of pedestrians. You can almost hear what they're thinking. Some look pensive, nagged, as though they can't get that pestering Nietzsche quote out of their heads; others appear to be in the silent throes of planning activist strategies; while still others look as if they're communing with a presence invisible to mundane mortals. You'll conclude that Berkeley hasn't changed all that much since the '60s, when it was the earth's axis for social change—things have simply become a bit more introspective.

That's not to say Berkeleyites aren't vocal. In some respects, the action has moved from the campus and People's Park to City Hall. There the town's residents—many of them former hippies, student intellectuals, and peace activists—seek to voice their opinions on issues from Columbus Day (Berkeley celebrates Indigenous People's Day instead) to the opening of a large video store downtown (too lowbrow and tacky). You can also find folks on a street corner or hovering near a retail establishment's door, passing out flyers and gathering petition signatures to defeat the latest unjust bill before the state senate. The *San Francisco Chronicle* once called Berkeley the "most contentious of cities," and it's a mantle most of its inhabitants either wear with pride or shrug off like an uncomfortable suit.

Don't draw conclusions just yet. Berkeley is dichotomous. It's also known for its overwhelming plethora of fine restaurants, hip boutiques, and the best furniture stores in the Bay Area. Arguably, that could be why its residents often wear looks of consternation or deep concentration—they might be trying to justify the coexistence of conspicuous consumption and heightened consciousness in the same city. Or maybe they're trying to decide where to eat.

MAJOR ATTRACTIONS

If you're a newcomer to Berkeley, start your tour of the town at the world-renowned **UC BERKELEY** campus (also known as Cal), the oldest and second largest of the nine campuses of the UC system. Driving through the university is virtually impossible,

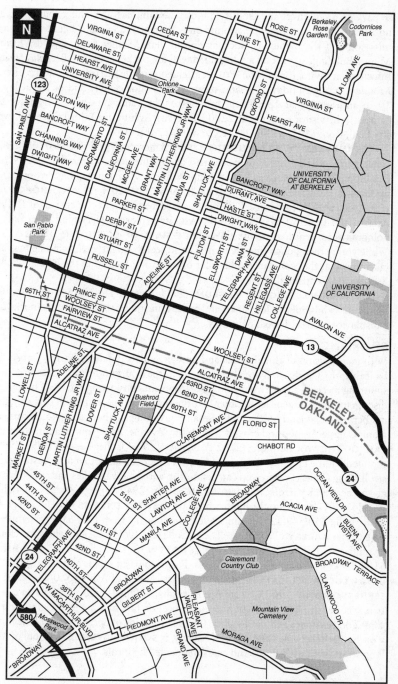

BERKELEY AND NORTH OAKLAND

so park on a side street and set out on foot. The campus isn't so huge that you'd get hopelessly lost if you wandered around on your own, but without a guide you might miss some of the highlights, such as Sproul Plaza, Sather Gate, and the Hearst Mining Building. So pick up a self-guided walking packet at the UC Berkeley Visitor Information Center (open Mon–Fri), or attend one of the free one-hour tours offered Monday through Friday at 10am (meet at the visitor center) and on Saturday at 10am and Sunday at 1pm (meet in front of the Campanile in the heart of the campus); the visitor center is at 2200 University Avenue at Oxford Street, University Hall, Room 101; 510/642-5215 or 510/642-INFO.

The **UNIVERSITY ART MUSEUM** (2626 Bancroft Wy; 510/642-0808) has a small, permanent collection of modern art and frequently hosts peculiar but riveting exhibitions by artists such as Robert Mapplethorpe. A vast array of anthropological artifacts is showcased at the **PHOEBE HEARST MUSEUM OF ANTHROPOLOGY** (510/643-7648), located in UC Berkeley's Kroeber Hall, at the corner of College Avenue and Bancroft Way. Hands-on exhibits exploring everything from bats to holograms are featured at the **LAWRENCE HALL OF SCIENCE** (510/642-5133). While you're there, duck outside to hear (and see) the giant, eerie wind chimes and take a peek at the Stonehenge-like solar observatory; located in the hills above UC Berkeley on Centennial Drive.

The **JUDAH L. MAGNES MUSEUM** (2911 Russell St; 510/549-6950) offers numerous exhibitions of Jewish art and culture, including a Holocaust memorial and a display of modern Jewish paintings.

SHOPPING

With its profusion of chichi stores and upscale outlets (Crate & Barrel, Dansk, Sur La Table, the Gardener, Sweet Potatoes, etc.), the Fourth Street area has become a shopping mecca—a somewhat ironic development considering the city's traditional disdain for the bourgeoisie. Another favorite shopping area is in south Berkeley, near the Berkeley/Oakland border, in the small Elmwood neighborhood, which stretches along College Avenue and crosses over Ashby Avenue. Poke your head into the tiny **TAIL OF THE YAK** boutique (2632 Ashby Ave, W of College Ave; 510/841-9891) for a look at the fabulous displays of Central American and other art treasures, then stroll along College, where you can pet the lop-eared baby bunnies and squawk back at the beautiful parrots at **YOUR BASIC BIRD** (2940 College Ave, N of Ashby; 510/841-7617); dip into the huge candy jars at **SWEET DREAMS** (2901 College Ave at Russell; 510/549-1211); munch on a fantastic fresh-fruit cheese danish at **NABOLOM BAKERY** (2708 Russell St at College; 510/845-BAKE); shop for clothes at numerous boutiques; and indulge in **BOTT'S** (2975 College Ave, S of Ashby; 510/845-4545) freshly made ice creams. For fresh pasta salads and sandwiches, try **ULTRA LUCCA DELICATESSEN** (2905 College Ave, N of Ashby; 510/849-2701) or **ESPRESSO ROMA** (2960 College Ave at Ashby; 510/644-3773), where you can sip strong coffee drinks, teas, fresh lemonade, beer on tap, or wine by the glass and eat some good calzones and sandwiches. On the other side of Berkeley, where the northwest border meets the little town of Albany, is **SOLANO AVENUE**, a popular, milelong street lined with shops and cafes frequented by locals.

Most folks around here agree that if you can't find what you want at **CODY'S BOOKS** (2454 Telegraph Ave; 510/845-7852), Berkeley's best bookstore, it probably isn't worth reading. Almost every night, nationally known literary and political writers appear at Cody's and at **BLACK OAK BOOKS** (1491 Shattuck Ave; 510/486-0698), a popular purveyor of new and used books. The four-story **MOE'S BOOKS** (2476 Telegraph Ave; 510/849-2087) specializes in used tomes and remainders. And a **BARNES & NOBLE** megastore (2352 Shattuck Ave; 510/644-0861), complete with a high-tech fountain and park benches for on-the-spot reading, offers discounts on the *New York Times* best sellers and hard-cover books and stocks hundreds of periodicals.

For some of the best bread in the Bay Area, go to Steve Sullivan's famous **ACME BREAD COMPANY** (1601 San Pablo Ave; 510/524-1327) or the **CHEESE BOARD** (1504 Shattuck Ave; 510/549-3183), a collectively owned bakery and vast gourmet cheese shop. If you're a bagel lover, two Berkeley bagel shops rival Brooklyn's best: **NOAH'S BAGELS** (3170 College Ave, 510/654-0944; and 1883 Solano Ave, 510/525-4447) and **BOOGIE WOOGIE BAGEL BOY** (1281 Gilman St; 510/524-3104), formerly Brothers' Bagels.

Like many university towns, this one seems to run on coffee. **PEET'S COFFEE & TEA** (2124 Vine St, 510/841-0564; 2916 Domingo Ave, 510/843-1434; and 1825 Solano Ave, 510/526-9607), with its sizable selection of beans and teas, is the local favorite. For an outdoor latte beneath the trees, try **CAFFE STRADA** (2300 College Ave; 510/843-5282) or the hip, crowded, college-hangout **CAFE MILANO** (2522 Bancroft Wy; 510/644-3100). **CAFFE MEDITERRANEUM** (2475 Telegraph Ave; 510/549-1128) churns out excellent cappuccinos and captures the bohemian flavor of Telegraph Avenue, still a favorite of students, street people, runaways, hipsters, professors, tarot readers, and street vendors. Or check out the homemade pastries and tasty lunch fare at **INTERMEZZO CAFE** (2442 Telegraph Ave; 510/849-4592), another popular Berkeley haunt. Some of the best beer in the Bay Area is brewed at the frat-packed **TRIPLE ROCK BREWERY** (1920 Shattuck Ave; 510/843-2739). In 1997, the **PYRAMID BREWERY & ALE HOUSE** (901 Gilman St; 510/528-9880) joined the fray with a state-of-the-art brewery and refined pub fare. For something completely different, treat your taste buds to a tour of **TAKARA SAKE USA** (708 Addison St; 510/540-8250), a sake factory that provides tastings of sake and plum wine.

PERFORMING ARTS

MUSIC: The Berkeley Symphony blends new and experimental music with the classics at **ZELLERBACH HALL** (510/841-2800) on the UC Berkeley campus. Modern rock, funk, and acid jazz are blasted at **BLAKE'S** (2367 Telegraph Ave; 510/848-0886). If you're feeling a bit more mellow, take a seat at the **FREIGHT & SALVAGE** coffeehouse (1111 Addison St; 510/548-1761), a prime Euro-folkie hangout. In the mood to dance? Drop in at **ASHKENAZ** (1317 San Pablo Ave; 510/525-5054). Live rock, jazz, folk, reggae, and other concerts are frequently held at UC Berkeley's intimate, open-air **GREEK THEATRE** (Gayley Rd off Hearst Ave; 510/642-9988), a particularly pleasant place for sitting beneath the stars and listening to music on warm summer nights. **CAL PERFORMANCES** (510/642-9988) presents up-and-coming and established artists of all kinds—from the Bulgarian Women's Chorus to superstar mezzo-soprano Cecilia Bartoli; the concerts are held at various sites on the UC Berkeley campus.

THEATER AND FILM: the **BERKELEY REPERTORY THEATRE** (2025 Addison St; 510/647-2949) has a national reputation for experimental productions of the classics and innovative new works, and the **BLACK REPERTORY GROUP** (3201 Adeline St; 510/652-2120) offers a range of plays, dance performances, and art by African Americans. Every summer the **CALIFORNIA SHAKESPEARE FESTIVAL** (701 Heinz Ave; 510/548-3422) performs in an outdoor theater in the Berkeley hills near Orinda (bundle up 'cause it's usually freezing). Film buffs will appreciate the **UC THEATER** (2036 University Ave; 510/843-6267), a revivalist movie house where the flicks change every night, and the **PACIFIC FILM ARCHIVE** (2625 Durant Ave; 510/642-0808), which shows underground avant-garde movies as well as the classics. For up-to-date listings of cultural events, pick up a free copy of *The Express,* the East Bay's alternative weekly, available at cafes and newsstands throughout the area.

PARKS AND GARDENS

For more pastoral diversions, stroll through the **BERKELEY ROSE GARDEN** (Euclid Ave, between Bay View and Eunice Sts), a terraced park with hundreds of varieties of roses and a great view of San Francisco. Or visit the 30-acre **UNIVERSITY OF CALIFORNIA BOTANICAL GARDEN** (Strawberry Canyon on Centennial Dr; 510/642-3343), where you'll see a spectacular collection of cacti from around the world, a Mendocino pygmy forest, and a Miocene-era redwood grove. The gigantic **TILDEN REGIONAL PARK** (off Wildcat Canyon Rd; 510/843-2137), set high in the hills above town, offers miles of hiking trails plus a steam train, a merry-go-round, and a farm and nature area for kids. Tilden also boasts a beautiful **BOTANICAL GARDEN** (510/562-7275) specializing in California native plants.

RESTAURANTS

Ajanta / ★★

1888 SOLANO AVE, BERKELEY; 510/526-4373 This brightly lit and attractive restaurant is one of the East Bay's best Indian restaurants. The dining room is a serene and exotic space, with intricate woodwork, golden fabrics, and graceful reproductions of murals found in India's Ajanta cave temples. The lamb rib chops, *murg ularthu* (boneless chicken simmered in a sauce made with onions, mustard seeds, fennel, garlic, and ginger), and prawn curry are a few of the standout dishes usually featured. There are always about half a dozen vegetarian dishes to choose from, including the wonderful *baigan ki boorani* (pan-fried eggplant slices topped with a garlic-lemon-yogurt sauce). *$$; AE, DC, DIS, MC, V; local checks only; lunch, dinner every day; beer and wine; reservations recommended; www.ajantarestaurant.com; near the Alameda.*

Bette's Oceanview Diner / ★★

1807-A 4TH ST, BERKELEY; 510/644-3230 The charm of Bette's Oceanview Diner doesn't have anything to do with the ocean (there's not even a view here). What this small, nouveau-'40s diner does have is red booths, chrome stools, a checkerboard tile floor, a hip wait staff, the best jukebox around, and darn good breakfasts. On weekends expect a 45-minute stomach-growling wait, but consider the payoff: enormous, soufflé-style pancakes stuffed with pecans and ripe berries, farm-fresh eggs scrambled with prosciutto and Parmesan, outstanding omelets, corned beef hash, and the quintessential huevos rancheros with black beans. If you can't bear the wait, pop into Bette's-to-Go (BTG) next door for a pre-breakfast snack. Later in the day, BTG offers superlative focaccia sandwiches and California pizzas. *$; MC, V; local checks only; breakfast, lunch every day; beer and wine; no reservations; between Virginia St and Hearst Ave.* &

Cafe Fanny / ★★

1603 SAN PABLO AVE, BERKELEY; 510/524-5447 Alice Waters's diminutive corner cafe can handle fewer than a dozen stand-up customers at once, but that doesn't deter anyone. On sunny Saturday mornings the adjacent parking lot fills with the overflow. Named after Waters's daughter, this popular spot recalls the neighborhood cafes so dear to the French, but Fanny's food is much better. Breakfast on crunchy Cafe Fanny granola, jam-filled buckwheat crêpes, or perfect soft-boiled eggs served on sourdough toast with a side of house-made jam, and sip a cafe au lait from a big authentic French handleless bowl. The morning meal is served until 11am and all day on Sunday. For lunch, order one of the seductive sandwiches, such as egg salad on crunchy Levain bread with sun-dried tomatoes and anchovies or the simple but delicious grilled eggplant with olive paste. Many fans combine a visit here with a stop at Fanny's illustrious neighbors: Acme Bread Company on one side and Kermit Lynch Wine Merchant on the other. *$; MC, V; checks OK; breakfast, lunch every day; beer and wine; no reservations; www.cafefanny.com; between Cedar and Virginia Sts.*

Cafe Rouge / ★★

1782 4TH ST, BERKELEY; 510/525-1440 Opened in 1996, this Fourth Street bistro offers everything from duck braised in white wine and smoked trout with frisée and leeks to hot dogs and cheeseburgers. Maybe it all makes a little more sense when one realizes that those aforementioned burgers and franks are the creations of Niman Ranch, so they're the most upscale versions you're likely to have. In fact, chef-owner Marsha McBride, a Zuni Cafe alumna, insists on high quality in all the ingredients, so it's hard to go wrong with anything on the small but beguiling menu. Her passions are oysters and charcuterie, but there are also creative salads and pastas, great grilled steaks, and juicy spit-roasted chicken. Desserts are absolute knockouts, including a seasonal warm quince bread pudding and a Jonathan apple puff pastry tartlet. Many of the house-smoked charcuterie items are available in the market in the back of the airy, bilevel restaurant, which boasts a long, curved zinc counter, skylights, and gold walls punctuated by red-paper wall sconces and modern artwork. *$$$; AE, MC, V; no checks; lunch every day, dinner Tues–Sun; full bar; reservations recommended; www.caferouge.net; between Hearst Ave and Delaware St.*

Cambodiana's / ★★

2156 UNIVERSITY AVE, BERKELEY; 510/843-4630 There aren't many Cambodian restaurants in Cambodia. As such, it took a forward-thinking Assyrian priest—Father Nazarin—to convince the local immigrant community that opening a Cambodian restaurant in Berkeley would be a successful endeavor. Today there are several Cambodian restaurants in the Bay Area, but Cambodiana's is still the best of the bunch. Owner Sidney Sok Ke and his wife, Carol Bopha Ke, the restaurant's talented chef, have assembled a menu organized around six regional sauces (based on tamarind, ginger, lemongrass, lamb juice, curry, and anchovy), each designed to complement delectable renditions of chicken, salmon, rabbit, lamb, prawns, quail, beef, and trout. Try the deboned quail stuffed with ground pork, shrimp, and garlic or the wonderful grilled lamb chops marinated in a mixture of garlic, lemongrass, galangal, paprika, and soy sauce. The country-style smoky eggplant, roasted and tossed with pork, shrimp, green onion, and garlic, also wins raves. *$$; AE, DC, MC, V; checks OK; lunch, dinner Tues–Sun; beer and wine; reservations recommended; between Shattuck Ave and Oxford St.*

César / ★★★

1515 SHATTUCK AVE, BERKELEY; 510/883-0222 This perennially packed tapas bar has proven without a doubt that the small-plates trend is here to stay. Right next door to the acclaimed Chez Panisse (César happens to be owned by Alice Waters's ex-husband), this 65-seat restaurant with a large communal table in the center of the room serves up delicious Spanish-style tapas. The no-reservations policy doesn't keep diners from coming to enjoy Maggie Pond's food in a convivial setting more reminiscent of a local bar than a restaurant. Start with the salty roasted almonds and a cool cucumber gazpacho. You can't go wrong here, as most of the 20 or so items on the menu are superb—especially the salt cod and potato *cazuela* (the Spanish version of brandade), which is served with slices of crunchy baguette. The *papas fritas* (fried potatoes) seasoned with cumin and garlic are delicious, as is the ham with sweet grilled figs. Dessert selections include a honey-sweetened, creamy *fromage blanc* served with peaches; bread pudding; and a rich *crema de chocolate*. *$$; AE, MC, V; no checks; lunch, dinner every day; full bar; no reservations; between Cedar and Vine Sts.*

Chez Panisse / ★★★★

1517 SHATTUCK AVE, BERKELEY; 510/548-5525 In the heart of Berkeley's gourmet ghetto, the most famous restaurant in Northern California is almost invisible from the street. Good-food lovers know where to find it, though; they just look for the small hand-carved sign in front of the vine-covered fence. Chef-owner Alice Waters has been at the forefront of the California cuisine revolution since 1971, when she started cooking simple French-influenced meals for groups of friends, then opened her legendary restaurant. Chez Panisse is divided into a fantastic (albeit expensive) prix-fixe dining room downstairs and a lighthearted (and more reasonably priced) upstairs cafe. Downstairs, the daily-changing dinner menu might begin with a bowl of olives and warm Acme bread, followed by aromatic, seasonal dishes such as an appetizer of thin-sliced salmon flash-cooked on a hot plate and served with an herbed flower butter, or a smooth corn-and-garlic soup flavored with a subtle touch of leek. An entree of boneless pigeon wrapped and grilled in vine leaves has a lovely smoky quality with a hint of mint and shallots; and a simple but sensational mixed-greens salad cleanses the palate before the appearance of a

THE CALL OF THE NOT-SO-WILD

JACK LONDON SQUARE is like a luxury SUV or a sailor in drag: gussied up, baubled, and bangled, when what it really wants to do is to load cargo. Beneath its tartish paint job lies the tattooed soul of a salty dog.

Back in the 1800s, when Oakland was little more than a township, the area at the end of Broadway was singled out to become a port that would rival—even surpass—the port of San Francisco; there was money to be made in the estuary muck. Soon docks sprang up, whaling ships lurched into Oakland, riverboats churned the water, and the locale gained a reputation as a rough and rowdy seafarer's gathering spot.

Nowadays there are a few places in Jack London Square where its beard stubble pokes through the blush. A ride on the Jack London Square Water Taxi or the Alameda/Oakland Ferry will take you past the real guts of the area: **THE DOCKS**. They were the places where, during the '40s, scores of women lent their hands to the wartime effort and where massive shipments from far-off lands are received to this day. A walk through the nearby produce district will reveal the grittier side of the area—the raw inner workings of a diminished though still vibrant industry. Heinold's First & Last Chance Saloon still stands; this is the bar where a young Jack London sold newspapers from a barstool and bent his ear to sailors' woolly tales.

It may not look as wild as it once was, thanks to the industrious efforts of makeup-artist developers, but explore—answer the call, pull back the wig—and you'll find a weathered mariner, ready to hum a sea shanty.

beautiful kirsch-infused Bavarian pudding. The warm, bustling upstairs cafe has a fine wine bar and seldom enough seats to go around. Its popular pizzas and calzones, baked in a wood-burning oven, often feature ingredients such as squid and roasted onion or simply mozzarella and the finest vine-ripened tomatoes in the state. Desserts include house-made ice creams and sherbets, fruit cobblers, tarts, and pies. *$$$; AE, DC, DIS, MC, V; local checks only; restaurant: dinner Mon–Sat; cafe: lunch, dinner Mon–Sat; beer and wine; reservations required; www.chezpanisse.com; between Cedar and Vine Sts.*

Kirala / ★★

2100 WARD ST, BERKELEY; 510/549-3486 A no-reservations policy often means a long wait at this small restaurant with the down-at-the-heels facade and plain-Jane decor. Expanded in 1999, it features an extensive sake bar—boasting more than 20 premium sakes from Japan—where you can enjoy a light meal. Once you snag a seat in the dining area or sushi bar, however, get ready to taste some of the best Japanese food in town. The sushi is fresh and ready in a flash of a knife; the gyoza and other appetizers are first rate; and the skewers of seafood, vegetables, and meats emerging from the robata grill are cooked to perfection and seasoned with a delicate hand. *$$;*

AE, MC, V; no checks; lunch Tues–Fri, dinner every day; beer and wine; no reservations; www.kirala.citysearch.com; near Shattuck Ave.

Lalime's / ★★

1329 GILMAN ST, BERKELEY; 510/527-9838 It's hard to pass Lalime's at night without stopping to stare at the goings-on through its fishbowl front window: the radiant yellow dining room boasts high ceilings, colorful collages on the walls, and a crush of sleek patrons leaning intimately over candlelit, white-linen-cloaked tables. The menu changes monthly, but if they're serving the soup made with Finn potatoes, golden beets, and ginger, or the roast garlic and shiitake mushroom ravioli, don't hesitate—they're always delicious. Desserts, such as the creamy house-made anise ice cream, mango flan, and chocolate cake with brandied cherries, are equally splendid. Lalime's prix-fixe dinners are often a good bet: one might feature seared spearfish marinated in fresh lime and curry and served with a blood-orange and fennel salad, followed by grilled chicken breast accompanied by crisp polenta triangles and a sweet onion, red pepper, and raisin relish, and, for dessert, a candied pecan tart with a buttery crust. The witty, efficient, and exceptionally knowledgeable staff can direct you to the gems on Lalime's extensive beer and wine list. *$$$; AE, MC, V; no checks; dinner every day; beer and wine; reservations recommended; www.lalimes.com; between Neilson and Peralta Sts.*

O Chamé / ★★★

1830 4TH ST, BERKELEY; 510/841-8783 Even jaded Berkeley food fanatics are bewitched by the fare in this exotic restaurant. Chef David Vardy spent years studying Buddhist-Taoist cooking in Taiwan, as well as Kansai and Kaiseki cuisine in Japan. (Kansai is the regional cuisine of Osaka; Kaiseki, created to complement the Japanese tea ceremony, consists of small dishes that can be consumed in a couple of bites.) Vardy developed an ardent local following when he opened the Daruma Teashop in North Berkeley in 1988, serving an intriguing assortment of teas, bento box lunches, and his popular Nambu tea cakes—thin, sesame-based biscuits flavored with nuts or seeds. These and more elaborate works of culinary art may now be found at O Chamé, a soothing cafe crafted in the style of a rustic wayside inn from Japan's Meiji period. The à la carte menu changes often, but typical dishes include a very fresh vinegared wakame seaweed, cucumber, and crab salad; tofu dumplings with burdock and carrot; grilled river eel with endive and chayote; and soba noodles with shiitake mushrooms and daikon sprouts. O Chamé also offers a range of delicately flavored teas and sakes as well as several good beers. *$$; AE, DC, MC, V; no checks; lunch, dinner Mon–Sat; beer and wine; reservations recommended; near Hearst Ave.*

Rivoli / ★★★

1539 SOLANO AVE, BERKELEY; 510/526-2542 Chef Wendy Brucker first came to the attention of East Bay diners in 1992 when she took over the kitchen of the dining room at Berkeley's Shattuck Hotel. That venue was too stiff and formal for her California sensibilities—honed at places such as San Francisco's now-shuttered Square One and the eclectic City Restaurant in L.A.—so she transferred her talents to a much more suitable place: her own, where she could have the freedom to present her relaxed yet refined ideas about California-Mediterranean cuisine. Start your meal with bruschetta topped with goat cheese, sun-dried tomatoes, and basil (a cliché, perhaps, but a wonderfully tasty one) or their renowned and expertly fried portobello mushrooms with arugula and aioli (definitely not a cliché). The grilled sage brined pork loin with honey-roasted figs and baked eggplant and fennel is the essence of good country cooking. Along with her husband and partner, Roscoe Skipper, Brucker deserves kudos for assembling a tantalizing menu that changes every three weeks. The wine list offers several good choices under $20. *$$$; AE, DC, DIS, MC, V; local checks only; dinner every day; beer and wine; reservations recommended; www.rivolirestaurant.com; between Peralta Ave and Neilson St.*

Spenger's Fresh Fish Grotto / ★★

1919 4TH ST, BERKELEY; 510/845-7771 Weary of minimalist restaurants with painfully modern furniture, vying for the title "Most Tragically Hip Eating Establishment"? Tired of somber wait staff who look like Banana Republic poster children? Yet you still want great food? Spenger's Fresh Fish Grotto is confirmation that a classic never goes out of style. This unassuming restaurant is situated in Berkeley's famous Fourth Street shopping district and was there long before it was chic—since 1890, actually. The famous have dined there—Robin Williams, Joan Baez, Clark Gable, Spencer Tracy, and Ernest Hemingway, to name a few. The decor is restored rather than renovated and speaks to a seafaring time long gone. The wait staff is equally charming, having been chosen for their knowledge and dedication rather than their looks. But naturally, it's the food in which you're most interested, and Spenger's will satisfy you on every level. The menu changes twice daily, based on fresh catch availability, but you can always expect simply prepared seafood with just the right amount of detail. Appetizers include tender fried calamari and stone crab claws with jalapeños, cilantro, and Key lime juice. Main courses may include such wonders as *monchong* blackened with Cajun spices, served with jasmine rice and Thai coconut curry sauce, or mahimahi, pan seared with a macadamia nut crust, served with mashed potatoes and spicy Jamaican hot rum butter. Regardless of what's on the menu for the day, you can be sure it will be fresh and beautifully prepared. After indulging in one of the homemade desserts, stroll on over to the bar to check out the proudly displayed Star of Denmark, a 34-carat diamond ring once given to Hawaii's Queen Kapiolani, and ponder the everlasting appeal of yet another classic. *$$$$; AE, MC, V; checks OK; lunch, dinner every day; full bar; reservations recommended; www.spengers.com; off University Ave.* &

LODGINGS

The Berkeley City Club / ★

2315 DURANT AVE, BERKELEY; 510/848-7800 Architect Julia Morgan called this lovely edifice with the grand Moorish flourishes her "little castle" (her "big castle" was Hearst Castle in San Simeon, the crowning achievement of her architectural career). The 1927 building, with its hallways graced by soaring buttresses and its tall lead-paned windows, garden courtyards, and handsome sandstone-colored facade, was designed as a women's club, and Morgan wanted it to rival the poshest male enclave. Today both genders are welcomed through its stately portals, not only as members who enjoy the club's fitness and social activities but also as bed-and-breakfast guests. The club's 40 rooms are simply appointed, small, and old-fashioned (if the rooms were as grand as the public areas, this would be a three-star hotel), but all have private baths and many boast views of the bay, the nearby UC campus, or the Berkeley hills. If you need a bit more elbow room, try to book one of the two suites. Overnight guests have access to the club's dining room and fitness facilities, including a 25-yard-long indoor pool that even William Randolph Hearst wouldn't have minded taking a dip in. Daily rates include a buffet breakfast; weekly and monthly arrangements are available, too. *$$; MC, V; checks OK; breakfast every day, lunch Mon–Fri, dinner hours vary for members and B&B guests only; full bar; berkeleycityclub.com; between Dana and Ellsworth Sts.*

The Claremont Resort and Spa / ★★★

41 TUNNEL RD, BERKELEY; 510/843-3000 OR 800/551-7266 With its towers and cupolas gleaming white against the green and golden Berkeley hills, this proud prima donna of a hotel holds fast to its Edwardian roots. It's hard to hurry here: the posh lobby with its plush furniture and alabaster chandeliers is made for loitering and gaping, while the 22 acres of gorgeous grounds—with flower beds, rows of exotic palms, and even a modern sculpture garden—invite leisurely strolling. The only folks scurrying about are those rushing the net on the Claremont's 10 championship tennis courts or feeling the burn in one of the spa's aerobics classes. Amenities include everything you'd expect in a grand hotel, including concierge and room service, a fully equipped business center, and extensive spa facilities. This is the place to treat yourself to a rejuvenating massage or beauty treatment or, better yet, opt for a Spa Trio that includes a luxurious body wrap, facial, and massage all in one. Parking at the resort and transportation to the airports and San Francisco are available for a fee. In addition to the tennis courts, guests have access to fitness classes, spa treatments, two heated pools, saunas, and a hot tub. Three restaurants grace the premises: the Paragon Bar & Grill, which offers casual fare including burgers, pastas, and fresh fish along with live music and a hopping bar scene; the Bayview Cafe, which is located by the pool and serves sandwiches, salads, and grilled fare; and Jordan's, the Claremont's California–Pacific Rim flagship restaurant, which serves breakfast, lunch, and dinner in a casually elegant setting known for its stupendous views. *$$$; AE, DC, DIS, MC, V; checks OK; claremontresort.com; at the intersection of Ashby and Domingo Aves.*

Rose Garden Inn / ★★

2740 TELEGRAPH AVE, BERKELEY; 510/549-2145 This attractive bed-and-breakfast surrounded by beautifully landscaped lawns started out as a restored Tudor-style mansion furnished with wonderful old furniture and period antiques. Then it swallowed the house next door and added a couple of cottages and a carriage house, giving the Rose Garden Inn's empire enough space for 40 guest rooms. The best rooms are in the Fay House, which has glowing hardwood walls and stunning stained-glass windows. All of the rooms in the Garden and Carriage Houses have fireplaces and overlook the inviting English country garden in back (room 4 in the Carriage House is the best). Of course, the rooms facing away from Telegraph

Avenue are the most tranquil. Each guest room has a private bath, a color TV, and a phone; some have balconies and views of San Francisco. *$$; AE, DC, DIS, MC, V; local checks only; www.rosegardeninn.com; between Ward and Stuart Sts.*

Emeryville

This tiny town slivered between Oakland, Berkeley, and the bay was once a dowdy industrial area, but a dozen years of manic redevelopment has turned it into one of the most intriguing urban centers in the Bay Area; computer jockeys, artists, and biotechies now abound here in their live-work spaces. Emeryville's town center is a nouveau ultramall called the **EMERYBAY PUBLIC MARKET**. The center offers great ethnic food stands, stores, a 10-screen cinema, and the hot **KIMBALL'S EAST** (510/658-2555), a jazz and blues club with national headliners; take the Powell Street exit from Interstate 80. Nearby is one of Emeryville's biggest attractions: the Swedish home store **IKEA** (4400 Shellmound; 510/420-4532). You really can't miss it. The bright blue behemoth seems to have engulfed every previously undeveloped lot in town.

RESTAURANTS

Bucci's / ★★

6121 HOLLIS ST, EMERYVILLE; 510/547-4725 Located in a beautifully restored former warehouse, Bucci's is all brick and glass, with soaring ceilings, an open kitchen, and a small patio garden. At lunch, biotech execs and multimedia artists nosh on rich focaccia sandwiches and crisp thin-crust pizzas topped with prosciutto, roasted peppers, provolone, mozzarella, and cherry tomatoes. Dinner offers more elaborate fare from a daily-changing menu, which might include a tender roast duck served with a rich butternut-squash risotto or delicate cannelloni stuffed with spinach, walnuts, roasted red peppers, and cheese and served in a lemon cream sauce. The desserts and espressos are topflight, and the full bar specializes in classic cocktails. *$$; MC, V; checks OK; lunch Mon–Fri, dinner Mon–Sat; full bar; reservations recommended; www.buccis.com; between 59th and 61st Sts.*

Hong Kong East Ocean Seafood Restaurant / ★★★

3199 POWELL ST, EMERYVILLE; 510/655-3388 With its green pagoda-style tile roof topped with writhing gold dragons and its white imperial lions guarding the front door, Hong Kong East Ocean looks more like a temple than a restaurant. Indeed, its worshippers are legion, thanks in large part to its superior dim sum. For the full dim sum treatment, come on the weekend, when the dining room swarms with dozens of carts pushed by Chinese waitresses who have a limited grasp of English, and when most of your fellow diners will be well-heeled Chinese. (During the week, you can order the dim sum from a menu—an efficient but boring departure from the traditional method.) Best bets are the crystal buns (delicate steamed dumplings filled with plump shrimp, chopped water chestnuts, cilantro, and ginger); crisp, baked *bao* (buns) filled with sweet red pork and topped with crunchy sesame seeds; and shrimp embedded in a noodle-dough crêpe served in a savory sauce. Besides dim sum, Hong

Kong East Ocean offers authentic and exquisitely prepared Cantonese-style lunches and dinners: try the whole black cod dressed in a satiny soy-ginger-garlic sauce; the addictive, peppery deep-fried squid topped with chopped chilies and scallions; or anything that includes the feathery egg noodles. *$$; AE, MC, V; no checks; lunch, dinner every day; full bar; reservations recommended; at the end of the Emeryville Marina.*

Oakland

There's no question that Oakland has gotten a bad and, in many respects, undeserved rap. After all, it was once ranked 12th on *Money* magazine's Best Places to Live in the United States list and third by the *Wall Street Journal* for fastest-rising real estate prices in the nation. But just ask Oakland residents what they love about their city—where to shop, where to eat—and you'll get a prideful response. They'll likely point you in the direction of charming yet somewhat eccentric **ROCKRIDGE**. They might give you directions to **PIEDMONT AVENUE** or Victorian Row. They'll tell you that if you follow Broadway to the bay, you'll hit Jack London Square. They may even let you know which neighborhoods boast some of the most amazing historic architecture in the Bay Area, or that the view from the Mormon Temple can't be bested. What they probably won't do is "dis" their city—Oaktown, as it is sometimes affectionately called.

With a resident celebrity list as diverse as its culture—Gertrude Stein, Maya Angelou, Bruce Lee, R&B group En Vogue, Amy Tan, and, of course, Jack London, all of whom either called Oakland home or were born there—this city seems to have something about it that fosters self-expression. Even Mayor Jerry Brown—yes, the former California governor—has recognized the creative spirit that seems to run through the city's veins. He's declared promotion of the arts part and parcel of a citywide renaissance and made it one of his primary focuses for his term in office.

In *Oakland: Story of a City* by Beth Bagwell, an anonymous Oaklander captured the mystique of the city best: "Oakland now is like a great old blues singer. She knows how to moan and cry, but the bad times behind her make her know how to savor the good times. The old-time Oaklanders, and the port, and the big corporations building new skyscrapers downtown are like instruments in a band, and all together now we're blowing some pretty good jazz."

MAJOR ATTRACTIONS

Oakland's premier tourist destination is **JACK LONDON SQUARE**, a sophisticated seaside spread of boutiques, bookstores, restaurants, hotels, cinemas, and saloons that is refreshingly void of the touristy schlock that pervades San Francisco's Pier 39. Must-see stops along the promenade include **HEINOLD'S FIRST & LAST CHANCE SALOON** (56 Jack London Sq; 510/839-6761), a decidedly funky little bar crammed with faded seafaring souvenirs, and the overhauled **USS POTOMAC** (510/839-8256), the 165-foot presidential yacht that served as FDR's "floating White House."

The sunken building that holds the **OAKLAND MUSEUM** (1000 Oak St, between 10th and 12th Sts; 510/238-2200), a spectacular specimen of modern architecture

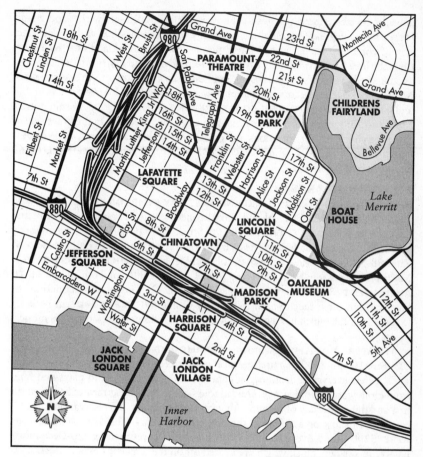

DOWNTOWN OAKLAND

designed by Kevin Roche in 1969, features innovative displays of the art, history, and ecology of California and also boasts beautiful terraced gardens.

Tots will get a kick out of **LAKE MERRITT'S CHILDREN'S FAIRYLAND** (699 Bellevue Ave; 510/452-2259), a kid-size amusement park that supposedly inspired Walt Disney to construct Disneyland. Kids will also thrill to the beasts at the **OAKLAND ZOO** (9777 Golf Links Rd; 510/632-9525).

SHOPPING

In genteel North Oakland, the Rockridge neighborhood running along College Avenue boasts numerous bookstores, cafes, antique stores, expensive clothing boutiques, and a gourmet's paradise that rivals North Berkeley. Stroll through the **ROCK-RIDGE MARKET HALL** (5655 College Ave at Shafter Ave, across from the Rockridge BART station; 510/655-7748), a chic multivendor market offering fresh pastas, gourmet cheeses, chocolates, fresh-cut flowers, delicious deli sandwiches and salads, breads from the great Grace Baking Company, exquisite produce, and a wide selection of wine. Grittier but just as interesting is downtown Oakland's **CHINATOWN** (tour the area between 7th and 10th Sts and Broadway and Harrison), which is not as congested (with cars or tourists) as San Francisco's Chinatown. An assortment of Mexican bakeries and taquerias tempt passersby along E 14th Street, between 2nd and 13th Avenues. The **PACIFIC COAST BREWING COMPANY** (906 Washington St; 510/836-2739) offers a lively bar scene and good microbrews. On the other side of town are your best bets for books and coffee near Oakland's downtown: **WALDEN POND BOOKS** (3316 Grand Ave; 510/832-4438) and the **COFFEE MILL** (3363 Grand Ave; 510/465-4224).

PERFORMING ARTS

MUSIC: The highly regarded **OAKLAND EAST BAY SYMPHONY** (2025 Broadway; 510/444-0801) offers classical and choral concerts at the Paramount Theatre and the **CALVIN SIMMONS THEATER** (10 10th Street; call 510/238-7765 for symphony schedules). You can catch the hottest jazz in town at **YOSHI'S** (510 Embarcadero W; 510/238-9200; see review, below), the bluest blues at **ELI'S MILE HIGH CLUB** (3629 Martin Luther King Jr. Wy; 510/655-6661), and a little of both at the **FIFTH AMENDMENT** (3255 Lake Shore Ave; 510/832-3242). Gospel acts abound in the East Bay, but often they're hard to find; try calling **REID'S RECORDS** in Berkeley (510/843-7282), which has a bulletin board where folks post the latest local musical events.

THEATER AND FILM: Downtown's **PARAMOUNT THEATRE** (2025 Broadway at 21st St; 510/893-2300), an architectural masterpiece built in 1931 and restored in 1973, offers everything from organ concerts and rock concerts to plays and films from Hollywood's Golden Age. Guided tours of the 3,000-seat theater are given the first and third Saturday of each month, excluding holidays. No reservations are necessary—just show up at 10am at the box office entrance. The **GRAND LAKE THEATRE** (3200 Grand Ave; 510/452-3556), a beautifully restored Egypto-Deco movie palace, shows new films, which are kicked off on the weekends by a live organist's dazzling performance.

DANCE: The **OAKLAND BALLET** (2025 Broadway; 510/465-6400) jumps and twirls at the beautiful art deco Paramount Theatre, and at various Oakland venues dozens of innovative contemporary and African dance troupes kick up their heels, including **DIMENSIONS** (510/465-3363) and the **FUADIA CONGO DANCE COMPANY** (510/562-0831).

SPORTS AND RECREATION

Those hotshot boys of summer, the Oakland A's, are usually knocking 'em dead at the **OAKLAND COLISEUM** (from I-80 take the Coliseum exit or, better yet, avoid the freeway crawl by taking a BART train; 510/638-0500). And the sparkling Oakland Coliseum Arena—renovated to the tune of $102 million—is the home of the tall guys: the **GOLDEN STATE WARRIORS** (510/986-2200).

Pretty **LAKE MERRITT,** one of the largest saltwater tidal lakes in the world, is home to flocks of migrating ducks, geese, and herons and provides a great place for a leisurely stroll or jog; the lake is bounded by Grand Avenue, Lake Shore Avenue, and Lakeside Drive. For fun on the water, rent a sailboat, rowboat, paddleboat, or canoe at the lake's **SAILBOAT HOUSE** (510/238-3187). For the ultimate urban escape, head for the hills to **REDWOOD REGIONAL PARK** (off Joaquin Miller Rd; 510/636-1684), where miles of fern-trimmed trails wind through redwood groves and oak woodlands.

RESTAURANTS

Asmara Restaurant and Bar / ★

5020 TELEGRAPH AVE, OAKLAND; 510/547-5100 Asmara has a split personality: the comfortable restaurant is full of East African kitsch, while the adjacent bar—stark white and brightly lit—is a sterile jolt to the senses. Eritrean expatriates seem to prefer the bar, while locals enjoy the restaurant's African decor. Both groups, however, often get caught up in the communal spirit of the place, sharing their meals with fellow diners and using pieces of spongy injera bread to scoop up tasty *ziggni* (beef marinated in a surprisingly mild berbere sauce made with jalapeño and other chile peppers) and *yegomen alicha* (mustard greens simmered with spices). Make the most of this culinary adventure by getting one of the combination dinners. $; AE, DIS, MC, V; no checks; lunch Fri–Sun, dinner Tues–Sun; full bar; reservations recommended; at 51st St.

Bay Wolf Restaurant / ★★★

3853 PIEDMONT AVE, OAKLAND; 510/655-6004 Located in an attractive Victorian house with dark wood wainscoting and pale yellow walls, Bay Wolf first became a local favorite under the direction of co-owner and executive chef Michael Wild. Almost 30 years old, this East Bay institution is beginning to show its age. The dark space is in need of a fresh coat of paint and the food sometimes lacks its early inspiration. Nevertheless, fresh ingredients and careful preparation of seasonal dishes keep Bay Wolf at the top of everyone's list of favorites. Typical first courses might include a spiced scallop and endive salad or a rich, smoky asparagus and hazelnut soup with lemon cream. Main courses vary from tender grilled duck with spiced nectarines, escarole, and shell bean ragout to a flavorful seafood stew bubbling with cracked Dungeness crab, prawns, rockfish, and mussels. Desserts change every two weeks, but a couple of summer offerings included an irresistible berry pudding chock-full of seasonal berries along with a warm chocolate pudding cake drizzled with crème anglaise and cocoa sauce. The carefully selected wine list offers a number of moderately priced vintages, and more than 10 wines are available by the glass. Service is efficient but a little stiff in the evening; the staff loosens up during the day. $$$$; AE, MC, V; checks OK; lunch Mon–Fri, dinner every day; beer and wine; reservations recommended; www.baywolf.com; between 40th St and MacArthur Blvd.

Caffe 817 / ★★

817 WASHINGTON ST, OAKLAND; 510/271-7965 Visit the downtown Oakland farmer's market on Friday morning, then rest your weary bag-laden arms at Caffe 817. This tiny restaurant bears the stamp of its design-conscious owner, Sandro Rossi, an electrical engineer who saw potential in this high-ceilinged space and hired local craftspeople to fashion its avant-garde furnishings. Despite its lofty decor, the cafe has modest ambitions: cappuccino and pastries are mainstays in the morning, and Italian sandwiches, simple salads, and fresh soups and stews are on the midday menu. The sandwich fillings are what you might call contemporary Italian-American: roast beef with arugula, grilled mozzarella with artichokes, prosciutto with herb butter and pears. But the rice-and-borlotti-bean soup is a classic Tuscan dish. If all this good fare inspires you to make your own Italian classics at home, head next door to G. B. Ratto International Grocers, a favorite East Bay source for arborio rice, olive oil, beans, and other imported foodstuffs. *$; AE, MC, V; checks OK; breakfast, lunch Mon–Sat; beer and wine; no reservations; between 8th and 9th Sts.*

Citron / ★★★

5484 COLLEGE AVE, OAKLAND; 510/653-5484 An immediate hit when it opened in 1992, Citron has settled in for the long run. The intimate dining room, which, true to its French name, is bathed in soothing shades of lemon yellow, sets the stage for chef Chris Rossi's equally small menu of contemporary French-Mediterranean fare. Rossi's menu changes every two weeks. Recent appetizers included a grilled corn and sorrel soup with soft-shell crab, as well as a yellowtail carpaccio with a citrus-red onion salad. One taste of the chicken with 40 garlic cloves and you'll think you've been transported to Provence. Then again, if it's Italian fare you're craving, look for Rossi's chanterelle mushroom soup and ricotta fritters, or the lamb osso buco served on a bed of flageolet-bean and sun-dried tomato ragout with a sprinkling of pistachio gremolata garnish. You can now sip your glass of Viognier under vine-covered trellises on the newly completed patio. Or slip right next door to Rossi's latest creation, À Côté, which opened in 2001 and serves delicious French tapas in a warm and beautifully lit dining room. *$$; AE, DC, DIS, MC, V; checks OK; dinner every day; full bar; reservations recommended; www.citron-acote.com; between Taft and Lawton Sts.*

Grasshopper / ★★

6317 COLLEGE AVE, OAKLAND; 510/595-3557 This casual little restaurant at the far end of College Avenue specializes in small Asian plates. The somewhat austere interior with concrete floors and high ceilings seems well suited for the equally restrained but well-composed dishes. Some standouts include tea-smoked quail; a spicy grilled Japanese eggplant topped with miso glaze; a zingy lemongrass skirt steak salad; and lamb chops with fresh ahi sashimi, pluots, and cucumbers. Grasshopper offers more than a dozen sakes to pair with the intriguing and ever-changing flavors of the 20 or so dishes. Noise levels can be off the charts, but don't let that stop you from staying for dessert: the tropical sorbets and granitas are sure winners. *$$; AE, DC, DIS, MC, V; no checks; lunch Tues–Fri, dinner Tues–Sun; beer and wine; reservations for parties of 6 or more; at Alcatraz Ave.* &

Jade Villa / ★★

800 BROADWAY, OAKLAND; 510/839-1688 Ever since Lantern restaurant closed, the title of Oakland's top dim sum house has been transferred to Jade Villa, a behemoth of a restaurant that takes up nearly a quarter block in Oakland's Chinatown.

During the lunch hour the place is packed with Chinese families sitting at large, round tables. The ornate dining room offers a tempting array of dinners, but the real reason you should come here is for the dim sum, served from early morning to midafternoon. Sip a cup of aromatic tea as servers circulate through the room pushing carts laden with assorted delicacies. They'll pause by your table and lift the lids of tiered metal steamers to let you inspect the barbecued pork buns, stuffed dumplings, wedges of green pepper filled with shrimp, and lots of other tasty treats. Hold out for at least one order of the steamed prawns-in-shell, the best dish. You'll be charged by the plate, and you can afford to experiment here—two people can eat with abandon for about 20 bucks. *$$; AE, DC, DIS, MC, V; no checks; lunch, dinner every day; beer and wine; reservations recommended; at 8th St.*

Jojo / ★★★

3859 PIEDMONT AVE, OAKLAND; 510/985-3003 Any restaurant daring enough to set up shop next to Bay Wolf had better have some sturdy culinary legs to stand on—and like a farm-bred, French country milkmaid, Jojo has just the gams for the task. With its light Dijon mustard–colored walls, sage green wainscoting, and olive with black filigree chiffon curtains, it's a statement in subtlety. The menu is—you guessed it—French country. And, thankfully, it's not so pretentious as to be printed in French. The simple yet well-developed fare changes every three days or so and includes starters like crab-and-goat-cheese tart with a warm bacon vinaigrette, as well as wonderful entrees such as a seafood stew with shrimp, clams, chicken, and sausage or flatiron steak served with anchovy mustard butter. For dessert, one simply must indulge in the chocolate soufflé cake with espresso crème anglaise and candied walnuts. Only eight months into their venture, co-owners and chefs Mary Jo Thoresen and Curt Coingman garnered *San Francisco* magazine's Best New Restaurant award for Jojo. Aside from the food, the one other attribute Jojo shares with France is the way the wait staff glides across the room with immovable plaster-of-Paris expressions. Get one of them to crack a smile and your evening will be complete. *$$$; AE, DC, MC, V; no checks; dinner only Tues–Sat; beer and wine; reservations recommended; www.jojorestaurant.com; between 40th St and MacArthur Blvd.* &

Le Cheval / ★★

1007 CLAY ST, OAKLAND; 510/763-8957 With everyone in the restaurant shouting to be heard, the din in Le Cheval is impossible to ignore. The egg-carton acoustic material on the ceiling doesn't help since it's about three miles away from the dining room floor—it's like trying to sound-dampen a stadium with velvet curtains. Nevertheless, people still flock to Le Cheval for the best Vietnamese food in the Bay Area—a title bestowed upon it by the *East Bay Express* newspaper. The menu is mind-bogglingly long, the seasonings are exotic, and the family-style portions are beyond generous. You could really pick just about anything off the menu and experience gastronomic euphoria, but be sure to sample some of the range of appetizers, which include imperial rolls, roast quail, marinated beef in lemon, or "bun"—similar to imperial rolls but of the do-it-yourself variety. Whatever you choose from the main course menu—whether prawns stewed in a clay pot or chicken with bamboo shoots—you'll be so content it won't matter that you can't hear

SAN JOSE, SOUTH BAY, AND THE PENINSULA
THREE-DAY TOUR

DAY ONE: Afterlife day. Check in to your room at the predictably luxurious **FAIRMONT** hotel in San Jose. You'll be glad you did since you'll be spending the day at some of the most peculiar sites in the Bay Area. Fuel up with a cappuccino at **CAFE MATISSE** before your first stop at the **EGYPTIAN MUSEUM AND PLANETARIUM**. This attraction features incredible mummies, Egyptian artifacts, scale models of temples, and accurate reproductions of tombs. But that's not the unusual part. The unusual part is that the museum is run by the Rosicrucian Order—not unlike the Theosophic Society—which takes rather seriously the mysterious tenets of ancient Egypt. Don't worry, you won't be converted. Drop in at **71 SAINT PETER** for lunch. From there, head on over to the **WINCHESTER MYSTERY HOUSE** for more otherworldly fun. After you've been thoroughly spooked, go back to your accommodations at the Fairmont—where the doors do open up to rooms—and relax for a bit before heading off to **ORLO'S**. Housed in a mansion built by faith healer Mary Hayes Chynoweth, it's the perfect place for an ethereal dinner.

DAY TWO: Day of the cat. Start your morning with breakfast at the hotel. No trip to the Silicon Valley would be complete without a side trip to **LOS GATOS**. Located off Highway 17 just before the Santa Cruz Mountains, this enclave put both charming and chichi on the map. All you really need to do is find a place to park, which could take awhile, as there is primarily on-street parking, and start walking. Brimming over with stylish boutiques, exclusive gift stores, and home accessory shops, this town will keep your credit card humming for some time. Try **I GATTI**—"the cats"—for lunch before sojourning through pesto-thick traffic to your room at the **GARDEN COURT HOTEL**

yourself chew. $$; AE, MC, V; *no checks; lunch, dinner every day; full bar; reservations recommended; near 10th St.* &

Mama's Royal Cafe / ★

4012 BROADWAY, OAKLAND; 510/547-7600 Die-hard regulars don't even question the 40- to 60-minute wait required on weekends to get a seat at this 20-year-old Oakland landmark known simply as Mama's. A combination of good food served in large portions and a schizo decor (picture a '40s-style diner/noodle house with pagoda door frames and Rosie-the-Riveter-era ads on Formica tabletops) attracts the bohemian/boomer crowd in Doc Martens and Tevas for some of the heartiest breakfasts in the East Bay. Unfortunately, the prices are kinda high, the service is suhloooow (leave the antsy kids at home), and the waiters sometimes serve up a little attitude with your home fries. But who cares when the menu includes 31 types of omelets and such breakfast specials as fresh fruit crêpes and burritos with chipotle tortillas? Rumors abound of a ghost who haunts the third dining room, which purportedly was once a barbershop where a local mobster was cut down midshave. $;

in Palo Alto. After you've had a chance to unwind from the drive, treat yourself to an amazing dinner at **MANRESA**. You will have earned it.

DAY THREE: The garden-variety day. After a breakfast of Italian pastries at **IL FORNAIO** in the Garden Court Hotel, if you haven't yet done your share of shopping, you can start your day with more retail therapy in Palo Alto's **STANFORD SHOPPING CENTER**. This shopping experience is a cut above the rest—the center retains its original outdoor layout, and its gardens are meticulously tended. For lunch, indulge in the exceptional fare at **MAX'S OPERA CAFE** (650/323-6287), located in the shopping center. However, if gardens get your heart pumping, you could skip Stanford Shopping Center and go directly to Woodside and **FILOLI ESTATE AND GARDENS** (86 Canada—pronounced con-Ya-da—Rd; 650/364-8300). This palatial mansion and its surrounding gardens were built in 1915 by Mr. and Mrs. William Bowers Bourn II, founders of the Empire Gold Mine. Filoli stands for "fight, love, live"—to fight for just cause, to love your fellow man, to live a good life—just in case you were wondering. Both the sprawling house and the spectacular gardens are open for tours, but take your time and journey back to a way of life long gone. A light, casual lunch at the **QUAIL'S NEST CAFE** on the Filoli grounds will be the perfect respite between tours and strolling. If all that fresh air has built you an appetite, head into downtown Woodside (you'll practically miss it if you blink) to dine at the recently revamped **VILLAGE PUB**. Don't let the name of the restaurant mislead you—a top-notch American-inspired menu featuring crispy sweetbreads and decadent strawberry shortcake is what you will find in this chic and luxurious establishment. Linger over an after-dinner cordial before heading back to your room at the Garden Court to relax.

cash only; breakfast every day, lunch Mon–Fri; beer and wine; no reservations; at 40th St. &

Nan Yang Rockridge / ★★

6048 COLLEGE AVE, OAKLAND; 510/655-3298 When Nan Yang opened in 1983, restaurants offering a full spectrum of Burmese delights were virtually nonexistent. Chef-owner Philip Chu assembled the menu by tracking down recipes from monasteries, street vendors, festival food booths, and family homes to create the first Burmese restaurant in the Bay Area. His noble efforts have been rewarded with rave reviews and long lines of customers clamoring for his fare—especially his ginger salad, a crunchy, textural delight with 16 ingredients including split peas, fava beans, shredded cabbage, coconut slices, sun-dried shrimp, garlic oil, roasted peanuts, and shredded ginger. The generous curry dishes come with giant chunks of beef, chicken, or fish; there are also plenty of seductive vegetarian variations. On sunny days, opt for a table on the front patio. *$$; MC, V; no checks; lunch, dinner Tues–Sun; beer and wine; reservations recommended; just S of Claremont Ave.*

Oliveto Cafe and Restaurant / ★★★

5655 COLLEGE AVE, OAKLAND; 510/547-5356 Oliveto has always been a top East Bay destination, thanks in part to chef Paul Canales and chef-owner Paul Bertolli's obvious passion for the Italian table and careful interpretations of Italy's rustic cuisine. Trimmed with granite, olive wood, and custom ironwork, the restaurant has the air of a Florentine trattoria, and the well-dressed, well-heeled stockbroker-and-filmmaker crowd cements the impression. House specialties include the fresh fish dishes, such as petrale sole piccata served on a bed of sautéed spinach and topped with a caper, white wine, and butter sauce. Meats from the wood-fired rotisserie and grill range from Watson Farm lamb to the house-made pork sausage and grilled rabbit. Downstairs, the more casual cafe draws a crowd of commuters (a BART station is across the street) and neighbors from morning till night. You'll see tense-but-chic workaholic singles sizing each other up over small, crisp pizzas and sophisticated salads like the panzanella with cherry tomatoes and fresh mozzarella. A woodburning oven rotisserie and high-end liquor cabinet (i.e., hard alcohol and a few mixed drinks) only add to Oliveto's popularity. *$$$; AE, DC, MC, V; no checks; cafe serves light breakfast, lunch, dinner every day; restaurant serves lunch Mon–Fri, dinner every day; beer and wine; reservations recommended; www.oliveto.com; at Shafter Ave, across from the Rockridge BART station.*

Pho Anh Dao / ★

280 E 18TH ST, OAKLAND; 510/836-1566 Essentially a one-dish restaurant, Pho Anh Dao specializes in pho, the Hanoi anise-scented beef and noodle soup that many Vietnamese eat almost every day. This aromatic meal-in-a-bowl has everything in its favor: it's cheap (less than $4), delicious, plentiful, and healthful. The essential garnishes arrive on the side: Asian basil, sliced green chiles, a lime or lemon wedge, and bean sprouts. Add as much of them as you like and then, with chopsticks in one hand and a soup spoon in the other, dive in. Pho aficionados ask for raw beef so they can "cook" it in the hot broth a slice at a time. Good pho takes hours to make, and Pho Anh Dao does it right. *$; cash only; breakfast, lunch, dinner every day; beer only; no reservations; between 2nd and 3rd Aves.*

Pizza Rustica Cafe / ★

5422 COLLEGE AVE, OAKLAND; 510/654-1601 Housed in a salmon-colored postmodern building with blue Corinthian columns, this jazzy nouveau pizza joint has a cramped, noisy dining room with tiny, knee-bruising tables, bright pop art on the walls, and California pizzas made with a light, crunchy cornmeal crust or a traditional peasant-bread crust. The traditional Mediterranean-style pizzas are impeccable, but pizza adventurers should try one of the more exotic offerings: the Thai pizza is prepared with roasted chicken in a spicy ginger and peanut sauce, mozzarella, julienned carrots, scallions, daikon, peppers, and sesame seeds; and the Ambrosia features sun-dried tomatoes, artichoke hearts, roasted garlic, kalamata olives, and a mix of fontina, mozzarella, and Parmesan cheeses. Check out the upstairs retro-tropical Conga Lounge, where you and 14 of your closest friends (minimum of 15 people) can nibble on pies in a kitschy Polynesian setting replete with fake palm trees. *$; AE, MC, V; no checks; lunch, dinner every day; beer and wine; no reservations; between Kales and Manila Sts.* &

Soizic Bistro-Cafe / ★★★

300 BROADWAY, OAKLAND; 510/251-8100 Just two blocks from Jack London Square in the produce and fishmonger districts, this handsome converted warehouse with 18-foot ceilings and a second-floor loft dining room is owned and operated by Hisuk and Sanju Dong, former owners of the now-closed (but it was wonderful) Cafe Pastoral in Berkeley. Hisuk is an architect, and Sanju is a painter and the head chef. They've created a Paris salon straight out of *The Moderns,* with warm, golden colors and rich details. Named after a French friend of the owners, Soizic (SWA-zik) offers a wonderful mix of Mediterranean-style cuisine: a terrific eggplant entree is layered with sun-dried tomatoes, goat cheese, and mushrooms and is served on a bed of polenta topped with a balsamic-kissed tomato sauce; tender smoked-chicken sandwiches are dressed with sun-dried tomatoes, watercress aioli, and spinach; and a hefty bowl of fresh New Zealand mussels is served steaming in a savory saffron broth with diced tomatoes. The fare is quite memorable and reasonably priced, too. Celebrate the occasion with the bistro's legendary dessert: a creamy ginger custard. *$$$; MC, V; local checks only; lunch Tues–Fri, dinner Tues–Sun; full bar; reservations recommended; www.soizicbistro.com; near Jack London Sq.* &

Spettro / ★★

3355 LAKESHORE AVE, OAKLAND; 510/465-8320 Would you consider it creepy to savor pasta and pizza amid the dearly departed? Well, welcome to Spettro (Italian for "spirit"). This restaurant's otherworldly theme is a bit unsettling at first (there is an assortment of macabre gravestone photography gracing the walls), but your appetite will return once you get a whiff of the dishes being concocted in the kitchen. Run by the owners of the now-defunct Topless Pizza, Spettro has given rebirth to some of Topless's pies and added an ever-changing menu of international dishes for variety, such as a vegan peanut pigeon stew prepared with tofu instead of pigeon, smoked chicken and oyster gumbo, and Brazilian feijoada with black beans and linguiça on a bed of rice. But why the dead theme, you ask? One of the owners is the daughter of an anthropologist, and she used to get her kicks as a tyke tracing gravestones. Whatever. The chatty staff is very much alive, and since the wait for a table can be as long as an hour on the weekend (reservations are available only for parties of six or more), they will ply you with cider and wine to raise your own spirits. *$$; cash or checks only; dinner every day; beer and wine; reservations for parties of 6 or more; at Trestle Glen St.*

Tsing Tao / ★

200 BROADWAY, OAKLAND; 510/465-8811 A favorite Sunday-night destination for local Chinese-American families, Tsing Tao delivers high-quality Cantonese cooking. Avoid the standard dishes that seem aimed mostly at non-Chinese and ask about the chef's specials of the day—that's where you'll find the good (i.e., authentic) stuff. For the Chinese equivalent of Mom's meat loaf, try the steamed pork patty flavored with heavily salted fish, and pair it with the tender mustard-green hearts glazed with a rich broth. Another winning combo: stir-fried crab with scallions and ginger (ask the price first—it can be high here) and stir-fried baby pea shoots, a springtime delicacy. The fish tanks sometimes hold live sturgeon, a bony fish the kitchen subjects to a two-part preparation: the bones and head are turned into a milky broth, and the fillets are steamed. *$$; AE, MC, V; no checks; lunch, dinner every day; full bar; reservations recommended; at 2nd St.*

Yoshi's / ★★★

510 EMBARCADERO W, OAKLAND; 510/238-9200 Business at this jazz-club-cum-Japanese-restaurant—once a premier destination for live jazz on the West Coast—hit a sour note in the early '90s, and the owners were ready to permanently close its doors. Then along came the City of Oakland to the rescue. Fronting a sizable chunk of the $5.1 million construction bill, the Oakland Redevelopment Agency and the Port of Oakland lured Yoshi's from its humble though pleasant Rockridge neighborhood to a glitzy new spread at Jack London Square. Architect Hiroshi Morimoto has fused traditional Japanese materials and elements with a sleek, modern design, and the results are fantastic. Equal attention was paid to the separate 300-seat amphitheater, a semicircular room equipped with a state-of-the-art sound system—there's nary a bad seat in the house. And then there's the food: textbook Japanese all the way, including sukiyaki, tempura, seafood, vegetarian cuisine, and a sophisticated ash-wood sushi bar. Prices are reasonable, particularly for combo dinner specials that include rice, miso soup, and an entree. But let's be honest: You're here to hear America's top jazz and blues bands, as well as occasional big-name talents such as Herbie Hancock and John Lee Hooker, right? Right. Here's the scoop: There are typically two gigs every night at 8pm and 10pm, and ticket prices range from about $15 to $26. Monday-night headliners are local artists trying to hit the big time, which in the past have included jazz heavies Charlie Hunter, Miles Perkins, and Joshua Redman. Sunday matinees have been added to the lineup, and the tickets for these daytime gigs are a bargain. *$$$; AE, DC, DIS, MC, V; no checks; lunch, dinner every day; full bar; reservations recommended; www.yoshis.com; 1 block W of Broadway.* &

Zatis / ★★★

4027 PIEDMONT AVE, OAKLAND; 510/658-8210 Zatis is a real find, discreetly tucked into a narrow spot near a bagel shop and Peet's coffeehouse on Piedmont Avenue. It's hardly noticeable during the day; only at night does the elegant ice-blue neon light entice you to step through the doors, where the aroma of roasted garlic and olive oil will certainly convince you to take a seat and stay for a while. The light seduces, and the jazz soothes. Think intimate (about 15 tables), and think Valentine's Day. Got the picture? Start with the savory filo triangles stuffed with perfectly seasoned chicken and spinach, or dip into the roasted garlic with Gorgonzola and flatbread. Then try the vegetarian eggplant entree stuffed with kalamata olives, jalapeños, and artichoke hearts and baked in a spicy tomato sauce; the grilled fillet of wild salmon served with red potatoes and fresh seasonal vegetables; or any of the chef's specialties of the day. The exceptionally professional wait staff is welcoming and efficient. *$$$; AE, MC, V; no checks; lunch Mon–Sat, dinner every day; beer and wine; reservations recommended; between 40th and 41st Sts.* &

LODGINGS

Lake Merritt Hotel Clarion Suites / ★★

1800 MADISON ST, OAKLAND; 510/832-2300 OR 800/933-HOTEL This art deco masterpiece standing right next to downtown Oakland looks out over Lake Merritt—a large, landscaped lake that's a mecca for joggers, walkers, and rowers. Built in 1927, the vintage white stucco hotel was restored in 2000 to its original opulence with stunning light fixtures, richly patterned carpeting, plush furniture, and lush flower arrangements. Most of its 50 rooms are standard suites appointed in the charming manner of studio apartments circa 1930 (with a modern-day nod to microwaves and coffeemakers). Every room has satellite TV, a modern bathroom, a stocked mini-refrigerator, and a phone, and some units face the lake. Other amenities include fax and copy services, a concierge, weekly wine tastings, and a continental breakfast served downstairs in the Terrace Room, which is adorned with scenes of Lake Merritt during the mid-'50s. If you're a business exec, you'll be happy to know the hotel provides a complimentary shuttle to whisk you to the nearby Oakland Financial District. *$$$$; AE, DC, DIS, MC, V; no checks; at Lakeside Dr.* &

Waterfront Plaza Hotel / ★★

10 WASHINGTON ST, OAKLAND; 510/836-3800 OR 800/729-3638 This small luxury hotel perched on the water's edge at Jack London Square is not the fanciest hotel you'll ever stay in, but it comes with all the essential amenities at a reasonable price. And Jack London Square is brimming with great stores, restaurants, and attractions, including popular Yoshi's (see review, above). Heck, you can even catch a ferry to San Francisco or a shuttle to downtown Oakland from the lobby. Each of the 144 rooms is attractively outfitted with pine furnishings, pleasing prints, quilted comforters, and color schemes of beige, copper, and blue. Be sure to request a room with a deck and a view of the harbor (an extra $20), and in the winter months ask for a unit with a fireplace. Additional perks include business and fax services, a fitness center, and a heated pool and sauna overlooking the harbor. Adjacent to the hotel is Jack's Bistro, where you can munch on wood-fired meats in a dining room with a view of the marina. *$$$$; AE, DC, DIS, MC, V; no checks; www.waterfront plaza.com; in Jack London Sq.* &

Alameda

LODGINGS

Garratt Mansion / ★★

900 UNION ST, ALAMEDA; 510/521-4779 Surrounded by lush gardens and located just five blocks from the beach, this three-story 1893 Colonial Revival manse is a picture-perfect example of Victoriana, with gorgeous stained-glass windows, hand-carved interior woodwork, and a wealth of wonderful architectural details. All seven spacious guest rooms have sitting areas, and five have private baths and phones. Favored boudoirs include Diana's Room, a large second-floor suite with a fireplace, a separate sitting room, a bamboo canopy bed, and a private bath with a claw-footed tub and stall shower; and the Captain's Room, with a blue and gold nautical motif, gold stars on the ceiling, a Venetian mask on the wall, leopard-print chairs, and a cigar-box collection. Innkeeper Betty Gladden serves guests a full breakfast with fresh orange juice and coffee and lays out platters of home-baked cookies in the late afternoon. *$$$; AE, MC, V; checks OK; www.garrattmansion.com; between Encinal and Clinton Aves.*

Fremont

RESTAURANTS

Pearl's Cafe / ★★

4096 BAY ST, FREMONT; 510/490-2190 As you approach Pearl's Cafe, you wonder if you've taken a wrong turn or if you've fallen prey to some cruel guidebook joke. Located near a couple of mini-malls that are going through arduously slow resurrections, and housed in a converted '60s tract home that looks as though it has been attacked by a band of marauding crayons, Pearl's is, well, a pearl in the rough. Once you're inside, though, you'll feel more at home—or garage—since that's what the front dining area once was. Oddly enough, the decor has an Old World feel with its beautifully crafted pine seating areas. The seasonal menu is an equally surprising turn of events. For starters there's the Brie, apples, onions, and thyme baked in pastry with roasted garlic and spiced walnuts, or the grilled spicy prawns and sweet potato–fennel fritters with aioli and caramelized tomato relish. Main course specials include such inventive dishes as the grilled salmon with squash fritters and a fragrant saffron dipping sauce; the peppered filet mignon with cherry demi-glace and blue cheese mashed potatoes; or an herb-roasted chicken with fresh figs and goat cheese over a citrus-infused risotto. After you've finished off your meal with one of the wonderful homemade desserts, you'll wander back to your car, perhaps a bit disoriented but certainly content. *$$$$; AE, MC, V; no checks; lunch Tues–Fri, dinner Tues–Sat; beer and wine; reservations recommended; www.pearls-cafe.com; near the intersection of Fremont Blvd and Washington Ave.* &

LODGINGS

Lord Bradley's Inn / ★★

43344 MISSION BLVD, FREMONT; 510/490-0520 OR 877/567-3272 Rebuilt after the devastating earthquake of 1868 that flattened large sections of the East Bay, this atmospheric Victorian-style hotel offers a good sense of what it must have been like to live in the Bay Area during the 19th century (though it's considerably more comfortable). The 10 individually decorated guest rooms have antique bedsteads and private baths, and a few of them have been completely redecorated from floor to ceiling. In the morning you'll be treated to a breakfast of fresh and dried fruit, croissants, and muffins with orange butter. During your stay, hike up Mission Peak—the highest prominence hereabouts, with panoramic views of the South Bay. Lord Bradley's also hosts outdoor weddings among the olive trees and roses. *$$; AE, DC, DIS, MC, V; no checks; www.lordbradleysinn.com; at Washington Blvd, next to Mission San Jose.*

San Jose and the South Bay

Nowadays, the answer to Dionne Warwick's question "Do You Know the Way to San Jose?" might well be "Dionne, honey, you've been away too long."

The rolling fields and orchards and the small-town spirit of the South Bay memorialized in Warwick's '60s hit song are gone—swallowed up by office complexes and shopping malls. The bumper crops San Jose peddles now are measured in gigabytes. With skyscrapers and stadiums springing up in unlikely places over the past few years, and traffic rerouted for construction, it's become somewhat the East Berlin of the Bay Area—constantly expanding its concrete girth—though nowhere near as bleak. There are a few undeveloped spots, rare and strangely beautiful against the backdrop of chrome and glass. And many of the ethnic neighborhoods—vibrant and alive with Latin rhythms or Asian austerity—remain intact.

ACCESS AND INFORMATION

Do yourself an enormous favor: fly into **SAN JOSE INTERNATIONAL AIRPORT** (408/501-7600) if your final destination is anywhere near San Jose. Now that the dust has settled from the dot-com bust, Silicon Valley's traffic problem is not as bad as it was in recent times (although you can still find yourself languishing in the same spot for up to 30 minutes—especially during rush-hour traffic). Even if your final destination is downtown, it still may take you forever to get there from the airport, but you'll have shaved off another two or more hours if you've arrived at San Jose International Airport instead of San Francisco International or Oakland International. **SHUTTLE SERVICES** include On Time Airport Shuttle (650/207-0221), San Jose Express (408/370-0701), and Silicon Valley Airporter (408/482-4415). There are plenty of **TAXIS** available.

The **VTA** (Valley Transportation Authority; 408/321-2300) runs the buses as well as the 24-hour light rail system that serves San Jose, Santa Clara, Sunnyvale, and Mountain View. **CALTRAIN** (800/660-4287) provides service from Silicon Valley to San Francisco.

San Jose enjoys the distinction of almost always being several degrees warmer than the rest of the Bay Area regardless of the season. Its valley location, with the Santa Cruz Mountains on the west and rolling hills to the east, locks in a temperate climate—and sometimes it's downright hot. You'd be safe dressing fairly lightly, even in winter, when the barometer drops to a bone-chilling 64-or-so degrees. But be sure to bring a sweater or other layering piece any time of year, especially if your travels will take you to other parts of the Bay Area, as the evenings can be on the cool side.

The San Jose McEnery Convention Center is affiliated with the **VISITOR INFORMATION BUREAU** (150 W San Carlos St and 333 W San Carlos St, Ste 1000; 408/977-0900; www.sanjose.org).

San Jose

While some San Jose residents mourn the continuing loss of open space and grittiness to the onslaughts of new construction and gentrification, others seem puffed up with understandable pride at the city's energetic new look and feel. First-class restaurants, an upscale state-of-the-art light rail system, a flourishing arts scene, a dazzling sports arena, and, most recently, an exquisitely designed multi-use shopping complex all contributed to the city's revitalization, furthering its emergence from the long cultural shadow cast by San Francisco, its cosmopolitan neighbor to the north.

MUSEUMS

The **SAN JOSE MUSEUM OF ART** (110 S Market St; 408/294-2787) provides a handsome setting for contemporary European and American art. The **EGYPTIAN MUSEUM AND PLANETARIUM** (at the corner of Park Ave and Naglee St; 408/947-3636), run by the mystical Rosicrucian order, presents a collection of Egyptian artifacts, mummies, and re-creations of tombs in a pyramidlike structure (the British Museum it's not, but it's educational, funky, and fun). The lively and ever-so-loud **CHILDREN'S DISCOVERY MUSEUM** (180 Woz Wy; 408/298-5437), painted in Easter-egg purple, offers kids the opportunity to explore exhibits of urban life: traffic lights, fire engines, a post office, a bank, and even a sewer (spanking clean and minus any errant rats or Ninja turtles). A Wells Fargo stagecoach, a farmhouse, and rural diversions like corn-husk doll-making help youngsters experience what the valley was like when it produced major crops instead of microchips. The **TECH MUSEUM OF INNOVATION** (201 S Market St; 408/294-8324) is a terrific hands-on science museum where adults and kids alike can play with robots, gain insight into genetic engineering, or design a high-tech bicycle; it's located across from the San Jose Museum of Art.

Fans of the supernatural might enjoy a tour of the **WINCHESTER MYSTERY HOUSE** (525 S Winchester Blvd; 408/247-2000), an odd, rambling mansion with an intriguing history: After inheriting $20 million from her husband's repeating-rifle company, Sarah Winchester became convinced that the ghosts of people killed by Winchester rifles were coming back to haunt her. Her paranoia led her to continually have additions built onto her home over a period of 38 years to house their restless spirits. The lovely—if somewhat unorthodox—Victorian mansion is a 160-room labyrinth of crooked corridors, doors opening into space, and dead-end stairways.

For anyone who loves to shop, the dazzling new **SANTANA ROW** (400 S Winchester Blvd; 408/551-4600) is not to be missed. Plopped down in an unlikely suburban locale, this ready-made European townscape boasts everything from Gucci and Escada to Pasta Pomodoro and Ann Taylor Loft. Along with well-known designers, numerous one-of-a-kind boutiques offer such chichi items as custom-made leather shoes and pricey handmade jewelry. Although you'll encounter droves of well-heeled shoppers with bags under their arms, there are plenty of other diversions with lower price tags. With countless restaurants, cafes, and even a Borders Books, you can avoid the retail temptation and simply people-watch in the Spanish-style palazzo. When you've worked up an appetite, enjoy dining Parisian-style at the southern outpost of the celebrated Left Bank restaurant. Or, if you're in the mood for Mexican, Cazuelas serves up delicious molés and inventive tapas at reasonable prices. At night things continue to buzz at the Vbar in the Valencia Hotel, and the

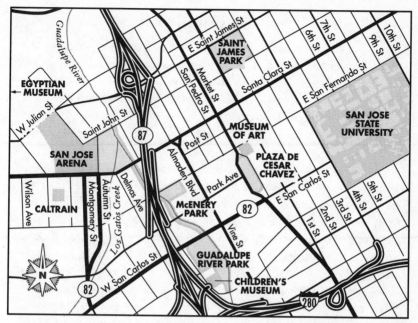

DOWNTOWN SAN JOSE

hip Blowfish Sushi offers tempuras, fresh sushi, and premium sakes until late in the evening.

PERFORMING ARTS

San Jose has a thriving community of theater, ballet, and opera groups, most of which may be found at the **SAN JOSE CENTER FOR THE PERFORMING ARTS** (255 Almaden Blvd at Park Ave; 408/277-3900). The **SAN JOSE CIVIC LIGHT OPERA** (408/453-7108) puts on musicals and other frothy diversions, while **OPERA SAN JOSE** (408/437-4450), the **SAN JOSE CLEVELAND BALLET** (408/288-2800), and the **SAN JOSE SYMPHONY ORCHESTRA** (408/288-2828) offer more classical cultural enrichments. **LOS LUPEÑOS DE SAN JOSE** dance company (42 Race St; 408/292-0443) reflects the Spanish heritage of the city. For drama, the **SAN JOSE REPERTORY THEATRE** (101 Paseo de Antonio St; 408/367-7266) offers innovative productions of new works and classics. The **SAN JOSE STAGE COMPANY** (490 S 1st St; 408/283-7142) primarily showcases American contemporary drama and comedy, while the **CITY LIGHTS THEATRE** (529 S 2nd St; 408/295-4200) follows the more experimental route.

PARKS AND GARDENS

KELLEY PARK is a pleasant place for a picnic and a stroll around the **JAPANESE FRIENDSHIP GARDEN** (corner of Senter Rd and Keyes St; 408/277-3664), complete with a koi pond and a teahouse. If you have little ones in tow, they're sure to be beguiled by the old-fashioned, low-tech charms of **HAPPY HOLLOW** next door, a

YOUR PC'S BIRTHPLACE

Two of the biggest babies on record were born in Silicon Valley—Microsoft and Apple—and despite the dot-com collapse three years ago, this area is still considered the unofficial high-tech capital of the world. Of course, where there are babies, there are albums to document their first steps, first words, what they might become. Such is the **TECH MUSEUM OF INNOVATION** (201 S Market St, San Jose; 408/294-8324; www.thetech.org) or, more simply, "The Tech"—a cache of technology's past, present, and future.

One look at the orange and cobalt blue museum building will make you chuckle at the now outmoded notion that "techie" was synonymous with "geek"—this is not a gathering place for nerds with taped glasses and pocket protectors. Instead, its modern facade seems to beckon the tragically hip to enter and get in touch with their inner programmer. The interior architecture follows suit, drawing one in, then catapulting the attention upward via a dramatic curved staircase and a massive supporting column lathered in gold leaf.

The Tech is divided into three levels. The ground level features an **IMAX DOME THEATER**—no museum is complete without one these days—and the Techstore, as interesting as the museum itself. The upper level contains the **INNOVATION AREA,** where you can, among other things, design and ride a virtual roller coaster or tour a computer chip lab, and the **LIFE TECH AREA**—an utterly fascinating look at technology's role in studying, diagnosing, and treating the human body. The squeamish and the recently lunched should avoid the video display that shows how a computer-generated image of the human body and all its internal organs is created by using a cadaver. The upper level also includes an interactive area called **IMAGINATION PLAYGROUND** that dispels the notion that high-tech endeavors are always sedentary. A **Sneaks and Spies** exhibit boasts hideouts equipped with the latest and greatest surveillance equipment, so that visitors can be James Bond for a day. A **SHADOWS AND SANDS** display projects your movements on screen for an interactive media experience. The lower level is where you can catch a glimpse of technology's future. From robotic dogs with amazingly realistic movement—you can special-order one if you're willing to pay $3,500—and a robotic submarine you can pilot to a model Mars rover you can ride, it's a techie playground. Be sure to take a ride on the **SEGWAY HUMAN TRANSPORTER**—the stand-up scooter that is propelled by the way you shift your weight. Finally, the **CENTER OF THE EDGE** area showcases rotating exhibits of the newest state-of-the-art technology.

—*Brian Tacang*

zoo and amusement park aimed at the toddler-through-early-grade-school set. **GUADALUPE RIVER PARK** is undergoing extensive renovations that will include a 3-mile stretch of picnic areas and paved walkways that will extend from the Children's Discovery Museum to near Highway 880 and the San Jose Airport; call the **SAN JOSE DEPARTMENT OF PARKS AND RECREATION** (408/277-4661 or 408/277-5998) for more information.

NIGHTLIFE

Once the red-light district, the area around Market and First Streets has gradually developed into a clean, hip home for many nightclubs and a slightly more alternative scene. If you gotta dance, you'll find live rock and recorded dance tunes in the **CACTUS CLUB** (417 S 1st St, two blocks south of the Fairmont hotel; 408/491-9300) and in the **B HIVE** (372 S 1st St; 408/298-2529). For live jazz and a bit of alternative rock, head to **AGENDA** (at the NW corner of S 1st St and E San Salvador St; 408/287-4087). Live rock, dance classics, and cheap draft beer are featured at **TOONS** (52 E Santa Clara St at 2nd St; 408/292-7464). For a mix of music—modern rock, swing bands, DJ-spun rock, and '70s disco—check out **THE SPY** (400 S 1st St; 408/535-0330). Coffee and attitude are dished out at **CAFE MATISSE** (371 S 1st St; 408/298-7788).

RESTAURANTS

Agenda / ★★★

399 S IST ST, SAN JOSE; 408/287-3991 At this chic and beautifully designed restaurant in the city's SoMa district (yes, San Jose's got one, too), stylish types sip cosmopolitans at the sculptured wood bar, Silicon Valley execs talk shop at tables flanked by arty souls, and jazz buffs check out the live (and very loud) band. A giant androgynous angel presides over all, stretching its da Vinci-esque flying-machine wings across an exposed brick wall. If you turn your attention away from your surroundings, however, you'll notice that the inventive food is what really takes flight here. That's apparent as soon as you spread a piece of feather-light focaccia with a delectable basil- and olive-infused tapenade. Under executive chef Brad Kraten, the food has taken a decidedly American turn. Look for offerings such as a cheeseburger on a house-made focaccia roll with applewood-smoked bacon and white cheddar cheese. Eclectic combinations continue to reign on this inspired menu, with dishes ranging from spicy tuna tartare to delicate English pea-filled ravioli, from barn-burning pot stickers to comfort food like garlic mashed potatoes. Portions are generous, but try to save room for dessert; choices that seem passé on paper, such as chocolate mud pie and crème caramel, turn out to be retro revelations. Service is savvy but a bit slow, which gives you a chance to soak up the scene and consider the rest of the evening. *$$; AE, DC, MC, V; no checks; dinner Tues–Sat; full bar; reservations recommended; at San Salvador St.*

Chez Sovan Restaurant / ★★

923 OLD OAKLAND RD, SAN JOSE (AND BRANCHES); 408/287-7619 This restaurant specializes in Cambodian cuisine and exceptionally friendly service. For a full review, see the Restaurants section of Campbell. *$; AE, MC, V; no checks; lunch*

Mon–Fri; beer and wine; reservations recommended; www.chezsovan.com; between Berryessa Rd and E Hedding St.

Eight Forty North First / ★★

840 N 1ST ST, SAN JOSE; 408/282-0840 This restaurant with the no-nonsense name caters to the San Jose power elite—say, isn't that the mayor exchanging pleasantries with a justice from the municipal court? The food is eclectic, with Italian and Asian touches influencing the contemporary American menu. Starters include a spicy sauté of honey prawns nesting on a bed of Chinese cabbage; a grilled portobello mushroom atop Asiago cheese, roasted garlic, and sweet peppers; and a curried spinach salad with apples, peanuts, and golden raisins. Entrees include pastas (such as linguine with chicken and broccoli topped with a creamy sun-dried tomato sauce and a sprinkle of feta and walnuts), fettuccine with smoked salmon, clams, artichoke hearts, and basil, and other temptations from the deep. A panoply of meat and poultry dishes range from ostrich medallions to a grilled coconut and macadamia crusted mahimahi served with a tropical fruit salsa. By now, you've probably gotten the idea that chef/co-owner John Petricca takes chances here; sometimes he hits the mark and sometimes he misses. Still, his concoctions are always interesting, and you can wash them down with a selection from the extensive (and pricey) wine list. *$$$; AE, DC, DIS, MC, V; no checks; lunch Mon–Fri, dinner Mon–Sat; full bar; reservations recommended; www.840.com; between Mission and Hedding Sts.*

Emile's / ★★★

545 S 2ND ST, SAN JOSE; 408/289-1960 Catering to an older, well-heeled crowd and expense-account execs, Emile's has been one of San Jose's finest restaurants for nearly three decades. Chef-owner Emile Mooser offers a California version of the cuisine he learned in his Swiss homeland, and his menu features classic French, Swiss, and Italian preparations as well as *cuisine minceur* (a somewhat leaner style of French cooking). Using fine stocks and the best seasonal ingredients available, the kitchen does a particularly good job with fish and game. Entrees on the seasonal menu may include a giant, open-faced ravioli with prawns, scallops, and fish in a lobster-brandy sauce; a fillet of beef with a roasted garlic and cabernet sauvignon sauce; or even such exotica as wild boar with fresh fruit compote. The *roesti*—a crunchy Swiss version of hash browns—is wonderful. Almost everything is made on the premises, from the house-cured gravlax to flawless desserts like the justly celebrated Grand Marnier soufflé. Emile's wine cellar contains more than 300 selections, ranging from the very reasonable to the very, very expensive. *$$$; AE, DC, DIS, MC, V; no checks; dinner Tues–Sat; full bar; reservations recommended; www.emiles.com; between Williams and Reed Sts.*

Gombei Restaurant / ★★

193 E JACKSON ST, SAN JOSE; 408/279-4311 Among the many worthy restaurants in San Jose's Japantown, tiny, lively Gombei stands out with its unparalleled noodle dishes and the near-volcanic energy of its devoted patrons and youthful staff. The menu offers everything from teriyaki and domburi to Gombei's renowned udon— the Japanese equivalent of Jewish chicken soup, which arrives in a huge ceramic